D1509114

All Our Children

All Our Children

The American Family
under Pressure

by Kenneth Keniston and
The Carnegie Council on Children

Harcourt Brace Jovanovich   New York and London

MERCYHURST COLLEGE
HAMMERMILL LIBRARY
ERIE, PA 16546-0001

301.427
K 355   Cop 1

Copyright © 1977 by Carnegie Corporation of New York

All rights reserved. No part of this work may be reproduced, stored
in a retrieval system, or transmitted, in any form or by any means,
electronic, mechanical, photocopying, recording, or otherwise, without the prior written permission of the publisher.

This book is solely the work of the Carnegie Council on Children
and does not necessarily reflect the views or opinions of Carnegie
Corporation of New York, or of its trustees, officers, or employees.
Printed in the United States of America
Library of Congress Cataloging in Publication Data

Keniston, Kenneth.
  All our children.

  Includes bibliographical references and index.
  1. Family—United States.   2. Children in the United States.
3. Child development.   4. United States—Social conditions—
1960–   I. Carnegie Council on Children.   II. Title.
HQ536.K43   301.42′7   77-74800
ISBN 0-15-104611-5

BCDE

Other Books
of the
Carnegie Council on Children

Council Books:

Small Futures: Inequality, Children, and the Failure of Liberal Reform by Richard H. de Lone for the Carnegie Council on Children

Growing Up American by Joan Costello and Phyllis LaFarge for the Carnegie Council on Children

Background Studies:

Child Care in the Family: A Review of Research and Some Propositions for Policy by Alison Clarke-Stewart

Handicapped Children in America by John Gliedman and William Roth

Minority Education and Caste: The American System in Cross-Cultural Perspective by John U. Ogbu

Acknowledgments

This book is the product of four years of lively collaboration among Council members, Council staff, and many outside advisors. The members of the Council have discussed at length the ideas and recommendations put forward, with Council members actively drafting and rewriting major sections of this book.

A crucial role in bringing the book to completion was played by Jill Kneerim Grossman and Christopher T. Cory, who brought extraordinary skills as writers and coordinators to the task.

Special thanks go to the Carnegie Corporation of New York for its generous and unintrusive support, and to its officers—in particular Barbara D. Finberg, Frederic A. Mosher, Alan Pifer, and David Z. Robinson—for their thoughtful advice. We are also grateful to Leo Molinaro, a member of the Council during our first three years, for his lively pragmatism.

Carnegie Council on Children

Kenneth Keniston, Chairman
Catherine Foster Alter
Nancy Buckler
John Putnam Demos
Marian Wright Edelman
Robert J. Haggerty, M.D.
William Kessen
Laura Nader
Faustina Solis
Patricia McGowan Wald
Harold W. Watts

Preface

Creation of the Carnegie Council on Children in 1972 by Carnegie Corporation of New York was not a hasty step taken in response to a suddenly perceived social crisis, as is the case with many national commissions.

The foundation had moved from a general interest in research on learning to a more specialized focus on the cognitive development of the very young to a concern with preschool education for all children, especially for those with disadvantaged backgrounds. Yet could the inquiry end there? Increasingly, we found ourselves asking whether the ability of children to learn was not linked to many other facets of child development, and whether child development itself was not heavily influenced by its social context.

We decided to explore these questions by commissioning a special group to examine the way children grow up in America, concentrating on the time span from conception to about age nine—or, as we put it, from minus nine to plus nine. To lead this new enterprise we enlisted the services of Kenneth Keniston, a person who combines significant scholarly achievement with a deep appreciation of public policy issues, a man who is not a specialist in early childhood but who cares deeply about young people. The selection of such a non-specialist was a quite deliberate preference on our part since he would come to the subject fresh, without preconceived ideas. For the membership of the Council, we worked with Professor Keniston to put together a group of men and women with a wide range of experience, interests, and talents, individuals who could bring a realistic, practical outlook to the work but who were nonetheless imbued with a sense of compassion toward children and of optimism toward the chances of improving their lot.

To this body we put some extremely difficult questions. What, we asked the Council's members, is the relationship between the nature of contemporary American society and child development? What do children need? What do their parents need? What has happened and is happening to the American family? Is it still viable?

What attitudes do Americans really have toward children? What is the status of children in our national life? Who "owns" and is responsible for children? Their families? Society at large? What rights do children have? Who is responsible for protecting those rights?

We had no illusion that our charge to the group was easy. We were not asking just how services for children could be improved (important as that is) but how the nation could develop a wholly new attitude toward children. Those terms of reference, we understood, would probably take the Council into areas of social policy not normally considered to be the province of child development, realms likely to be fraught with controversy.

The task did prove to be long and arduous, with periods of strain and discouragement and sharp clashes of philosophy. But there were also moments of joy, humor, and satisfaction of shared accomplishment. It is our earnest hope that this report and the Council's other studies will be widely read and debated and that the debate will move us decisively toward the formulation of new national policies affecting the status of children in American life.

I wish on behalf of the foundation—but, more important, on behalf of millions of the nation's children, born and yet to be born—to thank Kenneth Keniston and his colleagues on the Council and its staff most warmly for their devotion to this task. However wide the audience their work reaches, I believe that the Council's members would be the first to say that what they have achieved is only a beginning. The effort to make this a better world for children, and hence for all human beings, must continue and be intensified manyfold.

Alan Pifer
President
Carnegie Corporation of New York

Contents

Part One
Children and Families:
Myth and Reality

Introduction . . . xiii
1   The Transformation of the Family . . . 2
2   The Stacked Deck:
      Odds Against a Decent Life . . . 24
3   The Technological Cradle . . . 48

Part Two
What Is to Be Done

4   Premises for Change . . . 74
5   Jobs and a Decent Income . . . 82
6   Family Work and Wage Work . . . 120
7   Services Families Need . . . 132
8   Children's Health . . . 154
9   Protection of Children Under the Law . . . 182
10 Converting Commitment into Politics . . . 212
    Council Members . . . 223
    Council Staff . . . 227
    Notes . . . 229
    Index . . . 245

Introduction

In the United States, when we look at children and plan policies and programs in their behalf, we usually neglect half the picture. We see the characteristics and problems of individual children and families with enormous perceptiveness but too often overlook the social and economic influences that define and limit the range of choices parents of every social level can make for their offspring.

American social science habitually has studied the psychological, social, and intellectual development of children in relative isolation from the social context in which they live. Parents have been studied in much the same way. Although social scientists, politicians, and social theorists often pay lip service to the role of underlying social forces in children's lives, we have found little systematic study of these factors. Experts, lay people, parents, and children themselves seldom think concretely about the impact on children's lives of such things as the jobs parents have and the unemployment rate.

In this book, we attempt to describe some of the anxieties, worries, and obstacles that a changing society is creating for American parents and children. We take up some of the ideas and myths that have led both to the strengths of our nation's perceptions of children and to its blind spots. Some traditional American views, we conclude, severely hamper our national efforts to help children and parents. They obscure the "ecology of childhood"—the overall social and economic system that exerts a crucial influence on what happens to parents and children. Until policy makers and planners shift their focus to the broad ecological pressures on children and their parents, our public policies will be unable to do much more than help individuals repair damage that the environment is constantly reinflicting. Abandoning the tendency to deal with children in isolation from their families or the society they live in is a prerequisite for policies that will really support families and children.

At many points this Council on Children talks chiefly about families, and we do so for a reason: 98 percent of American children grow up in families now and are likely to do so in the future, although increasingly in families that are being transformed into new patterns and shapes. Hence we believe families—and the circumstances of their lives—will remain the most critical factors in determining children's fate. To support children almost always requires supporting their families; to understand the development of children, the lives of their parents must be understood. Keeping a family going does not come easily. Yet throughout our work we have remained mindful that many, if not most, families show courage and stamina in contending with the demands of daily life. If we describe grim obstacles that face all families, it is not to say that they fail but that the understanding and reduction of some of the worst problems will make their lives and those of children freer and potentially more meaningful.

Our perspective may seem unduly broad to those who are used to thinking of children's needs primarily in terms of day care, education, and health care. Our approach may not be traditional, but our goals for children are. We want to ensure parents the widest possible range of choices for their children, so that raising children can be more rewarding than taxing and so that children can thrive and make the most of themselves in both the present and the future.

We are a small private commission, a group of eleven women and men chosen because most of us have devoted the better part of our adult lives to working with parents and children—sometimes simply as citizens working in our own communities, sometimes also as teachers, doctors, social workers, historians, lawyers, economists, psychologists, or anthropologists. We were not chosen as spokesmen for particular professions or constituencies but because we share a common concern with the needs of American children and their families. Most of us are parents ourselves; we are individuals from diverse backgrounds, professions, and perspectives; most of us are in our forties. All of us are Americans, born and bred in this country.

Since the creation of the Council in 1972, we have met for three-day sessions six or eight times a year, in Massachusetts, Wisconsin, Mississippi, Colorado, New York, Arkansas, California, Iowa, Illinois, Maryland, Mexico, and Washington, D.C. Our staff numbered twelve professionals during most phases of the work and was made up of psychologists, lawyers, political scientists, sociologists, policy analysts, and people with experience in social movements, government program management, and teaching. In addition to conducting our own deliberations, we have listened to community leaders, city planners, educators, health professionals, civil rights workers, politicians, and, in particular, parents. From time to time we have inspected programs for children first hand and talked to those who run them and participate in them.

We have not generated original scientific data. Instead we have tried to perform a different role: we have assembled, sorted, and assessed the often fragmented research on children in the United States, the experience of those working with children, and the history of childhood.

Besides the present volume, the Council's findings and perspectives appear in two other volumes. The effects of inequality on children and families provide the basis for a book called *Small Futures: Inequality, Children, and the Failure of Liberal Reform.* How factors outside of the family influence children are described in another book, *Growing Up American.* In addition to these three Council books, several background studies are being published in book form as reports to the Council. These books grew out of the study of specific institutions by individual staff members.

All of us on the Council have had, and continue to have, divergent viewpoints and important differences. But we have found ourselves in strong agreement on our basic attempt to help clarify and broaden the way Americans look at the factors that make a difference in children's lives.

We did not expect, at the start, to find ourselves considering at such length the economic and social forces that affect children and their parents. But we have learned from our work that much of the effort to help individuals—to which many of us have devoted our personal and professional lives—now seems unlikely to have a major social effect unless we *also* face and change the forces that make those individuals what they are and keep them that way. So, too, we have come to question the extent to which we can expect children to fulfill our own unfulfilled hopes and dreams, to redeem the frustrations of our own lives, or to rectify in the future social injustices that we ourselves do not have the heart or the knowledge to change in the present.

Since the trajectory of our investigations has taken us from individual children, where our competence lies, to broader issues about the organization and structure of the economic, social, and technological setting of childhood, we often find ourselves addressing questions for which we do not have special background and knowledge. We have done our best to remedy our ignorance when we could and to invoke the views of those wiser than ourselves in other areas. But we believe that to have avoided issues to which our analysis led us— on the grounds that we were not "experts"—would have been far more irresponsible, and far more of a disservice to children and families, than to address these issues as best we could.

This report is structured so that our readers can go through some of the same processes of analysis that we did ourselves.

In our first chapter, we take up the rapidly evolving family, greatly changed in powers and functions but still vital to the rearing of children. The theme of our second chapter is the tragically broken yet central promise of American society—the dream that all children who live in this country shall have an equal chance and a fair share of its benefits. Finally, we treat the incursions into family life of our rapid technological innovations, each with its ambiguous mixture of benefits and dangers.

To indicate the kinds of policy changes that might follow from rethinking children's issues along the lines we propose, Chapters 4 through 10 outline our general recommendations to both the public and private sectors. We call for a long-run strategy of increasing families' choices by supporting their income at decent levels through two means that must work together to work properly. First and foremost the nation should reduce its unemployment, making sure that parents have fair chances to get jobs—and jobs that are safe and flexible. It should also provide a backup through a clear, unified system of income supports, perhaps following various proposals for a so-called credit income tax. We urge some expansion of the services that all of today's transformed families require for their children, whether rich or poor, but we particularly urge better integration of the existing patchwork of services to make them less frustrating to use, more effective for their price, and more controllable by parents, not just professionals. We propose legal protections for both children and parents that emphasize supporting troubled families, and stronger requirements for controlling the side effects that technology exerts on family life.

In framing these recommendations, we have been constantly aware that our national resources are limited and that we cannot automatically count on unrestricted economic growth to solve the problems of children and families in our society. We have therefore proposed policy goals that we believe fall within the nation's capability to achieve in the next decade.

We believe that public policy should catch up with the pressures and changes that families are undergoing. Today virtually the last question we ask of any public policy is how it will affect children. It should become the first question.

Part One

Children and Families: Myth and Reality

All my people are larger bodies
than mine, quiet, with voices
gentle and meaningless like the
voices of sleeping birds. One is
my mother who is good to me.
One is my father who is good to
me. By some chance, here they
are, all on this earth; and who
shall ever tell the sorrow of being
on this earth, lying, on quilts, on
the grass, in a summer evening,
among the sounds of the night.

James Agee
A Death in the Family

1. The Transformation of the Family

American parents today are worried and uncertain about how to bring up their children. They feel unclear about the proper balance between permissiveness and firmness. They fear they are neglecting their children, yet sometimes resent the demands their children make. Americans wonder whether they are doing a good job as parents, yet are unable to define just what a good job is. In droves, they seek expert advice. And many prospective parents wonder whether they ought to have children at all.

None of this is altogether new or uniquely American. Within

forty years of their arrival in the Plymouth colony, the first white settlers were afraid their children had lost the dedication and religious conviction of the founding generation. Ever since, Americans have looked to the next generation not only with love and solicitude but with a good measure of anxiety, worrying whether they themselves were good parents, fearful that their children would not turn out well. Today, parents and other adults all over the world are concerned about the effects on the next generation of changing family values and new institutions.

What *is* new and very American is the intensity of the malaise, the sense of having no guidelines or supports for raising children, the feeling of not being in control as parents, and the widespread sense of personal guilt for what seems to be going awry. For when the right way to be a parent is not clear, almost any action can seem capricious or wrong, and every little trouble or minor storm in one's children's lives can become the cause for added self-blame.

The sense that it no longer is possible to raise their children the way they were raised is underscored for many parents by statistics documenting dramatic changes in family life and in the lives of the forty-nine out of every fifty American children who live in families. In 1948, for example, only 26 percent of married women with school-age children worked at anything but the job of keeping house and raising children.[1]* Now that figure has more than doubled: in March, 1976, 54 percent worked outside the home, a majority of them full time.[2] The increase in labor-force participation is even more dramatic for married women who have preschool children once considered too young to be without a parent during the day: the proportion of such mothers who work rose from 13 percent in 1948 to 37 percent in 1976.[3] In 1975, in only 34 out of 100 husband-wife families was the husband the sole breadwinner, compared with 56 out of 100 such families a quarter century ago.[4]

To be sure, changes in American family structure have been fairly continuous since the first European settlements, but today these changes seem to be occurring so rapidly that the shift is no longer a simple extension of long-term trends. We have passed a genuine watershed: this is the first time in our history that the *typical* school-age child has a mother who works outside the home.

Consider the number of children affected by divorce, a 700 percent increase since the turn of the century.[5] Today about one out of every three marriages ends in divorce, and more and more of them involve children. Although divorced people remarry at rates that are even higher—age for age, the marriage rate is higher among divorced people than among single people—it is now estimated that four out of every ten children born in the 1970's will spend a part of their childhood in a one-parent family, usually with their mother as head of the household.[6]

* The numbered notes section appears on page 229.

4

Accompanying rising divorce rates and the attendant splitting up of nuclear family groups are other significant changes in familial groupings. The proportion of first births to women who have no legal marriage partners has more than doubled—from 5 percent in the late 1950's to 11 percent in 1971 [7]—and almost one million of these mothers are setting up their own households with their babies every year. There has been an eightfold increase in the number of single persons of opposite sex living together in single households.[8] Communes are more common than they used to be. Each of these new forms demonstrates the flux in our cultural habits. But each one certainly deserves to be called a family as much as does the by now atypical family form, with husband as breadwinner and wife as homemaker.

Statistics only hint at the personal stresses that accompany these shifts. Whatever their reasons for working, mothers who go off to a job every day are likely to worry about harming their children by neglecting them. For many generations in this country, the ideal (though less often the reality) has been the stay-at-home mother, involved full time with her children until they enter school and, once the children are in the first grade, at home after school waiting for them. The evidence from social science suggests that a mother working does not necessarily produce disadvantages for a child.* But the worries persist, partly because of the practical problems in making good child-care arrangements during the working hours, partly because of the traditional view that an "adequate" mother is on tap for her children twenty-four hours a day, while an "adequate" father is one who earns so much money that his wife's earnings are not necessary to maintain a desirable standard of living.**

When mothers work outside the home, subtle changes take place in the relationships between the parents as well as between the parents and their children. Complete financial dependence of the wife on the husband becomes a thing of the past; new pressures are put on men to share in housework and child care; traditional marriage roles begin to shift and at times to collapse. Another part of the anxiety of parents springs from these shifts. Are fathers who vacuum the house "real men"? Do they provide "adequate" role models for their sons? And how can it be good for children when their parents return home at the end of the day exhausted from demanding or draining work? In the absence of widely accepted answers, the

* For a review of the research, see a background report to this Council, Alison Clarke-Stewart, *Child Care in the Family: A Review of Research and Some Propositions for Policy.* New York: Academic Press, 1977.

** The worries can be exactly reversed, of course, in a social circle where everyone believes strongly that women should work. There the widespread belief is that a woman who is *only* a mother is inadequate; she gets paid nothing for her full-time job and has trouble defining herself except in terms of her children and her husband's career.

response is likely to be worry and discomfort in the parents themselves and a fear of the "breakdown of the family" in those who observe these trends nationwide.

Rising divorce rates both reflect and lead to similarly complicated tensions. Divorce usually produces anger and a sense of failure for parents, issues of conflicting loyalty for children, and questions for everyone involved about whether the children will be harmed. What scientific evidence there is suggests that divorce is often better (or at least less harmful) for children than an unhappy, conflict-ridden marriage.* But this is scant consolation for parents and children who have to navigate the emotional transition from a two-parent to a one-parent family at the same time the split-up is spreading financial resources as thin as the self-confidence of family members.

When both parents work, or a single parent is not around regularly, who *is* raising the children? Not siblings, for one thing. As parents have fewer children, the days are over when young children in large families could be raised by older brothers and sisters still living at home. Although aunts and uncles, cousins and grandparents still do a surprising amount of child rearing and baby-sitting for working parents, they rarely live in the same house.[9]

Partly as a result, children now enter group settings outside their families earlier and earlier in their lives. These settings range from the daily group set up by a neighbor who takes in the children of three or four working mothers to the "developmental" day-care

* It is probably true, as Paul Bohannan and others [10] have argued, that amicable divorces where the parents become attached to new partners can provide children with positive new versions of family life, enriching their lives with multiple adult models. No one knows how common this outcome really is.

center with the latest curriculum and equipment, from nursery schools to Head Start programs.

Are these settings really good for children? If they are publicly sponsored, should parents worry that their children are being raised by the state—"collectivized" and "Sovietized," as critics have charged? If the settings are private and profit-making, are the children being shortchanged in the interest of a fast dollar? And in any case, do the children really get the kind of individual attention and concern that a loving parent could provide?

Television also plays a new role in the development of American children. By the age of eighteen, the average American child has spent more time watching television than in school or with his or her parents. The difference between television and a human companion is striking. One can reprimand or even fire a baby sitter who constantly talks of murder, mayhem, and violence, or how wonderful the latest toys, cereals, and candies are, but it is impossible for an individual parent to influence programs and advertisements that do the same thing. If what is broadcast consistently conflicts with the parents' values, they have virtually no recourse short of smashing or locking up the set—and if parents did that, what would *they* watch? The result, again, is a sense of uneasiness about the handy but uncontrollable electronic baby sitter that seems to play so large a role in raising children.

Some children in this country have no contact with adults for extended periods every day. They are either locked up alone in empty apartments or left for hours out on the streets, more prone than other children to getting into trouble. No one knows how many "latchkey" children there are, but the fact that they exist at all contributes to the general feeling that American families are in real difficulty.

The discomforts and anxieties of today's parents are not nightmares dreamed up from nothing: they reflect deep changes in family life and in society. Americans have not had an easy time comprehending these changes—or imagining how to deal with them—in large part because our reactions are shaped by an outmoded set of views about how families work.

The Myth of the Self-Sufficient Family

When we Americans perceive unsettling changes in social patterns, such as the tremendous shifts in family life, we commonly blame them on the individuals involved. One current reaction to changes in families, for example, is the proposal for more "education for parenthood," on the theory that this training will not only teach specific skills such as how to change diapers or how to play responsively with toddlers, but will raise parents' self-confidence at the same time. The proposed cure, in short, is to reform and educate the people with the problem. One kind of education for parenthood

7

takes the form of programs such as high school courses on "parenting" or lectures and demonstrations in hospitals for expectant mothers and fathers. In addition, a growing number of agencies and companies offer workshops, often at high fees, on "effective" parenting, or on how to stimulate children's development, or on how to increase their IQ's. A parallel for families defined as "disadvantaged" are federally funded "Home Start" courses that try to teach parents to play, "interact," and talk "more responsively" with their children. And of course by far the largest movement in parent education is the informal instruction American parents seek from newspapers, books, and magazines. No newspaper or family magazine is complete without one or more regular columns of advice on child rearing; drugstores have volumes of paperback counsel about every aspect of raising children.

Not that the experts agree. Burton White, a psychologist at Harvard, argues in a recent book [11] that the first three years are crucial in determining the rest of a child's life. His Harvard colleague, psychologist Jerome Kagan, says that the importance of the first three years has been overrated [12]—that late starts are not lost starts. Traditional child psychoanalysts advise parents to attend to their children's inner fantasies, fears, and dreams, while behaviorists counsel ignoring these and simply rewarding desired behavior.

Although the experts differ, they share one basic assumption: that parents alone are responsible for what becomes of their children. Of course, many parents can use information, advice, and counseling on everything from how to deal with illness to what can be expected of a moody teen-ager. But the columns and courses rarely mention the external pressures on parents' and children's lives—for example, the possibility that a harassed working parent who does not "interact responsively" with a child may not have much time or energy to do so after a long and exhausting day. It is not surprising that research on parent education in past decades [13] does not provide grounds for much optimism about the power of this approach to make significant changes in the family life of large numbers of people.

Naturally, if parents are considered solely responsible for what becomes of their children, they must be held at fault if things go awry. It is easy to leap from here to the conclusion that children's problems are caused entirely by the irresponsibility, selfishness, and hedonism of their parents. "Parents today are selfish and self-centered," one angry parent wrote us. "They aren't willing to make sacrifices for their children. But that's what being a parent is all about, so is it any wonder that the children grow up on drugs?" By this logic, everything from working mothers to the rising divorce rate can be blamed on the moral failings of those involved. Families on welfare are lazy, sponging chiselers. Parents who divorce are indulging themselves at the expense of their children. Working mothers neglect their children for a few dollars a day which they waste on clothes and vacations. If children get the outlandish idea from television advertising that there is a box or bottle with a cure for every problem, their parents must not be talking enough, guiding them enough, or supervising them enough. *Parents* are to blame; and if there is a solution, it must lie in reforming them.

Blaming parents and giving them advice both spring from the assumption that the problems of individuals can be solved by changing the individuals who have the problems. This implies a second assumption as well: that families are free-standing, independent, and autonomous units, relatively free from social pressures. If a family proves less than independent, if it is visibly needy, if its members ask for help, then it is by definition not an "adequate" family. Adequate families, the assumption runs, are self-sufficient and insulated from outside pressures.

These two assumptions form the core of the American myth of personal self-sufficiency. This myth has deep roots in American history, although it did not emerge in its full form until the early 1800's.

The notion of society as a voluntary assembly of independent and self-sufficient individuals who freely contract with each other to form a community or nation was at the heart of the Enlightenment-Age thinking that flourished in the American colonies 200 years ago. The revolution that freed Americans from British rule had a psychological impact that was particularly important in establishing the myth of family independence and self-sufficiency. The American colonies had never provided fertile soil for feudal ideas of hierarchy, interdependence, and mutual obligation—ideas that bound peasants, vassals, and serfs to lords, squires, and landowners in return for benevolent protection and support in times of crisis. After the Revolution, free from British rule and isolated from Europe by an ocean that took weeks to traverse, Americans felt truly independent. The expulsion of the Indians to the area west of the Mississippi under Jackson opened vast tracts of forests and prairie for farming and land speculation and helped confirm the view that any American possessed of a minimum of ingenuity and industriousness could become self-sufficient in short order.

There were moral, political, and economic lessons in the ideal of the self-made man who knew no master, depended on no one, and lived by his wits. First, this ideal assigned special virtue to personal independence. To depend on others was not merely a misfortune but virtually a sin. Being independent attested to the possession of *moral* qualities: industriousness, enterprise, self-control, ingenuity, and rectitude. The dependent were suspected above all of idleness (the cause, most Americans came to think, of "pauperism") and sensuality (manifest in such sins as intemperance with alcohol, sexual immorality, and general self-indulgence).

Politically, the ideal of self-sufficiency helped define the qualities of the new democratic man in America. He would be free to make up his own mind and beholden to no man and no superstition—

above all, to no foreign allegiance, Pope, or prince. He was not to rely on the state, nor was the state to interfere in civil society except when absolutely necessary to protect his basic rights. In the triumph of democratic ideas in the early 1800's, the active exercise of state power came to be seen not only as tyrannical but, perhaps even worse, as potentially weakening American independence and free spirit. Americans contrasted their democracy of free men to the allegedly decadent societies of Europe, where the political freedom, independence, and initiative of ordinary citizens supposedly was sapped by an overactive and authoritarian state. The ideal society— and most Americans believed that it was being realized in America —was like an assembly of free atoms: men who came together occasionally to vote and who expected the state to protect their freedoms, but who were otherwise on their own.

As an economic doctrine, the myth of self-sufficiency was built on images of the independent farmer and entrepreneur. The economic facts of life in seventeenth- and eighteenth-century America encouraged Americans to think of themselves as especially self-sufficient. The nation's economy was primarily agricultural. Before the development of large agricultural markets and specialized farm production, most farmers in the northern states were indeed largely able to provide for themselves, raising their own food and bartering their surplus or their labor for the necessities (few by today's standards) that they could not produce themselves. The myth was, in turn, closely connected to the work ethic, with its glorification of work not as a means to an end but as a good in itself. For children in particular, "industry"—industriousness—was a moral quality as well as a useful one. It showed good character; it established a presumption that the child was neither idle nor sensual, the two great vices to be avoided. But children's industriousness, in addition to establishing their virtue, was a prerequisite to adult economic self-sufficiency, which was thought possible for all those willing to work hard. The emerging capitalism of the early nineteenth century provided enough examples of success apparently achieved through industriousness to make this aspect of the myth believable.

In the early nineteenth century, the doctrine of self-sufficiency came to apply to families as well as individuals. Until then, families had been seen as fundamentally similar to the wider society, as "little commonwealths," in the Puritan phrase, governed by the same principles of piety and respect as the community at large. In the early 1800's, however, the more prosperous, urban classes pioneered a redefinition of the family. In their thinking—soon widely accepted as the ideal—the family became a special protected place, the repository of tender, pure, and generous feelings (embodied by the mother) and a bulwark and bastion against the raw, competitive, aggressive, and selfish world of commerce (embodied by the father) that was then beginning to emerge as the nation industrialized. A

contemporary essay title was typical: "The Wife, Source of Comfort and Spring of Joy." [14] The family's task—and especially the mother's —was to protect the children's innocence against the temptations and moral corruptions of the threatening outside world. No longer simply a microcosm of the rest of society, the ideal family became a womblike "inside" to be defended against a corrupting "outside."

In performing this protective task, the good family was to be as self-sufficient as the good man. Ideally, it needed no outside help to armor its inhabitants against the vices of the streets. To be sure, an urban father had to venture into those streets to earn the family's living, and at times had to dirty his hands. But the pure wife-and-mother stayed at home, in part as a sign of the father's success, but also to protect her children from sin and temptation.

As the nineteenth century passed, Americans came to define the ideal family as one that was not only independent and self-sustaining but almost barricaded, as if the only way to guard against incursions from the outside was to reduce all contact with the rest of the world to a minimum.

If anything, this pristine portrait represented upper middle-class life in the cities, but only a privileged few American families could afford the insulation of women and children that the myth decreed. Most families lived a very different kind of life. Indians, slaves, Mexicans, poor people, immigrants, and growing numbers of factory workers were rarely as self-sufficient and independent as the myth said they should be. The ideal merely defined them as groups to be changed, pitied, condemned, educated, uplifted, reformed, or Americanized.

Nonetheless this ideal, like many other ideals, became a myth— the myth of the self-sufficient individual and of the self-sufficient, protected, and protective family. And the myth prevailed. Even those who could not make it real in their own lives often subscribed to it and felt guilty about not meeting its standards. The myth determined who was seen as virtuous and who as wanting; it provided, and still provides, the rationale for defining familial adequacy and morality. This moralizing quality is one of its most important features. For this myth tells us that those who need help are ultimately inadequate. And it tells us that for a family to need help—or at least to admit it publicly—is to confess failure. Similarly, to give help, however generously, is to acknowledge the inadequacy of the recipients and indirectly to condemn them, to stigmatize them, and even to weaken what impulse they have toward self-sufficiency.

The myth of self-sufficiency blinds us to the workings of other forces in family life. For families are not now, nor were they ever, the self-sufficient building blocks of society, exclusively responsible, praiseworthy, and blamable for their own destiny. They are deeply influenced by broad social and economic forces over which they have little control.

The New Role of Parents

If parents' decisions are not wholly responsible for the changes, what is putting such a strain on families in America? Over the last centuries, families have not only been reduced in size but changed in function as well; expectations of what families do for their children have also been reduced. Mothers are no longer automatically expected to spend the whole day with their four year olds; fathers are no longer expected to train them in skills for a job. No one imagines that parents will try to manage a child's raging fever without help or teach a ten year old set theory in mathematics. As the forms of life have changed, institutions with a great deal of technical expertise have grown up to take over these functions, while parents have gone out to jobs that are less and less comprehensible to their young children. Conversely, children need training and experience to prepare them for a world already strikingly different from that of a generation earlier when their parents were growing up. As a result, families today have drastically changed in their functions and powers, especially in their power to raise children unaided.

Few people would dispute that we live in a society where parents must increasingly rely on others for help and support in raising their children. In a sense parents have had to take on something like an executive rather than a direct function in regard to their children, choosing communities, schools, doctors, and special programs that will leave their children in the best possible hands. The lives parents are leading, and the lives for which they are preparing their children, are so demanding and complex that the parents cannot have—and often do not want—traditional kinds of direct supervision of their children. And although most of these changes have come about because of changes in our social and economic system, not because of the selfishness or immorality or negligence of individual parents, the extraordinary thing is that the myth of the self-sufficient family persists.

Changing Family Functions

All generalizations about "the family" have numerous exceptions. There are and always have been many kinds of families in America, different for reasons of class, region, ethnicity, and individual inclination. Moreover, scholars know less than they would like about the actual experience of family members in earlier times and often disagree about how to interpret what they do know. Finally, changes in family life have come unevenly and erratically.

Nevertheless, the major developments of the last two centuries seem clear enough, and the most important is a shift in the functions of families. Three centuries ago, almost all families resembled one part of the myth: they were largely self-sufficient agricultural units. They owned and occupied the farms and plantations of seventeenth- and eighteenth-century America. Apart from nails, salt, and a handful of other goods, these family farms produced, sometimes with the help of neighbors, most of what they needed to live: their own houses, their food, bedding, furniture, clothing, and fuel. Barter was more common than purchase for acquiring the goods the family could not produce (except in those regions of the South where cash crops such as tobacco and indigo were introduced early), and working for wages was rare in North and South alike. Family members were "paid" in room and board; most of the extra manpower that family members could not provide was supplied by indentured servants, bound apprentices, trading work between families or, in the South, by slaves.

The most important difference between these early American families and our own is that early families constituted economic units in which all members, from young children on up, played important productive roles within the household. The prosperity of the whole family depended on how well husband, wife, and children could manage and cultivate the land. Children were essential to this family enterprise from age six or so until their twenties, when they left home. (Indeed, in most seventeenth-century American paintings, they are portrayed in the same kind of clothes adults wore—a sign of how much they participated in the world of adult responsibilities.) [15] Families not blessed with children usually faced economic hardship as a result, for boys were necessary to the hard work of cultivating the land and harvesting the crops, while girls were essential to the "homework" of storing and cooking food, caring for domestic animals, spinning, weaving, and sewing.

Children were, in short, economic assets. Early in life, most children began to pay their own way by working with and for their families. Many years later, when the parents were elderly, children paid another economic dividend: in a time when there was no government old-age assistance or social security, grown children were often the chief source of their parents' support.

In the course of the nineteenth century all this began to change. Farm families began to find that raising one crop for sale and using the proceeds of that sale to buy goods produced by others could give them a higher standard of living than could self-sufficient agriculture. The production of cash crops such as grain and cotton replaced agriculture intended chiefly to provide for the family; money became the medium for obtaining necessities the family no longer produced; and families became less self-sufficient. In addition, an influential minority of families ceased entirely to be productive units in which parents and children worked together. Instead, family members (especially fathers) went out to work for wages in factories and businesses. As commerce and factory work became more common, family life and work were sundered: what a worker produced and what he or she consumed were increasingly not the same thing. Money—in the form of wages, salaries, or, for the wealthy, returns on speculation and investments—provided a new and more tenuous link between work and family.

This shift was gradual and uneven. Even in the late 1880's most American families lived on farms, while in cities, family-run stores and shops were far more common than today. And on farms, children remained part of the family productive unit until mechanization made agriculture a business of adults. One reason the nation's schools have long summer vacations is that their schedules were established in a time when children were needed to help in the peak farm season.

In our time, the family economy has disappeared almost completely. While once almost all American family members worked together at a common economic enterprise on whose success they collectively depended, today most American adult family members work for pay, while children rarely work at all. No common economic task remains. Work and family life are separate enterprises; families consume as a unit but do not produce as a unit.

The economic "value" of children to families has changed as a result. If weighed in crass economic terms, children were once a boon to the family economy; now they have become an enormous economic liability. The total costs of housing, feeding, and clothing one child as well as educating him or her through high school now add up to more than $35,000 by very conservative estimates for a family living at a very modest level.[16] Moreover, as schooling has lengthened, the financial drain of having children is prolonged to an average of twenty years. Nor can children today be counted on for an economic return in the form of informal old-age assistance.

In the past then, the intrinsic pleasures of parenthood for most American families were increased by the extrinsic economic return that children brought. Today, parents have children *despite* their economic cost. This is a major, indeed a revolutionary, change.

Furthermore, as children more and more have come to be regarded in the economic hierarchy as "dependents" rather than contributors, child rearing itself has come to be seen as a nonproductive job. It yields no wages, and ever since the industrial revolution, people have come to value their work more and more for the cash income it produces.

A second major change in family functions is the removal of education from the family. To be sure, there were schools in colonial America, and a large proportion of boys, at least, especially in New England, attended them for at least a few years, giving the colonies an unprecedented literacy rate as compared to Europe. But over the course of a year children spent less time in schools than they do now, and most of them left school as soon as they learned to read, write, and cipher. And like everything else, most education went on at home, organized either around reading the Scriptures or around learning a trade. In both cases, and whether they were teaching their own children or apprentices, the major responsibility for education fell on parents, with schools playing a distinctly secondary role.

With the creation of the public "common school" in the middle of the nineteenth century under the leadership of Horace Mann, formal education began to replace family education rather than assist it. Compulsory, free public education was given many justifications, but among the most common was the argument that families—especially immigrant families—simply could not educate their children for a productive role in the growing, increasingly complicated American economy. Schools, it was claimed, could do what families were failing or unable to do: teach good work habits, pass on essential skills, form good character, and, in short, Americanize.

We will discuss more fully in Chapter 2 the hopes and myths that have animated our American commitment to schooling. For now, the point is that acceptance of the doctrine of common public schooling marked another inroad on traditional family functions. A public institution, armed with the power of legal coercion, was taking over and expanding traditional family prerogatives. This shift was, again, gradual and uneven. We feel its full force only today, with nearly universal institutional attendance now often starting at age four or five and continuing after high school for at least a year or two of college, that is, until age nineteen or twenty. For a total of fourteen to sixteen years, the average American child spends the better part of most weekdays not in the presence of his or her family, but in the presence of day-care workers or teachers and other children the same age. It is hard to imagine a more crucial change in the role of the family.

In addition to economic production and schooling, a long list of other "traditional" family functions has been largely taken over by people and institutions outside the family. Sociologists and historians have pointed to the family's shrinking role in the care of the aged, the "relief" of the poor, the imparting of basic religious attitudes and values, and the care of the mentally ill. We will consider only one of these, the care of the sick, because it illustrates another, broader change: the way rising expectations accompany changing family functions.

Even one century ago, most care of the sick was a family matter. Doctors were rare and their ministrations of dubious benefit; many children survived despite the leeching of their blood by doctors, not because of it. Except for smallpox, preventive inoculations were unavailable; bacterial infections either cured themselves or led to more serious illness and often death. Hospitals did not exist in most localities; where they did, their staffs could do little more than make patients comfortable and wait for an illness to run its course. There were no specialties like pediatrics.

When children fell ill, their families nursed them and, if the children survived, watched over their convalescence. Except for information dispensed in popular magazines, preventive medicine was formally unknown, its informal precursors consisting of little more than keeping a special family watch on children considered frail or sickly. When children died, as they did far more often than today, they died in bed, at home, with their families beside them.

Today the family plays a diminished role in health care. Parents still make the crucial first decision about whether to call the doctor, and in most cases they still give simple care. But for anything complex, the diagnosis is in the hands of experts, not parents, and one crucial role for parents in the complicated business of nursing a sick child is to see that the child "follows the doctor's orders." In part, therefore, it is accurate to speak of health-care specialists assuming yet another traditional family function, but to stop there misses a central point: today we expect far more of health care for children than our forebears could. Most of what we expect of specialists did not exist a century ago: immunization against most life-threatening diseases, effective and accurate diagnosis of even obscure and rare illnesses, safe and hygienic surgery when needed, prompt treatment of bacterial infections, and medical correction of many handicaps. All of these are now considered among the basic rights of children. We are rightly shocked when children suffer or die from any of the host of childhood illnesses or conditions that today can be prevented or cured.

Rising expectations for what we want to give our children are crucial for understanding the transformation of families. Much of

16

what we today consider the birthright of all American children and parents was simply unknown to our forebears. They did not need to rely on social workers to guide them, however tortuously, through welfare bureaucracies, because there were no welfare bureaucracies. They did not complain about inferior school facilities or poor vocational programs or inadequate compensatory education because few of these existed in any form, good or bad.

The point is obvious: at the same time that families have been shorn of many traditional roles with children, new expectations about children's needs have arisen and, along with them, new specialists and institutions to meet the expectations. Part of the change of family functions, which carries with it a new dependence on people and institutions outside the family, rests on the family's needs for forms of help and expert assistance that are the creations of the last century.

Not all the family functions that seem to have been transferred outside the family—or that romantics sometimes yearn to bring back—were there in the first place. It is often claimed that "extended families" (with three generations at home, aunts and uncles included) were the rule, and that they have now been replaced by "nuclear" families. But actually most Americans have always lived in families consisting only of parents and children, and in colonial days, just as today, most children moved away from their parents' homes to set up households of their own. Nor is the mobility that scatters kinfolk to widely separated regions a new thing; historical studies indicate that frequent moves to new places have always been the rule in American life.[17]

A New Job for Parents: The Weakened Executive

The genuine shifts in traditional family functions do not leave families with nothing to do. On the contrary, some needs and tasks appear even more concentrated in families than in the past. Among these is fulfilling the emotional needs of parents and children. With work life highly impersonal, ties with neighbors tenuous, and truly intimate out-of-family friendships rare, husbands and wives tend to put all their emotional hopes for fulfillment into their family life. Expectations of sharing, sexual compatibility, and temperamental harmony in marriage have risen as other family functions have diminished.

Most important, parents today have a demanding new role choosing, meeting, talking with, and coordinating the experts, the technology, and the institutions that help bring up their children. The specific work involved is familiar to any parent: consultations with teachers, finding good health care, trying to monitor television watching, and so on. No longer able to do it all themselves, parents today are in some ways like the executives in a large firm—responsible for the smooth coordination of the many people and processes that must work together to produce the final product.

17

This job is crucial for parents because they are usually the world's outstanding experts on the needs and reactions of their own particular children. Teachers, doctors, TV producers, all deal with a piece of the child, and are often more beholden to the interests of educational bureaucracies, medical societies, and the needs of advertisers and networks than to the child as a particular person with unique needs. Only parents are in a position to consider each influence in terms of a particular child and to judge how these outside influences should interact.

But, as an executive, the parent labors under enormous restrictions. Ideally, an executive has firm authority and power to influence or determine the decisions of those whose work needs coordination. Today's parents have little authority over those others with whom they share the task of raising their children. On the contrary, most parents deal with those others from a position of inferiority or helplessness. Teachers, doctors, social workers, or television producers possess more status than most parents. Armed with special credentials and a jargon most parents cannot understand, the experts are usually entrenched in their professions and have far more power in their institutions than do the parents who are their clients. To be sure, professionals would often *like* to treat each child in accordance with his or her unique needs, and professional codes of conduct urge that they do so, but professionals who really listen to parents or who are really able to model their behavior in response to what parents tell them are still few and far between.

As a result, the parent today is usually a coordinator without voice or authority, a maestro trying to conduct an orchestra of players who have never met and who play from a multitude of different scores, each in a notation the conductor cannot read. If parents are frustrated, it is no wonder: for although they have the responsibility for their children's lives, they hardly ever have the voice, the authority, or the power to make others listen to them.

What light does this analysis of changing families shed on the parental worries with which we began this chapter? Recall the "problem" of working mothers. Their entry into the labor force is not a product of selfish eagerness to earn pin money but is related to the disappearance of the family as an economically productive unit. Mothers on traditional farms played too vital a role in keeping the farm afloat to work for wages anywhere else. Stay-at-home mothers with wage-earning husbands, in contrast, are important to their families and indeed work hard at housekeeping and child rearing, but many find it hard to maintain the sense of self-worth that can come from doing work society values and pays for, and they do not contribute directly to the family cash flow.

The economic drain children now represent adds to the new economic pressures on families. Since most children now use family income for seventeen to twenty-five years and few yield significant income in return, the years of child rearing are the years of greatest financial stress on families; that stress helps push women out into paid jobs to maintain the family standard of living. This is particularly true of single-parent families headed by a woman; her work is a necessity if the family is to avoid welfare and the stigmas that accompany it. In 1974, the median family income was $16,928 if the wife also worked, $12,028 when she did not.[18] Many families are above the poverty line not because wages have kept abreast of needs and inflation, but because wives have gone to work to make up the difference. Mothers work outside the home for many reasons, but one of them is almost always because their families need their income to live up to their standards for their children.

At the same time, rising expectations have inflated most Americans' definition of a reasonable standard of living. A private home, labor-saving appliances, time and money for entertainment and vacations have all become part of normal expectations. Some of these components of a good life in turn make work outside the home more possible for those who can afford them: freezers can reduce shopping to once a week; automatic washers and dryers have eliminated long, hard hours at the washboard and clothesline, store-bought bread eliminates the need to bake. All of these add up to a greater opportunity to work yet in a circular fashion make the income from work more necessary.

We see the same circle connecting mothers' employment to schools. If a mother must work, having children in school for 200 days a year leaves her many childless hours during which she can work without neglecting them. School thus permits mothers to enter the paid labor force by indirectly providing the equivalent of "free" baby-sitting, making working possible without expensive child-care arrangements.

Finally, the changing nature of the job market has opened up millions of jobs to women. What sociologists call the "service sector" —jobs that consist primarily in providing personal services, help, and assistance such as nursing, social work, waiting on tables in restaurants, teaching, and secretarial work—is growing more rapidly than any other sector of the American economy.[19] Many jobs in this sector have traditionally been held by women. In a number of service jobs, qualities such as physical strength that favor men are irrelevant, and stereotypically "female" qualities such as helpfulness, nurturance, or interpersonal sensitivity are thought necessary and therefore employable. These jobs pay less than those usually taken by men—one reason for the poverty of female-headed households—but they are all that is available to most women, who have taken them for lack of anything else.

Most mothers work because they need the money. To be sure, other factors are important as well: for example, greater cultural acceptance of women being gainfully employed, and the new insistence on women's right to independence, security, and fulfillment in work. Birth control and increased longevity also play a role that is often overlooked. Whereas formerly many women kept on having children as long as they were fertile, women now have fewer children and space them closer together, so that on the average their last child is in school by the time they are in their late twenties or early thirties. Faced with the prospect of living to seventy-five instead of, say, sixty-five, a woman in her twenties today knows that the days are gone when her role as mother would occupy most of her adult years. A job, even when children are at home, is, among other things, a way of preparing for the decades when the nest is empty.

Over time, however, economic pressures and the way we define economic well-being have had the most pervasive—and most often ignored—influence on mothers working for wages. It follows that it is addressing the wrong issue to point to ignorance, selfishness, or immorality in explaining it.

Or consider the "problem" of the rising divorce rate against the backdrop of the changes in the family. The one crucial factor behind the increase in divorce rates is the reduction in the number of bonds that tie husband, wife, and children together. When family members had more tasks to perform together—and especially when they were united around work as a family—lack of emotional satisfaction with the marriage partner still left family members with much to do in common. Furthermore, parents by and large had less elevated expectations about finding complete emotional, sexual, and interpersonal fulfillment in marriage. Men and women alike were more willing to accept sexual dissatisfactions or frustrations in marriage; temperamental incompatibilities may have caused equal misery but less often led to divorce. A happy, long marriage was, then as now, a blessing and a joy; but an unhappy marriage was more likely to be accepted as simply a part of life.

Finally, in earlier times, the collapse of a marriage was far more likely to deprive both spouses of a great deal more than the pleasure of each other's company. Since family members performed so many functions for one another, divorce in the past meant a farmer without a wife to churn the cream into butter or care for him when he was sick, and a mother without a husband to plow the fields and bring her the food to feed their children. Today, when emotional satisfaction is the main bond that holds marriages together, the waning of love or the emergence of real incompatibilities and conflicts between husband and wife leave fewer reasons for a marriage to continue. Schools and doctors and counselors and social workers provide their supports whether the family is intact or not. One loses less by divorce today than in earlier times, because marriage provides fewer kinds of sustenance and satisfaction.

Even the presence of children in a family is less of a deterrent to divorce than in the past. One reason, as we have said, is that other people and institutions provide more continuity in children's lives when a marriage breaks up. Furthermore, many parents today believe what research usually confirms,[20] namely that preserving an unhappy marriage "for the sake of the children" may be doing the children more harm than good. And finally, the financial effects of divorce on children, though still very bad, are by no means as disastrous as they once were. The greater availability of jobs for women means that more middle-class children today survive their parents' divorce without a catastrophic plunge into poverty.[21]

The entry of women into the paid work force, moreover, has its own effects on divorce rates. A positive by-product of women's economic independence is that a woman who can earn a decent living herself does not have to remain trapped in an impossible marriage because of money alone. And a husband who knows that his wife can earn a good salary is less likely to be deterred from divorce by the fear that he will have to support his ex-wife financially for the rest of her life. Moreover, wives' employment subtly alters relationships of power and submission within marriage. A wife's new independence can strengthen the husband-wife relationship, but increased equality also can produce new stresses or cause old stresses and resentments to surface. Women who are less submissive by and large will put up with less and expect more. One consequence may be the realization that a marriage has not lived up to the high hopes of husband or wife and a decision to end it, particularly when cultural attitudes toward divorce make it far less socially shameful than it once was.

As we have said, none of these changes is the result of an increase in selfishness, ignorance, or weakness in parents. This is not to say that parents are perfect. But few of these changes are within the power of individual parents to influence. Nor do these changes equal the "breakdown" or the "death" of families, as some claim. Most Americans marry and most marriages produce children. Most divorced people remarry in time, as if to demonstrate that their discontent was with their former partner and not with marriage itself.

What has changed is the content and nature of family life. Families were never as self-sufficient or as self-contained as the myth made them out to be, but today they are even less so than they used to be. They are extraordinarily *dependent* on "outside" forces and influences, ranging from the nature of the parents' work to the content of television programming, from the structure of local schools to the organization of health care. All families today need and use support in raising children; to define the "needy" family as the exception is to deny the simplest facts of contemporary family life.

There is nothing to be gained by blaming ourselves and other individuals for family changes. We need to look instead to the broader economic and social forces that shape the experience of children and parents. Parents are not abdicating—they are being dethroned, by forces they cannot influence, much less control. Behind today's uncertainty among parents lies a trend of several centuries toward the transformation and redefinition of family life. We see no possibility—or desirability—of reversing this trend and turning the clock back to the "good old days," for the price then was high in terms of poverty and drudgery, of no education in today's sense at all, and of community interference in what we today consider private life.

At the same time, however, most American parents are competing on unequal terms with institutions on which they must depend or which have taken over their traditional functions. To be effective coordinators of the people and forces that are shaping their children, parents must have a voice in how they proceed, and a wide choice so they do not have to rely on people or programs they do not respect. Parents who are secure, supported, valued, and in control of their lives are more effective parents than those who feel unsure and who are not in control. Parents still have primary responsibility for raising children, but they must have the power to do so in ways consistent with their children's needs and their own values.

If parents are to function in this role with confidence, we must address ourselves less to the criticism and reform of parents themselves than to the criticism and reform of the institutions that sap their self-esteem and power. Recognizing that family self-sufficiency is a false myth, we also need to acknowledge that all today's families need help in raising children. The problem is not so much to reeducate parents but to make available the help they need and to give them enough power so that they can be effective advocates with and coordinators of the other forces that are bringing up their children.

2. The Stacked Deck: Odds Against a Decent Life

It is misleading to discuss recent changes in family life without emphasizing the fact that for generations some Americans have had to raise children under particularly appalling pressures. Although much of what is worrying American parents is shared by them all, the most grievous problems are those that especially afflict a large minority—the poor, the nonwhite and, in various ways, the parents of handicapped children.

The extraordinary stresses that stack the odds against the poor have been described again and again, and yet the poverty persists. In tar-paper shacks without plumbing in rural Maine there are children who risk freezing to death for lack of heat on subzero winter nights. In Cincinnati slums there are children who have never slept in a bed of their own or seen a doctor. Every day their parents face the dilemmas of raising a family without the means to do so decently.

We all know such families exist, but most people vastly underestimate their numbers in this rich, powerful, and productive land. Children who are excluded from the mainstream of our society are hidden from the view of the majority. They live in faraway hollows of Appalachia or on reservations in the desert, in white ethnic neighborhoods in central cities, in tenant-farmer shacks in the South, or in the barracks that house migrant workers in California. Yet their numbers are legion. We estimate that *a quarter to a third* of all American children are born into families with financial strains so great that their children will suffer basic deprivations. Far too many of these children will remain outside the mainstream all their lives unless we act in new ways to include them.

To be sure, even poor children in America live better than poor children in many other nations of the world. But although the cash income of poor Americans seems infinitely greater than that of poor families elsewhere, everything in the United States costs more and everything is geared to American systems of transport, distribution, and marketing, which use up cash more quickly. There are no extensive barter systems, for example, to stretch a family's cash, and jobs are frequently far removed from home; telephones and cars in many cases are a necessary part of employment. Moreover, the psychological pain—and the ethical shame—of American poverty are made greater by the fact that this country possesses the wealth and the energy to raise all children to a minimally decent standard of living. At the very least, it is clear that in the United States there exist glaring disparities between what the society offers most of its children and what it offers a substantial minority of them.

How Poor Is Poor?

What income is "decent" and adequate to family needs? How far below the median, above which half of American families live, does an income have to go before a family is too poor to do justice to its children? Although there will always be room for debate, we find strong reasons for setting the decency standard at 50 percent of median family income in any given year.

The official standard index of who lives in poverty in this country is the federal government's "poverty line." The government arbitrarily computes where the line will be drawn each year by taking the cost of a basic food "basket" for a family and multiplying by three. To illustrate, we will take 1974 figures, which have now been analyzed in some detail. Although later figures are also available, in 1974 the American economy was in relatively healthy condition. Unemployment that year averaged 5.6 percent, and the gross national product was growing. Using later data, when the economy was in a slump, would of course reveal even greater extremes of poverty and inequality than we see in the 1974 figures. In 1974, the poverty line for a nonfarm family of two parents and two children was drawn at just over $5,000, less than $100 a week. A family of this size earning $5,500, even when located in a metropolitan area where rent alone could scarcely have been less than $1,800 a year, was not considered by official standards to be living in poverty. The line for farm families is drawn at 85 percent of the nonfarm family figure.

In 1974 some 24.3 million persons—11.6 percent of the population—lived below the official poverty line. People over sixty-five and under eighteen were disproportionately represented among the officially poor; of all older persons, over 15 percent were poor, while 15.5 percent of American children under eighteen lived in poor households. Over 23 percent of persons of Spanish origin lived below the poverty line; 33 percent of children in families with five or more children lived below it; 37 percent of female-headed families with five or more children were poor; 41 percent of all black children lived in poverty; over 50 percent of black and Spanish female-headed families were poor.[1]

Although these figures in themselves represent a shocking proportion of the population, they may give an unduly rosy picture, for the official poverty line is drawn far below what most Americans actually believe constitutes poverty. Since 1946, in Gallup and Roper polls Americans have been asked what they consider the smallest amount of money a family of four in their community needs to get along, the figure below which a family could be considered "poor." Year after year their answer has been not the poverty line but rather a figure approximating half the median income for such a family.[2]

In 1974, half the median income for all American families (all ages, sizes, and types) was $6,420. Half the median for families of four was higher: $7,373.50 or almost one and a half times the official poverty line. If we adopt this figure instead of the poverty line as the threshold of serious deprivation, we find that more than a quarter of all American children are in difficulty. More than 60 percent of the 6.3 million white children living in female-headed households lack basic access to essentials, and for children under six in these households, the figure rises to 75 percent. Almost six out of ten black children grow up with less than this minimum; for black children in female-headed households, it is five out of six.[3]

What does it mean to live with an income at half of today's median? Is that *really* poor, or have the figures just been inflated for effect? Perhaps the best way to support our conviction that the higher estimates are in fact conservative is to start with a description of the standard of living for a family living at about the median income— a family with twice as much income as the family we are defining as "poor," and almost three times the income of a family the government recognizes as poor. Such a family of four, in 1974, would have had an income of $14,747, in many cases coming from two earners. This median income would be located almost precisely at the "intermediate" budget constructed that year by the Department of Labor for an urban family of four (husband, wife, and two children, aged eight and thirteen)—a family with an income of $14,333.[4]

Table 1 shows separate components of this typical "intermediate" budget, and careful examination will confirm that it leaves precious little room for frills or careless spending. Nearly 20 percent of total income goes for social security and income tax, and no allowance is made for emergencies or savings. While individual tastes and circumstances would lead to different allocations of the $11,540 of disposable income, it should be clear that any increase for one component involves hard reductions for others.

The Department of Labor's calculations assume that this family can get by with a toaster that will last for thirty-three years, a refrigerator and a range that will each last seventeen years, a vacuum cleaner that will last fourteen years, and a television set that will last ten years. They also assume that the family will buy a two-year-old car and keep it four years. In that time, they will pay for a tune-up once a year, a brake adjustment every three years, and a front-end alignment every four years. This theoretical breakdown of a median-income budget allows just enough entertainment money for the husband to take his wife to the movies once every three months, and for one of them to go alone once a year. The two children are allowed one movie every four weeks. A total of $2.54 per person *per year* is allowed for admission to all other events, from football and baseball games to theater or concerts.

This is not a poor family we are describing; it is a family squarely in the middle of the income distribution. Its budget—not to mention the budgets of all the families who live *below* this income level, one of every two in the country—leaves no room to prepare for economic or other adversity or to save for a rainy day or for a child's higher education.

Now let us try to construct a scenario for living with half as much on the bottom line. At this point $7,375 for a family of four begins to look like a very real poverty line. Table 2 suggests one way a family might allocate that sum in order to minimize immediate

Table 1 [5]	Intermediate Budget for Family of Four at Approximately the Median Income	
Category	**Annual Cost**	**Interpretation**
Food	$ 3,548	$68 per week or 81¢ per meal per person
Housing	$ 3,236	$270 per month for rent or mortgage, utilities, home furnishings, and maintenance
Transportation	$ 1,171	$98 per month for car payments, gas, oil and repairs or 80¢ per day per person for public transportation
Clothing	$ 1,095	$23 per month per person for shoes, clothing, cleaning, laundry, and repairs
Personal care	$ 310	$1.49 per week per person for haircuts, soap, shampoo, toothpaste, etc.
Medical care	$ 742	$62 per month for health insurance, prescriptions, dental care, and uninsured portions of medical costs
Family consumption	$ 786	$3.78 per week per person for all leisure activities: vacations, entertainment, books, newspapers, etc.
Other costs	$ 661	$55 per month for gifts, contributions, life insurance, business-related and miscellaneous expenses
Compulsory social security and disability insurance	$ 780	5.4 percent of total income
Personal income tax	$ 2,010	14.0 percent of total income
	$14,339	

damage to the nutrition and health of its various members. The results look bleak. For example, the allocation of $103 per month for housing can only be regarded as fanciful by many people actually living at that income level, and there is not enough transportation money to allow ownership of a dependable automobile. Yet many families have to spend twice the allocated sum to secure barely decent housing and must have a car in order to hold a job. They simply have to eat less, drop their health insurance, or let their teeth rot, because a disposable income (after taxes) of $532 per month can be stretched only so far. Few middle-class parents can claim that they could give their children a decent chance at life while living within this budget.

Such is the poverty line we are proposing—the line below which one out of every four American children is currently growing up. To the best of our knowledge, no official agency has tried to draw a

Table 2 [6]	"Optimistic" Budget for Family of Four at Approximately Half the Median Income (150% of the current official poverty line)	
Category	**Annual Cost**	**Interpretation**
Food	$2,485	$48 per week or $11.95 per person for a week's food (30 percent lower than intermediate budget)
Housing	$1,239	$103 per month for rent, utilities, and furnishings
Transportation	$ 455	$38 per month or 31¢ per day per person
Clothing	$ 660	$14 per month per person
Personal care	$ 186	89¢ per week per person
Medical care	$ 737	$61 per month for all doctor visits, prescriptions, and health insurance
Family consumption	$ 294	$1.41 per week per person
Other costs	$ 327	$27 per month (50 percent lower than intermediate budget)
Compulsory social security and disability insurance	$ 472	6.4 percent of total income
Personal income tax	$ 520	7.1 percent of total income
	$7,375	

credible scenario for living at such a marginal level; certainly no one has tried at the level that currently marks passage out of poverty (approximately one-third of the median). Insofar as a threshold can be a useful tool for analysis and policy design, the level of half the median represents a critical break-point. Below this level, economic pressure on the family becomes highly prejudicial to children's chances to grow, develop, and take advantage of opportunities that normally lead to a productive adulthood.

Besides those now living below half the median, there is another group of families suffering acute financial strain: families in which mothers are working only because their income is desperately needed. There are numerous families of this type living below the median but above poverty, with the father earning, say, $7,000, and the mother a minimum wage of perhaps $4,000. They are not counted in the charts and statistics on families suffering from income problems, yet they suffer all the same. Many mothers with young children must face the unpleasant choice of trying to feed, clothe, and house the family on the low wages earned by their husbands, or leaving their offspring in day care in order to go to work themselves. Some mothers, of course, choose to work no matter how comfortable the family's circumstances, but for those in the marginal income range, the decision to work is often made under economic duress. Needless to say, these pressured choices, difficult enough for the mother whose husband's income cannot support the family, become most difficult of all for the single parent who tries to be self-supporting.

No one knows how many working mothers would spend more time with their children if they faced a less coercive choice, but there are many children who are not receiving the kind of care that their parents' best judgment would allow. Such children, several million at least, must be added to those below decent income levels before we can estimate how many children in our country are actually at risk because of economic pressures on their families. Once we include this group, we can see that perhaps one child out of three lives in poverty (or is slightly better off only because his mother has been forced by economic necessity to divert her energies away from her children).

One final group of children and families must be mentioned here. For in this nation not only do families have grossly unequal resources but they have unequal financial demands as well. Some children simply cost more to raise, much more than the average child. These are the children distributed through the richest suburbs and the poorest ghettoes—the large and politically almost unnoticed minority of handicapped children.[7] About one American child in forty suffers from a serious handicap. In many instances, there simply is not enough money to pay for all the special services the handicapped child needs. Hence many families are forced either to

31

give the child up to an institution or to concentrate their financial resources on the disabled child to the detriment of able-bodied brothers and sisters, not to mention the parents themselves.

Damage and Deprivation

Of all age groups in America, children are the most likely to be poor. In 1974, more than 17 million American children were living below our figure of half the median.[8] For children, being poor means something more than eating simple meals and living in crowded quarters. The chances of dying in the first year of life are approximately two-thirds greater for the poor than for those living above poverty levels.[9] To cite a simple matter that middle-income families take for granted, low-income children aged six to eleven have an average of 3.4 decayed and unfilled teeth, but high-income children an average of only .7. Poor children (from families with incomes below $5,000) were four times more likely to be in "fair or poor" health in 1974 than children in families with incomes over $15,000—and the ratio has not changed substantially since.[10] Yet although poor children are more often in poor health, they are only half as likely as high-income children to have seen a doctor in the past year.[11] In Massachusetts, in 1971, 61 percent of children in foster care came originally from families with incomes under $5,000; only 6 percent came from families with incomes over $10,000.[12] (Again, we have no reason to think the situation has changed much since then.) In the 1960's, among all students in the brightest 20 percent of their age group, those in the economically poorest 20 percent had only one-fifth the chance of attending college of those who came from families in the wealthiest 20 percent. Bright, well-off children, in other words, were five times more likely to attend college than poor children who were just as smart.[13]

Particularly distressing is how many American children suffer not one but several of these disadvantages. For by and large, the worst harms we tolerate for American children occur together, each making the others more painful and more damaging. The children whose parents lack the security of a regular job are usually the same children who are undernourished and who live in inadequate housing. Poor prenatal care and more frequent infant deaths are closely connected with low income. Ineffective schools are most common for the children who need good ones.

Moreover, the harm is cumulative, becoming more severe as a child develops, since missed chances can seldom be made up. Inadequate prenatal care for pregnant women increases the chances that their children will be born premature, disabled, sickly, or dead. For the strong ones who survive this disadvantage, early malnutrition decreases the hope for robust physical vigor. Poor living conditions increase the chance of illness, and inadequate health care allows minor illnesses to escalate into permanent handicaps.

Now consider the special case of children who are not white. Here the statistics become truly chilling. Children in black families are four times more likely to be poor than white children; Native American children suffer even more terrible odds.[14] In large metropolitan areas and in the rural South, the infant mortality rate for minority children is almost double that of whites.[15] Nutritional deficiencies are over three times more common among black children (32.7 percent overall) than among white children.[16] In South Dakota, Native American children are ten times more likely to be placed in foster care than other children.[17] Where other types of data are available, they show the same trends: for example, minority children enter foster homes in disproportionate numbers, and they are more likely than their white counterparts to remain in the care of the state without being returned to their families or adopted.

The Theft of the Future

Poor children live in a particularly dangerous world—an urban world of broken stair railings, of busy streets serving as playgrounds, of lead paint, rats and rat poisons, or a rural world where families do not enjoy the minimal levels of public health accepted as standard for nearly a century. Whether in city or country, this is a world where cavities go unfilled and ear infections threatening permanent deafness go untreated. It is a world where even a small child learns to be ashamed of the way he or she lives. And it is frequently a world of intense social dangers, where many adults, driven by poverty and desperation, seem untrustworthy and unpredictable. Children who learn the skills for survival in that world, suppressing curiosity and cultivating a defensive guardedness toward novelty or a constant readiness to attack, may not be able to acquire the basic skills and values that are needed, for better or worse, to thrive in mainstream society.

In some ways we might even say that such children are systematically trained to fail. The covert lessons their environment teaches them about themselves are astonishingly consistent. Such children are smart enough to sense from an early age that the world of mainstream America defines them and their parents as no-good, inadequate, dirty, incompetent, and stupid. This sense of self, constantly reinforced, in fact is an accurate perception of the messages our society gives these children.

At school such children often do poorly and are labeled "culturally deprived" by professionals or "stupid" by their classmates.[18] Their parents are referred to as welfare chiselers, down-and-out good-for-nothings, a disgrace to the community, or—less cruelly but probably no less hurtfully—problem parents. Handicapped children may find themselves the objects of doubly handicapping messages: they are made to feel, on the one hand, that they cannot do things because of their physical condition and, on the other, that they are somehow to blame for not "overcoming" their fixed condition. Parents and children absorb these images, often reluctantly accepting them as true, and because the children find their models of the future in those closest to them, they draw unhappy conclusions about their own adult fate.

"What do you want to be when you grow up?" is not just a game grownups play with children; it is a serious aspect of the present during every day of childhood. At the heart of childhood play is constant imitation of adult roles, as if to try them on for size. The three year old struggling to learn how to tie her shoelaces is already thinking of the day when she will grow up and go to school, and her parents are thinking beyond that to what kind of future she can reach for as an adult. School, once she gets there, is built on deep-running institutional assumptions about her future; thus she, and her peers, are classified and sorted by means of grades and tests and "tracks"—whether vocational or liberal arts, problem student or gifted, or the more subtle rankings and hierarchies that are vivid in the minds of every person in the classroom, including the teacher. ("She's a winner." "He's dumb, but what can you expect? Look where he comes from.") Ideas about a child's future can open doors, or they can present impenetrable walls to achievement.

Expectations are at the center of this process. People willingly —and, for the most part, readily—learn skills they see they are going to be able to use. Conversely, they do not learn—or they quickly forget—what they do not believe is going to be functional or relevant to their life's pattern. Many of the insults and injuries of poverty and race can be overcome by a child who foresees a reasonable chance for a good life as an adult. But without that vision of a good life, founded on the child's perception of the actual lives and achievements of the adults he knows best, he is likely to expect failure of himself just as the world expects it of him.

These patterns may be easier to grasp in a situation distributed among both rich and poor: the problems of handicapped children. A child with cerebral palsy is stuck with the job of growing up in a world where it is likely that no one like him holds a position of authority, respect, or power. His parents are probably as traumatized by this lack of models as he is; his teachers, his friends, his counselors, even his doctors cannot separate their sense of his future from their complex emotional reaction to him, from their fear that he has no useful role to play as an adult. As a study done for this Council indicates,* this constriction of his future is probably the greatest liability the handicapped child suffers—greater, in short, than the physical limitations themselves.

Statistical surveys document the special danger of the fore-

---

* *Handicapped Children in America.* A report to the Carnegie Council on Children by John Gliedman and William Roth. New York: Academic Press, 1978.

34

closure of the future that affects nonwhite Americans. Black unemployment has been twice that for whites ever since World War II.[19] In 1976 the Bureau of Labor reported unemployment of 39 percent among black teen-agers in the inner cities, compared to 16 percent for whites of the same age.[20] And survey after survey has shown that blacks with the same education consistently earn far less than whites: for example, college graduates who were family heads in 1974 had a median income of $19,500 if they were white, only $14,000 if they were black.[21]

Of course black children, Mexican Americans, Puerto Ricans, and Native Americans do not read these statistics—but they don't have to. The most crucial facts for them are daily experience. And when daily experience shows a black, Mexican American, Puerto Rican, or Native American child that the adults with whom he lives, no matter how capable, have difficulty in gaining education and work, what can he conclude about his own future? Why should he remember what he learns in school when the process has no real use for him? Concepts like "unequal access," "job discrimination," and "promotion ceilings" filter down to become the stuff of daily life for children who have never heard the abstract terms.*

Whose Fault?

Were we a society committed to the perpetuation of a caste system, dedicated to the continuation of gross inequality, eager to waste human potential, or happy with the exclusion of a large minority of the next generation, these facts about exclusion and the theft

---

* "Ceilings"—or hiring and promotion limitations—on the jobs performed by the adults that minority children see around them, and the way those ceilings influence children, are documented in another report to this Council: *Minority Education and Caste: The American System in Cross-Cultural Perspective* by John U. Ogbu. New York: Academic Press, 1978.

of the future would cause us no concern. But in truth they violate our most central values as Americans. Indeed, if any single theme dominates the social and political history of our nation, it is the continuing assertion that American society will include as full citizens all those who live here. Our society, we have believed, should impose no special burdens that will limit a child in the exercise of freedom or the pursuit of fulfillment.

Even the most superficial reading of our history will show how far we have fallen short of this high ideal. Exclusion is in no sense new. Native Americans, slaves and their descendants, other non-whites, immigrants, women, many of the handicapped, and a host of others have been deprived of full citizenship over the years. Still, public figures, politicians, and educators have repeated, and continue to repeat, the same promise to each generation: all human beings are created equal; your children will become full members of the community of Americans.

Confronted with the unhappy facts of exclusion, we sometimes reassure ourselves by telling stories: the poor boys who made it, the blacks who became a "credit to their race," the women elected to high office, the handicapped who made "useful contributions" to our society. These stories are the heart of the novels of Horatio Alger; moreover, they are heard whenever someone from an excluded group "makes it." Just as we believe in the self-sufficient family, we also believe that any child with enough grit and ability can escape poverty and make a rewarding life. But these stories and beliefs clearly reflect the exceptions. It takes an extraordinary parent or parents to raise children who can make their way in the economy

despite growing up in the slums of Harlem, the backwaters of Appalachia, or the migrant camps of Colorado, and despite the cultural stereotypes that stand like roadblocks in their way. That some parents do succeed in this is a tribute to the elaborate nurturing networks of kith and kin that often exist in poverty-ridden neighborhoods [22] and to the parents' own miraculous tenacity, love, and inspiration. But such miracles occur too rarely. In fact, the brilliant exceptions may systematically mislead us, for they encourage us to overlook the vast numbers of equally talented children who will not be heard from. Meanwhile, this viewpoint implies that there is something wrong with the ones who do not escape.

Blaming the excluded for their lowly estate characterizes a range of thoughtless reactions to poverty, handicap, and the problems of minorities. Some suspect that the poor and nonwhite remain in the cellars of society because of some deep and possibly inherent defect of character or intelligence. For generations, theories of the hereditary inferiority of nonwhites have had wide popularity in America, rephrased anew in the scientific jargon of each successive era. Today, with our contemporary emphasis on IQ and cognitive abilities, some argue that poor people or nonwhites are inherently less able than more prosperous people or whites. In earlier times, social critics reached a similar conclusion about immigrants from Ireland, Italy, Poland, and Russia, contending that such groups were "inferior racial stock" and showed unmistakable signs of what was then called "racial degeneracy." One study in the first decades of the century claimed that 83 percent of all immigrant Jews were "feeble-minded." [23] (Since then, of course, Jews have proven a highly successful immigrant group.)

Beneath the belief in "inherited," "racial," or "genetic" inferiority lies an even deeper presumption: that the excluded remain on the peripheries of society because of their *moral* flaws. Each immigrant group in turn has been accused of moral deficiency, starting with the German immigrants who came before the 1850's and continuing through every major immigrant group (save the Anglo-Saxons), up to and including the blacks who have moved to the North from southern states in our own times. Immigrants frequently were seen—and still are seen—as unindustrious, sensual, licentious, lewd, lacking in self-control, given to sexual vices such as prostitution or bearing illegitimate offspring, and inclined to waste their earnings on everything from demon rum to purple Cadillacs. Their lack of industriousness—in today's terms, their laziness—supposedly made them eager parasites on the hard-earned subsistence of others: public wards, charity cases, welfare dependents. Their sensuality led to excessive self-indulgence, manifest in alcoholism, illegitimacy, and a high birth rate. As for the handicapped, they are usually defined in medical terms, as somehow "sick." Most sick people, of course, are expected to get well. Since this is not possible for most handi-

37

capped people, the medical definition itself frames an adverse reaction among many able-bodied people, as if there were something deeply wrong about any handicapped person who does not behave "normally."

In the late nineteenth century, the popular minister Henry Ward Beecher stated very bluntly a conviction still held (although in other terms) by many Americans: "No man in this country suffers from poverty unless it be more than his own fault—unless it be his sin." [24]

There is, as well, an allegedly more "liberal" way of explaining why some Americans remain effectively excluded from the prosperity, prestige, and power afforded others. In this view, the poor and nonwhite and handicapped are not so much vicious, sinful, or ailing as they are limited or unenlightened. "Circumstances" make them what they are. The corruptions and temptations of the cities, some nineteenth-century reformers claimed, "seduced" young girls into the paths of vice. The poverty of teeming tenements turned young boys into beggars, thieves, street musicians, or alcoholics. Unstable families, inadequate education, and faulty training in character encouraged "pauperism," willing dependence on others for a living. And the peculiar Old World customs of immigrants made them unfit for the American way of life. Unfortunately, a viewpoint which began as extraordinarily empathetic when expressed, for example, by Jane Addams, has itself degenerated into "blaming the victims" of poverty.

Today, these same ideas are expressed in different words, though they come to much the same conclusion. The excluded are now described as "deprived"—culturally, familially, and cognitively. It is not exactly their fault; they are "disadvantaged" or perhaps even "sick." Living in a "culture of poverty" [25] or growing up in families which are a "tangle of pathology," [26] they can hardly be expected to develop the same intellectual abilities, "ego strength," good work habits, or ambitious character traits as do white middle-class children. Above all, the problem lies in the families of these children, which do not provide the cultural enrichment, cognitive stimulation, positive role models, or responsive interaction that children need.

What unites all these explanations of exclusion is a tacit agreement that there is something wrong with the excluded children and parents. Some see the failure as personal, moral, even genetic; others see it as the result of a deficient environment, which is generally taken to mean a deficient family. But in either case, it is taken for granted that the immediate cause for being at the bottom lies in the characteristics of those who live there. Unless there were something wrong with the excluded, why would they remain on the outskirts of our allegedly open and dynamic society?

From this explanation follows the traditional solution to the problem of exclusion: reform, change, uplift, and educate the excluded. If certain children—largely nonwhite and poor—are deprived of the cultural stimulation available to their middle-class peers, then programs of cultural enrichment and intellectual stimulation must compensate for the alleged deficiencies of their families. Such programs multiplied in the 1960's.

There are, however, two sides to deprivation: the deprived and the depriving. Significantly, many sociologists of the 1960's assumed that the most serious deprivations were "cultural" and were actually the responsibility of parents. They rarely asked whether the basic deprivations of nonwhites and poor people in America might stem from wholly different sources. In the 1960's in particular, the term "culturally deprived" became a euphemism for poor and black. For many Americans, it was another stigmatizing label, a polite way of pointing to the alleged inadequacies of families facing terrible odds against escaping from the lowest rungs of our economy. Little real attention was paid to the economic and social forces that prevent some families from providing their children with cultural riches and intellectual stimulation.

The Myth of Equal Opportunity

Why have we so consistently built program after program, through a long lineage of charity and reform, on an inaccurate assumption? To answer this question, it is necessary to examine another American myth—the myth of equal opportunity. The United States, we have long believed, is a society fundamentally open to success through hard work and talent; personal qualities largely determine the position of respect, power, and wealth any individual ultimately achieves in his or her lifetime. The myth denies that the circumstances of birth—and in particular the social and economic position into which a child is born—have much effect in determining where the individual ends up in life. Parental wealth, power, status, and race are seen as irrelevant to one's final status. The poor can rise from rags to riches, while those born to wealth will fall to poverty if they lack talent and industry. According to this view, the social level at which any individual is found directly reflects his or her efforts and abilities.

The myth of equal opportunity flowered in the first half of the nineteenth century, based at least partly on the same facts of social life in colonial times that we discussed earlier. Unlike European countries of that era, colonial America did not support immense contrasts between the vastly rich and miserably poor. There were, of course, large economic differences between the leading merchants of such cities as Boston and Philadelphia and the indentured servant, persecuted Indian, or impoverished farmer. But most white American families fell somewhere in between, headed by men of "middling estate" who usually owned the land they farmed. Furthermore, for those dissatisfied with their fortunes, the availability of free land well into the nineteenth century made it possible to move to new settings in the hope that prosperity would soon follow.

The ideas that justified the American Revolution provided another basis for the same myth. The Revolution was premised on Enlightenment ideas of human equality—at least moral and legal equality for white males. Revolutionary ideas of liberty and social justice, coupled with the promise of the frontier and the middling estate of most Americans, made the ideal of equality grow and thrive. In the first decades of the nineteenth century, the right to vote was extended to all white men, making real for many of them the egalitarian dream of political democracy.

But by the end of the nineteenth century, some Americans began to sense that social and economic realities had diverged more and more from the ideal of equality. Though less severe than in Europe, there were nonetheless extremes of wealth and poverty in America. Wealthy merchants, land speculators, and new capitalist entrepreneurs emerged as a visibly wealthy class, while indigent farmers and recent immigrants who fed the swelling ranks of industrial labor constituted an impoverished class. More Americans began to realize, however dimly, that economic wealth conveyed political power even in a democracy, for the rich gained access to political decision makers and exercised influence on local, state, and federal policies which men of lesser means could not have.

As time passed it became clear that the connection between talent and work on the one hand and worldly success on the other was far from automatic. To many this connection appeared entirely spurious, for the children of the rich tended to grow up rich and powerful far more often than mere talent or energy or morality could have guaranteed. And the offspring of the poor had a way, more often than not, of ending up poor. It began to seem possible that power, privilege, and prosperity were transmitted not only by the direct inheritance of wealth but also by the subtler route of acquired manners, learned skills, and influential friends. Apparently, the "opportunity" that had brought the present adult generation to its current social position was not always equal: the cards were stacked in favor of children born with prosperity, power, and prestige.

It is to the credit of nineteenth-century Americans that they found inequalities of condition difficult to tolerate and much in need of justification. In virtually all other nations, greater inequalities—economic, political, and social—were simply taken for granted. For Americans the contradiction between national ideal and social fact required explanation and correction. Ultimately this contradiction did not lead to the abandonment of the ideal of equal opportunity but rather to its postponement: to the notion of achieving for the next generation what could not be achieved for the current one. And the chief means to this end was a brilliant American invention: universal, free, compulsory public education. This "solution" was especially important for children and families because it gave children a central role in achieving the national ideal.

A Dream Deferred: Equality and the Schools

Today the idea of free and universal public schooling seems commonplace; in the early nineteenth century, to its advocates and opponents alike, it seemed (and was) revolutionary. Although schooling before that time had been fairly widespread, it was chiefly a way of providing access to the Scriptures or the laws of the land or the skills of a trade. In the egalitarian mood of the early 1800's, however, schools assumed a new social function as the major vehicle for equalizing opportunity in the next generation. In short, if schools could be made free, compulsory, and universal, they might equalize the conditions from which all children started the race of life.

Horace Mann, the most articulate and influential advocate of such ideas, drew explicit connections between universal public education and the elimination of economic inequality. Mann fervently believed that education "prevents poverty" and termed the school "the great equalizer of all conditions of men . . . the balance wheel of the social machinery." [27] Thus the idea of an equal start for rich and poor was deferred for a generation. The dream would become real for the children; school would enable them to overcome the inequalities of their condition at birth.

Deferral of the egalitarian dream had several consequences. First, personal frustration and societal guilt engendered by inequalities of condition were translated into hopes for equality of opportunity. It was assumed that if opportunities were equalized, outcomes would be more nearly equal as well. Furthermore, faith that schooling would reduce inequalities in the next generation meant that present inequalities could more or less be rationalized away. For our children, Americans came to hope, things will be different. For the next generation, we will create *real* equality of opportunity, in contrast to the excessive inequalities that pervade our present society. Even if our social positions are humble, our lives constrained, our bodies drained, our minds numbed by outside forces, we can direct our hopes and energies to the success of our children, and our

41

sacrifices will pay off in their lives. Children, the repositories of the dream, will redeem our own personal disappointments and will thus help realize our collective vision of a more just society.

One unexpected aspect of this idea lay in the way it translated potential political discontent into personal discontent, and personal discontent into effort to improve one's children. Parents need not feel impotent in the face of social injustices (as in many other countries); on the contrary, American parents had the positive responsibility of "investing" in their children as a way of redeeming their own lower status. This view promised a more equal and just society in the future, and placed on individual families and schools the burden of creating that society by preparing children to gain whatever place they had the wits and will to earn.

The myth of equal opportunity through schooling was thus a major factor in defusing the social conflicts that have divided and at times broken apart other industrial societies. Social classes have always existed in the United States as elsewhere, but in our country they have rarely been seen as inherent features of our economic and social system. For over 150 years we have considered them temporary aberrations, cultural embarrassments that could and would be overcome in the next generation. Hence, the myth of equal opportunity indirectly helped forestall the development of any widely accepted critique of the American social and economic system. We Americans are probably more prone to define personal worth in terms of economic wealth than are the citizens of any nation on earth; at the same time, we have consistently rejected all theories which presume that conflicts over the distribution and control of wealth are an inherent consequence of our social and economic organization.

By defusing conflict and transforming personal and social discontent into "investments" in children, the myth of equal opportunity has undoubtedly contributed to the economic growth and social stability of America in the last century and a half. Those who believed that economic and political opportunities were equal but who nonetheless ended up on the bottom of the heap were led to blame themselves, or consider their plight as temporary—and often they worked all the harder. Those who doubted the actual opportunity open to them nevertheless worked on improving their own and their children's chances through individual effort and education. We have paid a price for the myth of equal opportunity, but we should nonetheless recall its useful purposes. The social unrest and guilt engendered by the tension between Americans' egalitarian ideals and unequal society were dissipated with a promissory note.

The Reality of Unfair Distribution

Few Americans would fault the ideal that all children should have a fair chance to attain whatever respect, riches, and rewards our society has to offer. Achieving that goal must remain high on our national agenda for children and adults alike.

But equal opportunity is more than an ideal. It is frequently presented as a factual claim: a claim that ours is (or soon will be) an open society; a claim that equal opportunity will by itself end the poverty and exclusion of millions of American children; a claim that by education alone we can eliminate unequal opportunity; a claim that people who do not make it in our society are people who are inadequate. Unfortunately, the myth of equal opportunity starts from a fundamental confusion that blinds us to the real forces that exclude more than a quarter of our children from a chance of entering our society as full citizens.

The most basic flaw in the myth of equal opportunity is a simple but common error of logic. Important as equality of *opportunity* is, its achievement in reality would not necessarily lessen inequality of *condition,* much less place the floor of a decent standard of living beneath all Americans.

Consider the extreme example of a society where 95 percent of all adults receive fixed salaries of $3,000 per year and the remaining 5 percent receive $1,000,000 per year. Nineteen of every twenty adults would be poor, and the twentieth would be very rich. Obviously, such a society would have gross and unjust inequalities of condition.

Now let us ask how in this society any child's chances of belonging to the wealthy 5 percent might be determined. The state might decree that all children born into rich families should continue to be rich as adults, leaving the children of the poor as poor as their parents. The accident of birth, regardless of merit, motivation, or social contribution, would thus determine adult status. There would be absolute *in*equality of *opportunity,* for no child could either rise above his or her parents' position or fall below it.

Other methods of allocating wealth would be possible, of course. For example, lots might be drawn for all babies, assigning one of every twenty to the top group and the remainder to the bottom. This lottery would provide absolutely equal opportunity: each child would have exactly the same chance as every other child of ending up on the top or the bottom, regardless of the accident of birth. Or—to take another example—suppose that instead of a lottery there was a competition during the first twenty years of life, carefully ensuring that for those twenty years, all children had the same kind of upbringing, schooling of the same quality, and so on. At age twenty, everyone would be impartially graded on the basis of merit, ability, and promise. The top 5 percent would then be guaranteed their $1,000,000 per year for life, while the losers would start getting their $3,000. Provided that the children of the rich received no special advantages in those first twenty years, this system, too, would provide equality of opportunity, based on some measure of skills. In neither case, however, would the distribution of wealth change at all; in both cases it would remain intolerably unfair no matter how access to the wealth were determined.

A less extreme example is closer to the reality of modern American life. As of 1975–76, the American economy could not provide employment for about 7 percent of the population who were actively seeking work. At least another 10 to 15 percent were employed only at poverty wages or had given up looking for work or could find only seasonal or part-time work. In this economy, increasing equality of opportunity would not have any bearing on the fact that 17 to 22 percent of employable Americans could not earn a decent living. Unless the economy were changed, whenever one worker found a decent job, another worker would have to lose one.

We noted earlier that more than a quarter of all children live in families that earn less than half the median income. Truly equal opportunity for all children would change the present state of affairs by changing the way poverty and wealth are transmitted from generation to generation. But, by itself, equal opportunity would still leave a quarter of American children living in families without adequate resources. Unless jobs at a livable income are available for all, an equal opportunity to compete for the jobs that do exist can only reshuffle—not eliminate—inequalities of condition. Although the ideal of equal opportunity is regularly invoked to deal with the problems of poverty and deprivation, these problems are not problems of opportunity at all; they are problems of distribution.

Distribution of the rewards—as distinct from the opportunity to compete for the rewards—is far more unequal than our national self-image seems to imply. The top fifth of American families receives approximately 41 percent of all family income; the bottom fifth receives approximately 5.4 percent.[28] If income from tax-exempt bonds, capital gains, and other sources not reported to the Internal Revenue Service is also counted as income, the top fifth of families receives nearly 48 percent and the bottom fifth slightly less than 4 percent.[29] And census bureau studies, as well as studies using other data, reveal that this has been the pattern, with very little fluctuation, since the end of World War II.[30] Indeed, some economists are not sure the pattern has changed much since as far back as 1900.[31] What Americans often perceive as change is, sadly, a modest reshuffling.*

Not even the kinds of people at the top have changed very much. Surveys of the social background of American corporate leaders, government officials, and others of rank and wealth have showed that the vast majority are not poor people who achieved a meteoric rise to success [32]; instead, they were largely born to wealth and

---

* If wealth alone is counted—as distinct from income—the discrepancy between the affluent and the poor is most glaring of all: the top fifth of American families owns 60 percent of the nation's wealth, while the typical family in the bottom fifth has no assets at all.

44

status. A study done in 1974 found that of every 1,000 children born into the top tenth of social and economic status, 326 are still there as adults (and many others are not far behind), while only 4 of every 1,000 children born into the bottom tenth ever achieve incomes in the top tenth.[33] Although a slight majority (55 percent) of white males moves up the economic ladder during the course of a lifetime, the most common trends for women and blacks are no movement at all or movement downward.[34] And even the figures for those who move up are deceiving. As we observe in another of our Council books, "Typists become secretaries, unskilled laborers become operatives, but very few typists become executives (with their own secretaries), and very few laborers become foremen or managers." *

Although most Americans believe that the "progressive" federal income tax helps to make income distribution more even, here, too, the facts are another story. The structure of loopholes flattens out the theoretically higher rates for higher incomes. And these loopholes are not merely the esoteric tax shelters of the rich but everyday deductions that benefit most people above the median, such as deducting interest payments and real estate taxes. Moreover, the flat rates of social security taxes (up to a ceiling of $16,500) and of state and local taxes fall more heavily on the poor, who pay a higher proportion of their incomes than do those with more money.[35] Ironically, it turns out that only two groups pay a tax rate significantly different from that of the 90 percent of people in the middle: the extraordinarily rich, who tend as a group to pay a higher percentage of their income in taxes even with their liberal use of loopholes, and the extraordinarily poor, who, although they pay little or no federal income tax, still are taxed disproportionately every time they go to the corner store or the gas station.

Given the enormity of the forces that work against greater equality and mobility, the best evidence is that the effects of schooling on equal opportunity, much less equality of condition, are marginal. Large-scale studies undertaken in the late 1960's by James Coleman, and in the 1970's by Christopher Jencks and others,[36] have indicated clear limitations in what the schools can do. These studies are complex in methodology and have been criticized by other researchers, but their essential findings seem unassailable. School performance, Coleman found, is massively influenced by the social, economic, educational, and cultural background of the child. Jencks went on to add that success in later life as measured by the criterion of income bears almost no relationship to test scores or academic achievement, once the characteristics of the child's family have been taken into account. In short, the main factors that "predict"

* *Small Futures: Inequality, Children, and the Failure of Liberal Reform* a report of the Carnegie Council on Children by Richard H. de Lone. New York: Harcourt Brace Jovanovich, 1978.

45

where a child will eventually end up in the economic and social hierarchy are related to the accidents of birth—family income, parental education, race, and so on. These factors also appear to determine most of the differences among children in school performance, IQ scores, and years of schooling actually completed. Furthermore, Jencks states that a substantial portion of schooling's effect on success is a function of credentials, not of learning.

To describe in detail how ten, twelve, or sixteen years of schooling often work to perpetuate the status of birth is beyond the scope of this report.[37] But in essence, the process is one of informal and formal labeling, which many (perhaps most) children eventually come to accept as an accurate reflection of their intrinsic worth and adult destiny. One of the crucial roles of schools as they actually work in America is not to equalize opportunity but to sort and classify children for roles in a stratified adult world. In performing this task, the schools rely on family background as one strong indicator of the child's future—which amounts to telling him to expect a future like that of his parents.

To be sure, schools help a large number of Americans get ahead—by, for instance, teaching English and other skills that immigrants need to hold jobs, and by giving ambitious children models of teachers (and of the heroes in literature and history books) around which to build their own aspirations. Moreover, schools perform important work in passing along the heritage of culture and in helping human beings to develop lively interests. But as agents of economic change, schools may be necessary but they are not sufficient. Immigrants, for example, have benefited as much from labor unions, which opened up jobs and raised salaries, as they have from learning English in school. Schools tend to perpetuate the existing system of economic and social status, and they do so by heading most of their students toward the social and economic tracks of their parents. Some children will move up or down the social ladder, but not many of them will, and usually not very far. For too many—and schools help ratify this result—the rule is from rags to rags and from riches to riches.

The Importance of a Continuing Promise

Although equality of opportunity will neither eradicate poverty nor accomplish the major goal of redistributing goods and benefits, we believe along with most Americans that it remains an important social goal. Children's chances for a good life should not be prejudiced by the accidental fact that they are born into rich or poor, white or nonwhite families. It is not reasonable to expect that schooling *alone* can create equality of opportunity when equality does not exist in the world of jobs, of social relations, or of politics. But it is perfectly reasonable to expect schools to *contribute* to the goal of equal opportunity instead of perpetuating the status of birth. In a complex society certain basic cognitive skills are essential to effective participation, and whatever disagreement there may be about the other functions of schools, there is certainly a consensus that their job includes the teaching of these basic cognitive skills to all children, regardless of background. It is a slander on any child to think that he or she cannot learn the skills needed to participate effectively in society. If the schools set this standard in what they demand for themselves and expect of children, they can increase the opportunities open to the excluded even if they cannot themselves guarantee complete equality of opportunity.

Our conclusions about the scale and persistence of poverty and exclusion in America—and about the consequences for families and children—can be summarized in a few words. One child out of four in America is being actively harmed by a "stacked deck" created by the failings of our society. To try to change those children who are born unequal is to avoid the more important task of changing the structural forces that keep them that way. Schools, the institutions traditionally called upon to correct social inequality, are unsuited to the task; without economic opportunity to follow educational opportunity, the myth of equality can never become real. Far more than a hollow promise of future opportunity for their children, parents need jobs, income, and services. And children whose backgrounds have stunted their sense of the future need to be taught by example that they are good for more than they dared to dream.

3. The Technological Cradle

GUY BILLOUT

Society has always had its
technologies, whether the primitive
but essential technologies of
cultivation, pot making, and irrigation
or today's advanced technologies of
computers, petrochemicals, and
nuclear fission. What distinguishes the
modern society of the United States
from those of history and prehistory is
the pervasiveness, rapidity, and
centrality of technological change in
the lives of ordinary citizens.
Every aspect of the experience

of children and parents in the United States today is radically affected by inventions that did not exist in the time of our grandparents. Our sophisticated technology delivers once unimaginable benefits to to-day's families—from kidney dialysis machines to convenience foods, from the automobile to the pocket calculator, from no-iron children's clothing to the telephone.

Although the advantages of modern technology to families are enormous, there are also costs. In the last decades, Americans have become increasingly aware of the unexpected side effects of tech-nological change. Some thoughtful men and women now believe that the harm we risk for future generations outweighs the benefits of con-tinued innovation. For many, the pollution of the natural environ-ment and the specter of atomic warfare are generating controversial scenarios that show children in jeopardy from chemical destruction four generations hence, if not sooner from nuclear holocaust.

If parents have little feeling of control over the conditions that seem to fuel the divorce rate or the forces that determine family income, they feel even less control over the processes of technology that are so deeply embedded in our society. How can parents exert real influence over food chemists who create synthetic flavors, colors, and texturizers for the food their children eat? How can they know which technological decisions made today will have harmful con-sequences for their children when they grow up?

Specific technological innovations have an impact on families that is never simple, usually hard to foresee, and sometimes very substantial indeed. Henry Ford's Model T had a revolutionary effect simply by giving families unimagined ability to travel where and when they pleased. But the mass-produced automobile has also produced unlooked for side effects: traffic jams, tens of thousands of highway deaths and over a million injuries a year, routine city weather reports indicating that "air quality will be unsatisfactory to-day," and the emptying out from the inner cities of those who can afford to live in the suburbs.

It is no easy task to predict how far the ripples of innovation will spread and what they will touch. For example, among all the concerns stemming from air travel, no one anticipated that airport noise would have ill effects on the cognitive development of children in schools located nearby.[1] For another example, the perfection of the pasteurizing process for milk and the development of commercial formulas close in composition to mothers' milk are two factors that have reduced the proportion of mothers who breast-feed their babies.[2] Yet another example can be seen in the development of new contraceptive devices that make it possible, for the first time in history, to avoid unwanted pregnancies. Although this represents an extrordinary advance from the standpoint of children, some of these contraceptives pose potential dangers to the health of the mother, the fetus, and—way into the future—even the adult who once was that fetus.

In discussing the benefits and the risks of life in a society characterized by advanced technology, our approach is more tentative than the one taken in the two preceding chapters. Advanced technology is so new to human history that it is difficult simply to know what the problems are. Furthermore, science and technology are far afield from the traditional concerns of groups that think about children. Yet we believe that the influence of advanced technology on the power and autonomy of parents, and on the physical health and future social world of children, is an issue that Americans will have to consider far more seriously than they have to date.

The problems around this subject are complicated and controversial. We do not have answers to the questions we raise. But we cannot write a book about the future of children in the United States without somehow considering the impact that technology has and will have upon them.

Television

One technological wonder we have come to take for granted is the television set in the living room. Unknown to previous generations, this flickering family member now occupies more waking hours of American children's lives than either their parents or their schools. Experts and lay people differ about just what television is doing to children, but no one doubts that it is doing something. The average child spends between two and four hours a day in front of the set, and by the age of sixteen can expect to have watched from 12,000 to 15,000 hours of television—the equivalent of watching twenty-four hours a day for fifteen to twenty solid months.[3] At the end of one typical year, this same average child will have seen 25,000 commercials.[4]

Programs such as *Sesame Street* and *Zoom* have shown that TV can teach children specific skills. Television also exposes children to far wider horizons than most parents or schools can; there are wildlife, nature, and science programs, discussions of feelings, and even a few realistic portrayals of other children. It is no longer startling to hear fourth graders talking about politics and world events or to find eight year olds nagging adult smokers with statistics from the American Cancer Society's anticommercials.

But rare are the parents who do not worry over what television may be doing to their children, and their worries are founded in reality. For one thing, the United States is the only nation in the world where there is little programming for children on weekday afternoons.[5] After school, American children watch reruns of outdated cartoons and adult programs, which often include violent serials and situation comedies. Indeed, children in this country watch more "adult" programs than programs designed specifically for them, although they have none of the experience and perspective that could help them understand how inaccurately these programs represent the real world. Far from typifying any reality most children will ever grow up to see, the medium portrays a narrow range of characters who face agonizing and dangerous dilemmas that they are able to resolve in an hour or less. An extraordinary proportion of the people portrayed on television spend their time committing crimes, avenging crimes, or catching criminals. Where are the middle-level white-collar workers, the garbage collectors, the department store clerks? And although 51.3 percent of our population is female, in family and prime-time viewing periods less than a third of the characters are women.[6] Where are the single mothers and the women executives?

To be sure, public television provides some worthwhile alternatives, with presentations of cultural events and occasional discussions of controversial topics. Yet all too often, public television stations are crippled by a lack of funds that makes them dependent on corporate, foundation, and government donations—a kind of support that cannot help but influence, however subtly, the choice of what subjects are explored on the air. For their part, commercial outlets occasionally broadcast special dramatic programs and public affairs presentations. Recently, the situation comedies have shed their suburban split-level stereotypes, replacing them with more serious and realistic people in diverse social settings. Commercial television also has become somewhat less timid about introducing believable characters, such as women and blacks who speak and act with confidence and authority. *Roots*, the series that showed slavery from the black point of view, attracted the largest audience in television history.[7]

But whether public or commercial, more realistic programs raise anxieties of their own. Many parents fear that such programming exposes the young to values, problems, and situations—such as crime, sexual experimentation, and moral relativism—that children cannot or should not deal with at an early age. And although programs designed for children are purportedly framed in youthful terms, in fact most stress fast action and violence at least as much as adult fare does. A growing number of research studies shows a connection between active, violent programming and children's behavior—in particular between televised aggression and aggressive behavior.[8]

Programming is not the only worry. The United States is one of only three nations in the world that permit commercials on television programs designed for children,[9] and the commercials often sell products that parents disapprove of. For example, although nutritionists worry about the growing amount of sugar in children's diets, much TV advertising aimed at children is for candies and highly sugared products. Are children able to resist it? Arrayed against the normal intelligence of, say, an eight year old is a commercial production budget of up to $100,000 for one minute, enlisting the skills of motivational researchers, script writers, producers, directors, musicians, jingle writers, camera people, and cartoonists.[10] As consumer advocate Robert Choate testified in Senate hearings, "In the 1930's, mother . . . fended off aggressive door-to-door salesmen eager to get junior's ear. Today she is told to protect the innocent while 22 salesmen per hour beseech her child over the tube, disguised as the friendly folk of cartoon, jingle and adventureland." [11] It is scant consolation that the number of ads on children's programs has since been reduced from twenty-two to an average of eighteen to twenty per hour.

In the early 1970's $400 million was spent annually on TV advertising to children.[12] Approximately $80 million is spent annually on TV advertising by the processed cereal industry alone.[13] Within its overall TV advertising budget of $29.4 million, General Mills spends $5.4 million promoting one dry cereal, Cheerios.[14] According to nutritionists, Cheerios is one of forty cereals characterized by "empty calories"—calories with little useful nutrition.[15] Much advertising of breakfast cereals, candies, and other sugar-laden products takes place during a time slot that the industry sometimes refers to as "the children's ghetto"—the hours from 8 A.M. to 2 P.M. on Saturdays, when 50 percent of all American children in the age group between two and eleven are watching television.[16]

On the grown-up programs they watch, children see advertisements that express another powerful set of values. These ads seem to promise that for every ill there is a simple cure in a package at the supermarket, drugstore, or appliance dealer. The TV set—along with other advertising media to which children are less exposed— subtly implies that the frustrations of parenthood can be dissolved with headache compounds, that marriage can be improved by a good laundry detergent, that success is to be judged by new cars and expensive vacations.

Quite apart from worries about the content of programs and commercials, television raises another, even deeper set of anxieties among its critics. Glued to the screen for hours every day, the child may come to experience life in an unrealistic way—as a series of quick takes, constant excitements, incessant movements, instant resolutions. Reading and self-directed activities may thus be discouraged, and the number and quality of children's social relationships may suffer. For many children, more time in front of the television set means less time actively involved with their famiiles. Even mealtimes may suffer, with the traditional gathering around the dinner table being replaced by TV dinners on trays in front of the set. "The primary danger of the television screen," the psychologist Urie Bronfenbrenner has said, "lies not so much in the behavior it produces as in the behavior it prevents—the talks, the games, the family activities and the arguments through which much of the child's learning takes place and his [or her] character is formed." [17]

No one knows for sure how damaging these trends are, but it is hard for parents to be completely calm about their children's viewing when everything from juvenile delinquency to the decline in College Board scores is attributed to television watching.

Confronted with these worries, defenders of television accuse the critics of attempting to arrest technological progress, of yearning for an idealized and nonexistent past. New media of communication, they argue, are both inevitable and desirable. Television broadens our horizons, opening out into the living room a whole new world of experience. In any case the medium only reflects the demands of its viewers, who could, if they wished, stop watching or change channels in order to watch something else. The "choice" is said to be that of independent consumers, who get just what they want.

In some sense, of course, television does cater to the preferences of viewers. Year after year, the largest single audience of Americans is riveted by fast action and a good deal of violence. Not that there are no audiences at all for other programs. In the spring of 1976, for example, the public television production *The Adams Chronicles* drew an average audience estimated at 7,000,000 people,[18] about seventy times the size of a jam-packed crowd at the nation's largest public arena, the Rose Bowl. Yet even such an audience is small compared with the 27,000,000 people who watched a typical broadcast of the moderately popular NBC series *Police Woman* during the same season.[19] It is that mass audience which most television aims for, regardless of the preferences of other groups.

The reason television executives pay such attention to mass audiences is taken for granted by most Americans. Most television is commercial, dependent on advertising for its operating costs and profits. Commercial messages from sponsors pay for programming; sponsors want the largest audience possible; and networks provide them with shows that attempt to attract such audiences. If this usually means appealing to the lowest common denominator, so be it. But, as a result, much of the content of television shows is shaped, as historian David Potter put it, by people whose first interest is not in the communication itself, much less in its impact on children, but in the sales of whatever product they are advertising.[20]

Is it really a situation of free choice for consumers, when so much of the available television fare involves warfare, mayhem, arson, and murder? Are children autonomous and rational consumers, when they have been conditioned to expect so heavy an emphasis on one basic type of programming? Do parents voluntarily choose to have their children exposed to hundreds of brilliantly executed advertisements per week? Are we dealing here with free choices made by the consumers of television, or are we witnessing the manipulation and limitation of choice?

And how was it decided in the first place that broadcasting in the United States would be organized primarily as a commercial rather than a public medium? No iron rule of nature decrees that television has to be set up primarily to make money. Most other democratic nations decided in the early days of television that the medium's educational potential made it too important to entrust entirely to profit-seeking private enterprises.[21] Some chose entirely public television, others a public-private mixture.

The major problem with the American system of broadcasting is that nobody planned it. Whereas other nations set up commissions to study, design, and control the system (which not only shaped the initial arrangements but continue to evaluate and advise), in the United States government regulation came only as the result of industry's contentions that broadcast interference was intolerable, and that the government should act as traffic cop on the airwaves. The unique aspect of the development of broadcasting arrangements in the United States is that here the radio spectrum was already occupied by a large number of broadcast entities before government entered the picture. It was not entirely clear that advertisers would dominate the system as it developed, for the first broadcasters were manufacturers of radios, offering free programming to encourage the sale of sets. During the 1930's, when educators argued strenuously that time should be reserved for public service use, broadcasters replied that this would not be necessary. According to the public trustee concept, they accepted an obligation to provide public affairs programming. Moreover, their leaders promised that prime-time hours would not be used for commercial purposes.[22]

Television thus illustrates the mixed blessings of technological change in American society. It is a new medium, promising extraordinary benefits: great educational potential, a broadening of experience, enrichment of daily life, entertainment for all. But it teaches children the uses of violence, offers material consumption as the answer to life's problems, sells harmful products, habituates viewers to constant stimulation, and undermines family interaction and other forms of learning such as play and reading. How can the balance be struck?

The ways in which the defenders of television respond to its critics are also instructive. On the one hand, they appeal to the inevitability and advantages of technological progress; on the other, they argue that the alleged shortcomings of television are merely reflections of consumer preferences in a free market. In short, they blame the family—following a pattern we have seen before.

Our New Diet

Television epitomizes the Jekyll-Hyde nature of technological effects on families in a society where child rearing has fallen more and more to people and forces other than parents. A similar mix of benefits and costs is associated with the changing diet of American children.

Beyond question, the safety and quality of the food consumed by infants and children has improved enormously. Milk is no longer routinely contaminated; vitamin D supplements have eliminated rickets; modern food-processing techniques provide fresh or frozen vegetables year round; the productivity and inventiveness of food growers, processors, and sellers puts an adequate and nutritious diet within the reach of most American families and enables Americans to pay a smaller share of their income for food than citizens of any other country.

At the same time, however, the amount of chemical pollution and additives in the air, the water, and the food supply—in short, in the total diet of the average American child or adult—has markedly increased. Chemical additives in food recently reached an average of four pounds per person per year, double the level of a decade ago.[23] Gross food additive use also has doubled in the past fifteen years—from 400 million pounds in 1960 to more than 800 million today [24]—and it continues to grow. In 1973, about 1,300 chemicals were routinely added to manufactured food; by 1975, the figure had risen to more than 3,000.[25]

Some additives are useful preservatives; others are "cosmetic," designed to improve a food's taste, appearance, or texture—and salability. New research questions the safety of many of these additives. Most of them have never before been part of the human diet, and even when there is no sign of immediate damage, scientists are concerned that the cumulative effect of some chemicals could eventually cause chromosome breaks, which in turn might produce mutations, birth defects, and cancer.[26]

As if additives are not worrisome enough, the overall balance of nutrients in the American diet has changed in ways that seem likely to make today's children less healthy than they might be as adults. Although the decade from 1955 to 1965 was a period of rising income and increased consumption across all income lines, a ten-state nutrition survey showed that the proportion of American families with good diets actually declined from 60 percent to 50 percent.[27] There was a marked decrease in the per capita use of milk and milk products, grain products, potatoes, vegetables, and fruits and a distinct increase in the use of meat and fats (as opposed to poultry and fish, which are lower in saturated fat than meat.)* The high-salt, high-fat, high-sugar diet that is becoming more and more the American norm as been implicated in a growing list of chronic adult diseases and disabilities: hypertension, arterial disease, and degenerative changes in the pancreas, liver, and bone.[30]

What are parents to do? How can they know what to feed their children when they hear so many warnings about chemical contamination or when they learn that additives like cyclamates or Red Dye No. 2, which the Food and Drug Administration classified for decades as "generally recognized as safe," are banned as potentially unsafe? If parents become convinced that the diet "everybody" eats is not good for their children, how can they obtain healthier foods when the selection at most supermarkets is weighted to foods of doubtful value and their children are clamoring for the high-sugar foods advertised on television? Despite the variety of products in American supermarkets, it is a demanding exercise in label reading (and guessing) to put together a low-salt, low-fat, and low-sugar diet that is relatively free of additives. Parents may want to buy for their children's lunches a plain, pure soup—without cosmetic additives or flavor intensifiers—but a reading of the fine print on the can reveals few if any such prepared soups. Parents can make their own, of course (as long as they avoid prepared ingredients such as bouillon cubes or canned carrots), but how many have the time? Such worries are currently making healthy profits for high-priced health food

* Poor diet may be due as much to the choices of foods we make as it is to income.[28] Reviewing nutrition studies over the past two decades, researchers concluded that "infants from high socio-economic groups may receive less adequate diets than those from low socio-economic groups." This is due to the higher amounts of sugar and fat in processed foods, which the more affluent buy in larger quantities than the poor.[29]

stores—and even there, it is sometimes uncertain how "organic" the products sold really are.

The arguments pro and con about our new technological diet run parallel to those about television. Defenders of the new diet recall the perils of food in the past and define changes in the diet as progress. Agricultural scientists and food technologists, they argue, are constantly seeking better, safer, and cheaper foods. To challenge their results is to challenge the advance of scientific knowledge and the technological applications of that knowledge. The basic logic of our technological society is progressive. Once again, critics of the products of advanced technology are defined as romantics or reactionaries, as "food freaks" eager to turn back the clock to a time when food was truly hazardous.

A second defense of the new technological diet is also familiar. When nutritionists caution against the dangers of a sugary, salty, fatty, high-additive diet for the future health and vitality of today's children, representatives of the food industries reply that parents and children freely choose this diet and that food processors sell only what the public demands. If sugar-coated cereals, highly salted potato chips, and artificially flavored, colored, and textured snack foods stopped selling, food companies would stop producing them. If parents want to feed their children some other kind of food, they are always free to do so. Or so the argument goes.

This appeal to the laws of supply and demand and the sovereignty of the consumer leaves out some important elements in the overall equation. Take children's "choice" of high-salt, high-sugar foods. For many years, the baby-food industry routinely sugared and salted infant foods—not because babies have any taste or need for large amounts of salt or sugar, but because mothers who taste baby foods before feeding their infants are more likely to buy baby foods that taste like adult foods. One of the results of an early infant diet high in sugar and salt is an acquired taste for both—a taste that in later childhood helps perpetuate and increase the American "demand" for highly sugared and salted products.[31] This is not a common demand in cultures where infant foods are not sweetened or salted.[32] By contrast, American children consume needlessly high amounts of salt and sugar, with potentially dangerous results for their health in adulthood, and at the clear and immediate expense of their teeth.

Human food preferences and hence "demands" have always been learned. Normally they follow the traditional eating habits of the society where children grow up. Today, however, that learning has a new ingredient: vigorous, systematic conditioning by companies whose main purpose is to maximize their returns and increase their share of the market. When children's tastes have been at least partly conditioned in infancy, can food manufacturers, who help create the tastes in the first place, legitimately speak about the free choice of

58

children and the ability of parents to determine what their children eat?

The argument that our new diet merely reflects consumer preferences runs headlong into another indubitable fact—the active role of government, often in close alliance with food producers, processors, and sellers, in defining the food choices open to Americans. Government-sponsored research and education programs have played a vital role, of course, in raising agricultural productivity and spreading new technologies. If agricultural price-support programs have kept the prices of some foods high and thus discouraged consumption, at the same time laws excluding agricultural workers from minimum wage guarantees have kept down the prices of other foods, such as lettuce, grapes, and apples. Government has discouraged certain kinds of food production by paying farmers not to plant, and has sometimes used and sometimes ignored its extensive powers to license and regulate food processing for reasons of safety and quality. Government control of food imports and exports directly influences the scarcity or abundance, and hence the cost and consumption, of basic family foodstuffs such as grain and meat. Federal, state, and local governments have consistently influenced the market to achieve goals that market forces alone could not have accomplished. Whether or not we approve of these goals, government is playing a massive role in determining what we and our children can choose or afford to eat.

Given the early conditioning of children's tastes, and given the money spent in persuading children to pressure their parents to buy frosted cupcakes or salted corn chips, it is disingenuous to claim that consumer "choices" and children's "demands" entirely determine the diet of young Americans. It is at least as accurate to talk of demand that is manipulated and of choices that are restricted or manufactured.

Nuclear Energy

Since television and food so immediately affect the lives of all American families, advocates for children commonly seize on these issues as focal points of change. In contrast, the current debate over the use of nuclear power plants would seem to have a less direct connection with children. Few children have seen a nuclear reactor. Nuclear-generated electricity apparently runs the toaster just as well as electricity from other sources. Yet in their arguments both proponents and opponents of greater commitment to nuclear power frequently invoke children—often in the form of "future generations."

In some cases, the new energy technology does have immediate effects on children. Children in certain parts of New Mexico drink water containing levels of radioactivity that may accumulate to harmful levels in their tissues by the time they are adults.[33] The radioactivity comes from the wastes of factories processing uranium.

More often, however, the debate over nuclear power and children involves long-term effects—effects that will become evident only when children become adults and parents in their own right. Many critics of nuclear power are concerned about a slow, insidious increase in the level of background radiation in the environment, especially if the number of reactors should multiply as rapidly as some energy experts propose. Such radiation, they assert, might eventually threaten the genetic integrity of the human race. Other critics point to the danger of catastrophic breakdowns in nuclear power plants, which could conceivably produce fallout endangering thousands.

There is also the long-term problem of what to do with wastes that will remain radioactive for centuries. Because nuclear reactors produce uranium that can be reprocessed into weapons-grade plutonium, the proliferation of nuclear energy everywhere poses a serious threat to worldwide security. Some critics even argue that the domestic police forces necessary to prevent sabotage and the theft of nuclear materials in an age of widespread nuclear power would have to be so large that they would create a virtual police state.

Because solar energy provides an alternative, the critics conclude that we need not undertake the risks entailed in "going nuclear." In any case, they maintain, nuclear energy can never be more than a short-term option since our domestic supplies of uranium are limited. When we run out—whether in thirty years or one hundred —we would be faced with OUEC instead of OPEC, a poor exchange indeed. Further worries center on what we could do with outmoded nuclear plants, since their radioactive parts could not be consigned to conventional wreckers.

There is, of course, another side to this argument. Advocates of nuclear power claim that the dangers of reactor accidents have been greatly exaggerated and that present energy sources like coal and oil pollute the atmosphere far more dangerously than nuclear energy. Furthermore, at present rates of energy consumption stocks of oil and natural gas will be practically exhausted within a generation. Since the technology needed to harness solar power for electric generation has not yet been perfected, nuclear or coal-generated power are the best available alternatives, and nuclear power is safer and cleaner than coal. Precisely in order not to let our children and grandchildren down, we must adopt nuclear energy as soon as possible; otherwise we can hardly sustain our economy and our standard of living. If solar energy or another source is eventually harnessed for electricity, then nuclear energy will have provided a bridge that allowed us time to develop it.

If we listen with an open mind to both sides of this argument, what course can we choose for the good of our children? Choose to limit nuclear power, according to partisans on one side, and we will bequeath to our children a world without the means to warm itself, light its houses, or move its transportation. Choose to develop nuclear energy, say voices that are also persuasive, and we will unnecessarily endanger our children's lives.

The arguments used by proponents of nuclear power invoke two familiar premises. First, the new technology is inevitable, promising cheap, safe, and virtually limitless benefits at risks that are (or can be made) negligible. Second, this innovation is necessary to meet the "needs" of consumers: nuclear reactors are, in the end, merely a response to what the public demands. As we have already noted, these same arguments are brought forward in discussions of television and the new diet—indeed, they permeate the entire debate about the effects of new technology.

Other dilemmas of technology reach into every corner of family life. X rays, to take just one more example, have brought great medical benefits but also dangers that were underrated for a long time.[34] For years X rays were even used to fit shoes. How many similar risks are we taking today without knowing it?

In principle, many technological threats to the future of children can be anticipated and corrected. The Food and Drug Administration, thanks to a courageous staff member, banned the drug thalidomide before a great many American babies were born with the deformities that crippled large numbers of children in Europe and Japan. After sustained protest from a group of concerned parents (Action for Children's Television), the National Association of Broadcasters amended its code to stop TV stations from inserting sixteen minutes of commercials into every hour of weekend pro-

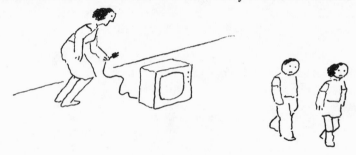

gramming for children when adult shows had three minutes less. The new limit set by NAB in 1974 was nine and a half minutes.

Yet for every technological side effect that is detected and modified, others surely are going undiscovered. The initial benefits of new technologies frequently are more apparent than the long-term drawbacks. The acceptance of technology outstrips the possibilities for systematic evaluation; technological growth outruns our present willingness to look carefully for possible adverse effects and our present ability to monitor and control such effects once they appear.

Two Myths: Technological Progress and the Laissez-Faire Economy

Why the lag? Part of the answer lies in the complexity of the issues themselves. But part lies in our unwillingness even to confront the problem, much less to try to resolve it. To explain this unwillingness, we need to look at two traditional myths that help obscure the existence of any problem at all.

One is the myth—one might well say the abiding faith—that enshrines technology as the engine of progress. For well over a century, our people have looked to machines, to invention, to the "practical arts" as the surest route to the Good Society and the Good Life.

Of course the founders of the republic had no inkling of the technological forces that would shape our modern America. Thomas Jefferson's vision of the future as belonging to sturdy yeomen-farmers reflected the common sentiment of his generation. However, even before Jefferson's death, the process of industrial development was well begun and gaining momentum. The establishment of the first "manufactories," the building of the Erie Canal, the launching of the first steamboat—this much was completed by 1825. The development of the steam locomotive, perhaps the single most vivid symbol of technological invention, followed within the decade. The Jeffersonian vision would never entirely disappear; indeed, a yen for the simple life and virtues of the countryside has survived as a nostalgic crosscurrent within the mainstream of our culture right down to the present day. But pride of place was rapidly claimed by technology. As early as 1831, one spokesman extolled this expression of man's triumph over nature in rapturous terms:

> Where [Nature] denied us rivers, Mechanism has supplied them. Where she left our planet uncomfortably rough, Mechanism has supplied the roller. Where her mountains have been found in the way, Mechanism has boldly levelled or cut through them. Even the ocean, by which she thought to have parted her quarrelsome children, Mechanism has encouraged them to step across. As

if her earth were not good enough for wheels, Mechanism travels it upon iron pathways.[35]

The power of technology to surmount natural barriers and boundaries has remained a central motif in American self-perceptions ever since. We have substantially defined ourselves by reference to this power, and we have encouraged other peoples around the world to think of us in the same way. To be an American has meant participation in a culture of triumphant self-assertion, of mastery within both the natural and social environment; and the means to this end has been, in large part, a distinctive national gift of technological ingenuity.

From the start, the strenuous commitment to technology was rooted in the vision of America as a land of plenty with limitless fresh air, abundant clear water, and plenteous food. The egalitarian values of the country seemed to require an economy of abundance, in which all people could express their particular energies and talents. The industrial revolution and the political revolution would thus go hand in hand; freedom from want was the necessary precondition for freedom of mind and spirit.

These beliefs served to mold a characteristically American version of the idea of progress. The country had embarked on a unique experiment in human betterment, and the ultimate prospect seemed dazzling. "It is an extraordinary era in which we live," said Senator Daniel Webster at ceremonies opening a new railroad in 1847:

> The world has seen nothing like it before. I will not pretend, no one can pretend, to discern the end; but everybody knows that the age is remarkable for scientific research into the heavens, the earth, and what is beneath the earth; and perhaps more remarkable still for the application of this scientific research to the pursuits of life. . . .
>
> The progress of the age has almost outstripped human belief; the future is known only to Omniscience.[36]

The wonderment, the pride, the extravagant hopes that Webster expressed have come down undimmed from one generation of Americans to another. Sometimes there was a hint of anxiety below the rhetorical surface, an echo of Webster's sense that events were moving so fast and so far that "no one can pretend to discern the end," but until recently our national faith in technology has remained strong. Many Americans, therefore, now receive the warnings of risk and danger inherent in our technological progress with a special sense of surprise, of indignation, and even of panic.

To move from faith to skepticism is difficult: we are asked suddenly to question what we have previously taken as given. The world of technology that pervades every aspect of our daily existence seems massively complex when we try to analyze it piece by piece. Our ignorance of the critical details, to say nothing of the underlying forces, feels unbearably profound; and even if we could design substantive plans for change, we may well doubt our capacity to implement them.

Most of us, most of the time, stand back from the technological dilemma. We have various strategies for reassuring ourselves, which in turn draw on still other elements of national myth. Consider, for example, our persistent tendency to assign responsibility and at times blame to those who are injured, or—if the victims are children—to those who care for them. It is the parents' responsibility to beware of the dangers and prevent them. *Caveat emptor*—let the buyer beware. If harm occurs, it is a result of the consumer's preference or failure to exercise proper caution. According to this argument, parents have no one to blame but themselves. And all too often, that is just what they do.

So deep is the belief in individual responsibility that some reformers and consumer advocates accept the same basic line of reasoning. The problem, they contend, is simply that consumers do not have enough knowledge. If parents had better information about nutrition, they would not feed their children sugar-coated cereals; if the alternatives to nuclear power were explored and demonstrated, voters would insist on safer energy-generating methods.

There is no doubt that American children can benefit from honest advertising, clear and full labeling, responsible evaluation of products, and better consumer education. These reform objectives assign ultimate responsibility to the consumer, where in some sense it belongs; but they rest on the assumption that the consumer is in control, or can readily become so, which does not accord with the facts. This assumption is a piece of a far broader American myth—the myth of the laissez-faire economy.

The laissez-faire idea was a reaction against earlier views that the crown or religion defined the common good and that self-seeking was the enemy of the public weal. ("Laissez-faire" essentially means "hands off.") Eighteenth-century liberals argued that the public interest cannot be achieved unless each citizen is free to pursue his or her own interests, subject only to the loosest possible legal constraints designed to protect the rights of others. Within a competitive market economy, they maintained, the impersonal operation of the laws of supply and demand would produce the greatest possible productivity at the lowest possible cost; thus the common economic good would drive out the bad. For example, when a householder considered the purchase of pins, he or she would decide between some that were uniformly straight, smooth, and sharp, and others that occasionally were bent, rusty, or dull. Superior merchandise would win the market competition as each individual strove to satisfy his or her needs by obtaining the best quality at the lowest cost.

Adam Smith, John Locke, and the others who developed this liberal doctrine were of course aware that people often behaved in ways that apparently ran counter to their own economic interests; but they attributed such behavior to occasional limitations of human rationality—for example, to people's ignorance of the real choices before them or to miscalculation of the consequences of their choices. Furthermore, the free market could hardly operate freely under the constraints of royal monopolies or laws restricting free trade. But such obstructions to rational choice were removable. The blinders of superstition could be lifted; people could be more fully informed and educated; the advantages of economic efficiency could be made apparent. State monopolies could be broken up, new laws could guarantee free trade. Human rationality, the prerequisite for the effective action of the free market, could thus be encouraged. Once people were able to calculate their own interests freely and accurately, everyone ultimately would benefit.

Popularized, simplified, and robbed of its original qualifications, the doctrine of laissez-faire became one of the key operating assumptions of American life. It provided an ideological justification for the expansion of the American capitalist economy in the nineteenth century. Economic self-seeking, once suspect, now was loudly praised. In economic life, not to act in one's own interest was to act in an economically "irrational" way—for example, not to sell at the highest possible price to the widest possible market, not to try to outdo one's competitors, not to minimize production costs by holding down wages. Such "irrationalities," if compounded, were said to threaten the entire structure of the market on which rested the common good.

The doctrine of laissez-faire also helped define the practical meaning of social responsibility in America as responsibility to one's self and family or, later, to one's corporation. Society had little need to define or protect any overall public interest that was not the sum of individual interests. It was widely agreed that those who interfered with the free exercise of individual self-interest were subverting the welfare of all—one cause, perhaps, of our tendency to sneer at "do-gooders." When the best way to help people is "minding your own business," *not* minding your own business becomes suspect.

The doctrine of laissez-faire reinforced an older idea that children were the exclusive responsibility of their parents. Even though children could not advance their own interests either economically or politically, and even when their interests could not be fully protected by their parents, the idea that government might intervene on their behalf ran headlong into the liberal view that the best government is the one that governs least. Government was expected to play a minimal role in family life. The state existed only to protect the basic rights of all citizens and to maintain the social and legal conditions necessary to the operation of a market economy; this meant enforcing the basic laws needed to ensure political stability, the integrity of the currency, and the observance of contracts.

The early liberals' image of a free market was suitable at best to a simpler society than our own—a society of individual sellers and buyers, producers and consumers, all interacting with roughly equal power. But early in the nation's life, corporations obtained the same legal status as individual entrepreneurs and thus became major actors in the marketplace. By the late nineteenth century, giant corporations had developed the capacity to prevent competition, to fix prices, to restrain free trade, and to influence "free" economic choices. Drawing on the liberal tradition, the Sherman Antitrust Act of 1890 was the first in a series of government acts designed to restore or preserve free competition and to prevent unfair pressures on small producers from larger ones.

One unifying goal of these governmental acts, up to and including the 1968 Truth-in-Lending Act, has been to restore the market of freely choosing individuals as envisioned by the early liberals. But the assumptions of laissez-faire, like the assumptions of technological progress as an unmixed good, have been eroded past all restoring by the build-up of new economic and social patterns. As we grope toward clearer understanding, it is time to recognize that these myths no longer help but hinder.

The Quandaries of Technology

In pointing to the quandaries for parents and children created by television, our new diet, or the debate over energy sources, our goal is not to show that technological innovations have made daily life more hazardous. The evidence suggests the opposite. But as we begin to realize that our world no longer fits the categories of technological progress and a laissez-faire economy, it is worthwhile to consider some emerging problems and some new approaches for solving them.

The same technology that creates new risks for American families has also vastly increased our capacity to detect risks. Modern techniques of testing chemicals permit the detection of some hazardous substances in heretofore unrecognizable quantities. The high technology that developed DDT was also able to find it in minute amounts in eggshells, the liver, and mother's milk, and then, through refined animal experimentation, to demonstrate that in high concentrations it could produce cancer. Accurate measurements of the upper layer of the earth's atmosphere have confirmed the theoretical suggestion that a common propellant in aerosol sprays, used in quantity, could reduce the ozone in that upper layer. From modern science come both the creation of monstrous atomic bombs and the discovery that the above-ground testing of these bombs was raising normal radiation levels, with an attendant risk to the genetic integrity of future generations.

The improved measurement of risk is not limited to areas of new discovery. The traditional natural flavoring in root beer has been shown to have cancer-producing properties; today's root beer, therefore, is artificially flavored and safer. Modern epidemiological research first pointed to the close association between smoking and several forms of cancer and heart disease. Medical research has shown that lead arsenate, once a common food additive, is highly toxic.

Part of our sense of hazard in connection with technological society springs from this improvement in our ability to assess a broad range of environmental risks. But to an unknown degree, the proliferation of new products may jeopardize us beyond even our growing capacity to measure and prevent our jeopardy.

As our understanding of risks and our capacity to measure them has increased, so has our insistence that we control them. Risks from unsafe design, which twenty years ago were considered simply part of buying an automobile, are now regarded as intolerable. The risks associated with bad air, water, foods, and food additives were scarcely considered a generation ago; now they must be carefully assessed. With many childhood diseases virtually eliminated, medical science turns to evaluating the synergistic effects of stressful and toxic environmental exposures on our children.

Living in a modern technological society raises our aspirations. In discussing changes in family life, we noted that families today rightly expect a level of health care that was not possible a century ago. A parallel process has occurred, justifiably we believe, in other areas. The list of "unacceptable" risks grows longer even as in some ways our lives grow less hazardous. While apparently protected from the traditional dangers of natural disaster, famine, and contagious disease that preoccupied earlier societies, we are concerned with even subtler and at times more elusive hazards; we fear that our growing powers over nature may—through greed, ambition, error, or poor judgment—unleash new forces that will destroy us all.

A second problem lies in the social costs of production. All production has costs to the producer—for example, such obvious internal costs as supplies, labor, rent, and heat. Social costs are harder to calculate and not always easy to attribute directly to the producer. The classic example is a factory that discharges its wastes into a river. Alone, the wastes might be dissipated; joined with the wastes of other factories, they leave the river polluted. Each producer can claim that its discharges are not responsible for the damage. Yet those who would fish or swim in the river or drink its waters are prevented from doing so.

In a pure laissez-faire economy, stopping pollution is difficult or impossible. Clearly, public intervention is called for, either to require producers to pay for the social costs of their production (for example, by a "pollution tax") or else to pass laws that forbid pollution. In either case, the previously external costs have been converted into internal ones, so that the producer must now take account of the social cost on the company's own balance sheets. An economy left to itself will not force that result.

A third problem is assessing risk. Innovation makes risk inevitable. A new product may itself be hazardous or have bad secondary effects; the process of production can injure workers or others; the research that leads to innovation can be dangerous to the public. A new food additive may enhance taste but produce cancer; a new drug may be effective against its target bacteria but destructive to healthy cells as well; a supersonic airplane may provide extremely rapid transportation but deplete the ozone layer of the atmosphere.

It is not possible to live without risk. To be among friends is to risk contagion, to drive is to risk highway death, to heat one's home is to risk fire. The problem is to assess the risk, to minimize it, and to estimate the trade-off between risks and benefits. The risk of catching a serious disease from friends is usually minute by comparison with the pleasures of sociability. But sometimes the risk is greater—when one member of the party is known to have an infectious disease, for example. And sometimes the risk is so great that the appropriate response is quarantine. Under some circumstances, even higher risks are worth taking: for example, chemotherapy for cancer damages healthy body cells as well as cancerous ones, but this risk is outweighed by the possibility of arresting an otherwise lethal disease.

In the past, the assessment of risks has been largely a matter of personal judgment, well within most people's ability. But today large new areas have emerged where common sense and tradition no longer serve as a guide. The issue of nuclear power plants is a case in point. Understanding the risks of nuclear power generation requires highly specialized knowledge. Weighing these risks against the benefits of nuclear power and comparing the entire equation to the risks and benefits of alternate power sources is even more complex. Both tasks are now beyond the range of ordinary citizens.

The nuclear power issue is but one of thousands where modern technology requires specialized knowledge to assess risk. Where public safety is at issue—as it usually is—the marketplace cannot be counted on to prevent unnecessary risks, for it works too slowly, and at times only after irreversible damage has occurred.

In an era when tens of thousands of new products appear each year and technology has advanced to the point where the risks have reached almost incomprehensible magnitude, the assessment of risks cannot be left to individual producers and consumers. Producers, even when they have the technical resources to judge risk, also have a vested interest in understating the dangers of potentially profitable products. And no consumer, no matter how great his technical expertise, can hope to evaluate the potential dangers in all the new products he faces each year. Clearly, then, the evaluation and control of risks must be a government responsibility.

In the relatively simple world envisioned by the early liberals, the primary objective was to eliminate the tyrannous powers of state monopolies and restrictions; once this was achieved, the consumer met the producers on terms of rough equality. The buyer could tell a rotten apple, a leaky roof, a bent pin. If dissatisfied, he took his business elsewhere and told his friends to avoid the producer.

Today, the independent competitive entrepreneur vending apples, renting a cottage, or selling pins has receded before the modern corporation. The individual consumer, of course, retains the right not to buy what the corporation produces, but he or she no longer faces the corporation as an approximate equal. In some industries, such as oil, prices are more or less fixed, either by impliict understandings among producers or by direct government edict. The consumer no longer faces an individual entrepreneur; instead he confronts the consumer relations department of a vast corporation. Furthermore, one mistake by one corporation can affect—sometimes threaten—the lives of thousands or even millions of consumers. For the consumer to confront the corporation on fair terms requires government mechanisms and institutions not included in the simple maps of the world of laissez-faire.

Faith in technological progress and a laissez-faire economy was born in a world of apparently unlimited resources. Since then, regulation has gone a long way toward altering the original laissez-faire model in the United States, although we recognize the changes all too dimly. At the same time, we are beginning to catch a glimpse of the limits to expansion.

It is clear that both the market and the regulators need to plan better. For better planning, a first ingredient is better information. For example, we do not currently have a catalogue of all fossil fuels that are known to exist or what the cost of recovering them would be. We do not know enough about the risks and possibilities of nuclear energy or solar energy. This lack of information makes it difficult to allocate resources wisely, whether in a laissez-faire or a planned economy.

Many of our policies—particularly our energy policy—have not been well planned. But in the social and economic environment of today's families, the need for coherent planning and public policies that relate to planning becomes inescapable. In short, if the government is going to interfere in the operation of the market, as it regularly does in the production of energy, its interference should reflect the most careful possible assessment of the public interest.

Groping Toward Solutions

These comments should make it clear that we do not view the problems of children in a society characterized by high technology as easy to resolve. Like most people today, we are of two minds about the advanced technology that shapes our lives. On the one hand, we enjoy it, use it to extend our powers, welcome the protection it has so far given us against a host of age-old dangers. But on the other hand, we realize that we all face new dangers, created by the very manmade technologies that in so many ways free and empower us. Safe as our daily lives may be compared to those of our grandparents, we live in a world where our national security is premised on a "balance of terror" involving atomic weapons that could destroy life on our earth. This paradox lies at the heart of our ambivalence about advanced technologies.

In the end, the fate of children depends on our ability to use technology constructively and carefully. The connection of children and technology is not simply a matter of seat belts, safe toys, safe air, water and food, additive-free baby foods, or improved television programming. These are all important issues, but to stop here is to forget that today's children will soon be adults. Technological decisions made today will determine, perhaps irrevocably, the kind of physical and social world we bequeath them and the kind of people they become. If the worst fears of the critics of television should be realized, our children would become mindless seekers of sensation, violence-prone illiterates. If the darkest worries about diet should prove true, our children would grow up laden with harmful chemicals and vulnerable to serious diseases. If the predictions of those who oppose nuclear power should be accurate, our children would, as adults, absorb radiation from the atmosphere, risk disaster from reactor breakdowns, and live under conditions of restrictive security needed to protect nuclear materials from theft.

None of these predictions need come true, and we trust that none of them will. In part, we must rely on the good sense of concerned citizens and on persistent efforts to inform them better. In part, we must have corporations with a high sense of social responsibility, even when the exercise of that responsibility produces no new profits or increases in the rate of corporate growth. And, most important, we will need to extend public vigilance through old and new agencies of government to minimize social costs, to assess better the risks of innovation, to regulate and control the risk of technological change, and to plan for the long-term future of society.

We have no magic formulas to guarantee any of these outcomes, but we are encouraged by the vigor of the consumer movement and unperturbed by its occasionally strident tone. We applaud the social responsibility of corporations that go beyond a concern for corporate image and public relations. And above all we approve the creation of effective government agencies to consider, assess, and guard against the hazards to coming generations of our often blind faith in advanced technology.

We conclude that educating parents about the risks of advanced technology is important, but not enough. By itself, consumer education assigns all responsibility to those whose children are harmed by innovations; it neglects the fact that no parent alone can possibly know enough to limit the risks of technology for children; it keeps us from the really important task of devising social institutions that can protect future generations from the hazards of the manmade environment. With technology as with family change and exclusion, blaming parents—and making them the focus of change—stands in the way of changing the society that largely determines the shape of family life.

Part Two

What Is to Be Done

The aim of a life can only be to increase the sum of freedom and responsibility to be found in every [person] and in the world.

Albert Camus
Resistance, Rebellion, and Death

4. Premises for Change

In the next chapters, we
move from analysis to an attempt
to open debate on solutions.

Since more than 98 percent of all
children in the United States
live with one or both of their own
parents, supporting the next
generation means, above all,
supporting today's parents. In any
foreseeable future, we believe,
the overwhelming majority of
American children will be—and
should be—brought up in families.
Children need adults who are
deeply attached to them, who

know them so intimately that they can distinguish a cry of hunger from a cry of fatigue and respond appropriately. Children need adults who will stick with them not because they are paid to but because they have a profound sense of commitment and love.[1]

This commitment is as common to single-parent families as to families with both a father and a mother. Such bonds can and do form in communes and foster homes and day-care centers. They often form between children and sympathetic neighbors or friends. Sometimes these relationships are essential, for there are always a few parents who find themselves unable to care for their children and others who have children before being able to feel truly responsible for them. Equally important, but less noted, is that some children are more difficult than others to care for, demanding a degree of patience, devotion, and responsiveness that only a few parents can muster. What is missing in such cases is the unconscious accommodation of needs and interests that normally bind parents and children together. The result is a mode of family life frustrating and destructive to parents and children alike. There will always be extreme situations where, no matter how much external support is provided for the family, the safety of the child requires removal and placement elsewhere. But the extreme cases are a tiny minority that, with more sensible public support, could be even smaller.

Despite the long-term reduction in familial roles and functions, we believe that parents are still the world's greatest experts about the needs of their own children. Virtually any private or public program that supports parents, effectively supports children. This principle of supporting family vitality seems to us preferable to any policy that would have the state provide children directly with what it thinks they need.

Our policy proposals depart from those traditionally advocated on behalf of children, for we do not focus primarily on services for children or on programs designed especially for "needy" children and families. Instead, we believe the goal of public action should be to change the context in which all families live, so that parents and children are freer to exercise their best instincts about the process of growing up. To this end, we propose that the nation develop a family policy as comprehensive as its defense policy.

In our concern with issues that are raised by forces largely beyond the direct control of individuals and families, we are not trying to let parents off the hook or make them feel they are not responsible for their children. If parents have the power to do so, we believe that most of them will accept the long-term responsibility of caring for and supporting their children. By eliminating factors that undercut family life and make it hard for parents to function as parents, we are trying to create an environment where a truly responsible job of raising children becomes something that can reasonably be expected from all.

Parenthood is deeply rewarding, but it is not easy and it is not cheap. We believe that those who choose to bear children must be expected to support and care for them, barring unexpected catastrophes. Programs that provide income support for families must also find effective (and nonpunitive) ways of ensuring that all parents, including those unmarried, separated, or divorced, contribute a fair share of their children's financial support. Today, far too many parents are unable to accept the full responsibilities of parenthood because there are no jobs or supports for them, or the jobs they can find do not pay a living wage. As we begin to remove these external barriers to parental responsibility, we can and should expect more of parents.

One way of reading the meandering history of social policy in the United States is to note the slow, erratic, but nonetheless definite trend toward broadening the definition of the basic rights of all Americans. The Constitution guarantees such freedoms as speech, religion, and assembly. In the nineteenth century, free public education became the right of all children. During this century, still other rights have been established, such as the right to a livable income in retirement (social security), the right to public compensation during periods of unemployment (unemployment insurance), the right to protection against the consequences of injuries incurred during work (workmen's compensation), and the right to a childhood without the burden of heavy wage work (child labor laws). Few of these basic rights have been fully extended to every segment of the population. But the trend toward broadening the basic rights of all citizens seems clear.

This concept—sometimes known as universal entitlement—contrasts with another principle of public policy which we have repeatedly found to be unsound—the concept of special programs for special people. (One observer has called them poor programs for poor people.) They are targeted at specific groups implicitly or explicitly defined as inadequate, who deserve help not by right but only because of the humanitarian kindness of the donors and only so long as the recipients demonstrate their worthiness, gratitude, and compliance. These programs—of which welfare is the classic example—stigmatize their recipients and commonly subject them to special investigations, tests, requirements, and restrictions. In the short run, special programs for the poor may remain necessary, but the long-range goal of family policy should be to include their recipients in programs that are universal.

With special reference to children, we believe it is time to make the principle of entitlement include access for every family to the resources that all families today need. This does not imply that the public has to pay for all these resources. Currently a good many families, at least most of the time, can afford to pay from their own incomes for all or most of the help and services they need, providing those are available. As we will later explain, in an economy which provided parents with adequate jobs as well as income supports for those unable to work, even more American families could afford to pay the full cost of essential child-rearing resources.

Our nation's professed belief in the importance of the family has not been matched by actions designed to protect the family's integrity and vitality. Although the sanctity of the family is a favorite subject for Fourth of July orators, legislators rarely address the question of how best to support family life or child development. We have no comprehensive system to guarantee adequate health care to families, as Canada and many European nations do. We offer inadequate income supplements to families, yet families bear the financial burden of rearing the young, who will make the future society in which we all have a stake. We have few programs or plans to help those who wish to be both parents and workers. We have been slow to improve the lives of parents who have suffered discrimination because of their color, and we have kept in positions of low earning power and prestige the people who most often care for children, namely women. We rarely even consider the effects of other national policy decisions on the lives of families and children. In brief, we have no explicit family policy but instead have a haphazard patchwork of institutions and programs designed mostly under crisis conditions, whether the crisis is national in scope (such as a recession) or personal (such as the break-up of a particular family).

We are not recommending that the nation abandon programs that try to relieve the harm done to families and children. In the short run, these are extremely important to the families they help. But we need to understand that the system will continue to produce victims faster than we can salvage them, until we move toward changing those deeper forces that are causing the damage.

Where is change most important? Earlier, we described the profound forces that limit real choices for parents. Change must begin in employment and income, family support services, and the law. In the chapters that follow, we hope to further national debate by recommending in these areas some possible solutions to the problems of families. In keeping with our view that a family's economic position is the single most powerful determinant of the opportunities open to families and to children, we support above all national policies to help equalize the impact of economic forces on our entire

citizenry. This will take a commitment to creating jobs and achieving full employment, so that no American child will suffer because a parent cannot find work or earn enough to provide a decent living. It is vitally important for children that their parents have the self-esteem and the wherewithal that a decent job and decent income provide. To make such a full employment policy meaningful for minorities and women, we must maintain and expand vigorous equal employment opportunity programs, beginning with strong leadership and enforcement at the federal level. To be consistent with a continuing national commitment to parents' responsibility for raising children—and most particularly to respond to the needs of the many single and married women whose financial contribution is necessary to the well-being of their children—we support a significant new push for more flexible and family-conscious work practices: flexible scheduling, part-time work, and time off for child rearing. Further, we support a revised and comprehensive back-up program of income supplements for the reduced number of parents who cannot work or who choose to stay at home and raise young children, so that no child or family in America is deprived of the basic physical necessities of life.

Second, we support a revised range of comprehensive and universally accessible public services to support and strengthen—not to replace—families in the rearing of their children. We have in the following discussion chosen to focus on the general dimensions of services for families, and on health care. Finally, we discuss and recommend some new kinds of attention to the statutes and regulations that protect or circumscribe American families.*

We have deliberately omitted a discussion of the importance of public education in the lives of children, for several reasons. In spite of its failings, schooling is the oldest and best established of "family services"; it is the function that families first turned over to public institutions. Its funding and governance are now firmly in the public domain, and its role in the lives of children has been thoroughly examined and debated in recent years. Second, while we share the public concern for many educational issues, we have come to believe that other forces operate at least as powerfully to determine a child's life chances; it is on questions of income, health, and family supports that much of a child's early development and later success will turn. For many years, schools have been seen as the primary agent of opportunity and equity in this society. But if we are to provide lives of dignity and stability for all children and families in this country, we must look beyond schools to other social and economic forces and institutions.**

In the pages that follow, we speak almost entirely of government actions. Government alone can no more solve all the problems of American families than it can share their pleasure in each other's company at the dinner table. But it can do some very important things to affect what happens at that table—much more than it is doing now.

---

* In many of our observations and recommendations, we have found ourselves part of an emerging consensus reflected in particular in the investigations of the Family Impact Seminar in Washington, D.C., in *Toward a National Policy for Children and Families* by the National Academy of Sciences (1976), and in *Here to Stay: American Families in the Twentieth Century* by Mary Jo Bane (Basic Books, 1976).

** The issue of how schooling functions to supply the labor force, and what impact this has on children, is discussed at length in *Small Futures: Inequality, Children, and the Failure of Liberal Reform*, a report of the Carnegie Council on Children by Richard H. de Lone. New York: Harcourt Brace Jovanovich, 1978.

5. Jobs and a
   Decent Income

The single most important factor that stacks the deck against tens of millions of American children is poverty. Other things being equal, the best way to ensure that a child has a fair chance at the satisfactions and fulfillments of adult life is to ensure that the child is born into a family with a decent income.

The traditional American view, as we have argued, is to see the excluded as ultimately to blame for their exclusion, and to place our hopes for a more just society on reforming and changing individuals, especially through schooling. But unless we also confront the economic deprivation that we now know to lie behind much of this exclusion, many of the billions of dollars we today spend on remedial, corrective, or compensatory programs for those who bear its scars will treat the symptoms, not the cause, of a deeper disease. We must also attack the causes of the deprivation—the lack of jobs for those who can, should, and want to work, and the lack of a minimal income for those who cannot work, or should not have to, and even for many who do. If our society is determined that the family is to remain the basic institution for rearing children, and if all children are to have a chance to develop and use their potential, then it is necessary for the economic status of American families to be more secure.

In this chapter we propose a combined program of jobs and income supports which would require that parents able to work do so and which would assure a decent, if modest, net income for all families with children. This plan guarantees a job to all heads of households and provides income supports for those who either cannot work or whose job opportunities, even with a job guarantee, fail to produce an income adequate to family needs. It views the care of young children as a legitimate work choice for parents and assures a "living" income to a parent who makes that choice. And it is addressed to the needs of all American families and children, not merely those who are stigmatized as inadequate by the fact of their unemployment or poverty.

Full Employment

Most Americans work for their living and prefer it that way. It could scarcely be otherwise in a society so firmly rooted in the work ethic. Indeed, in any society, work and human dignity are inseparable. Earning a living is virtually synonymous with being defined as an adequate person, and failure to earn a decent income has adverse effects on the adults themselves, on their ability to be effective, caring parents, and on their children's image of them and of themselves. Unemployment, low wages, and discriminatory barriers to employment that affect parents are directly translated into harmful effects on their children. Young children, whether or not they understand what their parents do, form an impression of whether the work world esteems their parents. A parent does not have to say a word to communicate a feeling of helplessness, powerlessness, worthlessness, or futility to a child. Everything we know about children suggests that, to a substantial degree, they grow up to think of themselves in relation to the world much as their parents do. When children absorb their parents' sense of worthlessness or powerlessness, they often exhibit what psychologists call "low self-concept." Low self-concept is often viewed as a strictly individual pathology caused by the "failures" of the family; we believe that more often it is caused by the pathology of the labor market.

With children in the forefront of our minds, therefore, we believe that a family policy in the United States must provide *all* parents with the opportunity to choose employment at decent wages, and that jobs must be flexible enough to take into account certain fundamental demands of family life. Parents who might be restricted to full-time child care if they had to live by the ordinary demands of the familiar forty-hour week should be able to find at least minimally satisfying part-time jobs or jobs on flexible schedules. It is consistent with almost any interpretation of American traditions and values to insist that parents' efforts to secure an adequate income for their family not be thwarted by the brute fact that there are no jobs for them.

The goals of a jobs component of a family policy must be to make employment available, fair, and humanly possible—available, that is, to anyone who wants it, open at every level to *all* groups of Americans, and accommodating enough so that it is possible for adults to work at the same time that they are being parents. (Flexible work practices are further explored in Chapter 6.)

We do not believe that the entire task of reinforcing deficient incomes can or should be accomplished by giving parents jobs; we also recommend below policies aimed at reducing some of the inappropriate pressures on parents to seek employment outside the home. Jobs are, of course, only one component of a sound family policy. But the denial of jobs to people who are ready, willing, and able to work is a tragic waste of their potential and of the social and economic benefits their work would produce for the society. When families enjoy economic security from productive work, the social dividends reach far into the future, when children reach adulthood and can make their own contribution.

We believe that with conscious and sustained effort it would be possible, over the next decade, to combine a full-employment strategy with a system of income supports so as to yield almost all American families with children a minimum income of at least half the current median in any given year—the line most Americans consider the true poverty line. To be effective, both parts of this program must work together: full-employment strategies must be combined with income supports, for each one of these reaches certain families that the other cannot.

Since World War II, this country has frequently tolerated a rate of unemployment far too high, often well above that of other industrial democracies. The heavy penalty this imposes on great numbers of Americans, as we have said, can mark their children for the rest of their lives.

Who is "unemployed"? There is, of course, the obvious group of people seeking jobs and unable to find them, officially estimated at 7.3 percent of the labor force in January, 1977. The actual figures, however, tell only a small part of the story. Official unemployment at any time counts only those willing and able to work who have sought work in the last four weeks and were employed less than one hour in the previous week. Many more are willing and able to work but have been discouraged from seeking jobs by outright discrimination or lack of opportunities.

Defining the ideal of truly full employment is tricky. To begin with, there is always bound to be a certain amount of what economists call "frictional" unemployment as firms go out of business, seasonal jobs dry up, or workers search for different jobs. Second, if the number of jobs increases far beyond the number now considered to be in the labor force, the size of the labor force would also be likely to increase as people currently not seeking work were encouraged to do so by the increased ease of finding work.

Should a full-employment program predicated on the right to a job guarantee jobs to second—or third and more—job seekers in a given household? This would be a gargantuan task for the nation to undertake. To be realistic, and since heads of household are the one group of earners most relevant to families with children, we have limited our proposals specifically to that group.

The United States should make it a goal of the highest national priority to reduce unemployment for heads of households to 1 or 1½ percent. When unemployment for heads of households reaches the 1-to-1½-percent range, the general unemployment rate must come down as well, probably to something in the range of 3½ to 5 percent.

Even with unemployment down to these levels, there will still be parents from time to time and place to place who want to work to support their families but cannot find jobs in the marketplace. These are most likely to be low-skill, low-income workers, always the most vulnerable to unemployment and its damages. Therefore, we believe that the United States must back up its commitment to children and families with a second plank in its full-employment policy: namely, to provide publicly guaranteed work for at least one parent in every family that contains a child—work that is safe, stable, full-time, and at wages no lower than half the average wage for full-time industrial workers for that year.

In late 1974, the average such wage was about $184 a week, or nearly $9,600 a year.[1] Half this wage, which is what we propose as a minimum for these back-up jobs, would be $4,800—that is, $92 a week or $2.30 an hour, which is the current minimum wage. In a strong full-employment labor market such as we had in the late 1960's, there is not a tremendous call on this back-up, but it should be available to any family head who has been without employment for over three months.

Literally millions of American children would be affected if national policy took this definition of full employment seriously. In concert with an income-supplementation policy as described below, full employment would mean that virtually no child in

America would grow up in a family with significantly less than the amount of money required to "get along."

It is very clear that the federal government is able to make choices that drastically affect the number of jobs available in the nation. Its tools for reducing unemployment consist in large part of fiscal and monetary policies that put more money into circulation, either by lowering taxes or by borrowing money to increase federal expenditures. The greater purchasing power that is produced by increased government spending indirectly creates more jobs. We are not recommending greatly increased deficit spending on a permanent basis. At full employment, or at the approximation we have established as a goal, the government will be taking in more taxes to cover expenditures. We do, however, advocate deficit spending when the economy is operating far below capacity, as it was in 1976.

Government can also increase employment by designing tax policies that give businesses an incentive to hire more people; it can undertake economic development programs; and, finally, the government itself can simply create more jobs in such areas as preventive health and protecting the environment—which is, of course, the most direct use of federal spending to lower unemployment.

Current policy includes elements of all these approaches but seldom if ever in the cause of achieving full employment and never on a wide, interlocking scale. Fiscal policies to stimulate private-sector demand, such as the 1975 tax cut, typically are adopted only in times of recession. Their contribution to a full-employment economy is offset, over time, by their equal and opposite countermeasures —fiscal and monetary policies that curb any resulting inflation by increasing unemployment. Furthermore, such measures by themselves in no way ensure improved allocation of jobs to areas of chronic unemployment, such as the inner cities. On the record so far, the best the Keynesian "new economics" can offer is not a full-employment policy but a seesaw employment policy, helping check cyclic ups and downs in the economy by trying to keep unemployment neither too far above nor too far below the rate considered "normal," which is too high to meet our criterion for a full-employment economy. This is not to suggest that fiscal, monetary, or tax policies do not have an important role to play, but simply that by themselves they are not an adequate approach to full employment.

Another means through which government can and ought to encourage fuller employment is economic development programs to increase available work in areas where there are high concentrations of unemployed persons, such as the inner cities. In such programs, government creates incentives for new industry to move in and establish an ongoing operation that will be self-supporting.

But probably the most direct way to reduce unemployment, and one of the most effective, is the creation of jobs by government action. This can take many forms, from laws and regulations that encourage self-employment to federal grants for school districts to hire consultants. To many people, "job creation" smacks of leaf-raking and boondoggling. But in fact, one student of such programs has remarked that the most successful job-creation program in American history is operated by the Department of Defense.[2] In addition to employing millions of soldiers, sailors, and marines, the Department of Defense hires hundreds of thousands of civilians as part of its management and planning functions. Contracts for the production of military goods and materials, for weapons research, and for "basic research" that might eventually lead to military applications have directly provided millions of jobs to Americans, and have indirectly stimulated the entire economy. So it is clear that the public sector already operates enormous numbers of programs that have a job-creating and employment-stimulating effect. For example, the decision to divert federal taxes on gasoline to the Highway Trust Fund, which in turn underwrote the construction of the interstate highway system, used public tax monies not only to build roads but to support a vast construction industry, with indirectly stimulating effects on the steel industry, the concrete industry, the automobile industry, engineers, surveyors, planners, and so on.

Controlling Inflation and Costs

Obviously, there is a tremendous reserve of unused human and productive potential in this country. In wartime, the vast reserves of unemployed, many of whom are currently considered "unemployable" or difficult to train, have been swiftly mobilized and redefined as productive and essential. We believe it is possible to mobilize these same reserves to meet the tremendous backlog of domestic needs for public service, preventive health care, child care, environmental protection and clean-up, and for rebuilding the urban core—needs surely as vital to the welfare of this country as spending for war or the possibility of war. But the nation has been deeply reluctant to do this, primarily out of fear of severe inflation.

In classical economic theory and in government practice, it has long been assumed that if unemployment is allowed to rise, inflation will drop. Recent years have shown this to be a highly questionable assumption. Both inflation and unemployment have been high, defying the "law" that unemployment provides a brake on inflation.

Furthermore, barring the catastrophe of a runaway inflation that leads to the collapse of markets and organized economic activity, the damage that inflation does to families and children is not comparable to the damage done by unemployment. Most parents depend on current earnings for all or most of their incomes, and those earnings generally keep close pace with prices. So long as they can find steady employment, family heads as a group are not likely to suffer anything worse than a temporary, fractional loss of purchasing power during a prolonged period of rising prices (and wages). A permanent and deliberate policy of less-than-full employment, on the other hand, places the lion's share of the lost purchasing power —with all its attendant human costs—selectively on those families who are least able to compete for available jobs. These include a large proportion of low-wage parents, often unprotected by unemployment insurance, with particular concentration on women, blacks, and other minority groups.

Obviously we cannot pursue the goal of full employment without devoting the closest attention to keeping inflation within reasonable bounds. But we stress that a full-fledged effort at full employment has never been tried. We are confident that if full employment is their primary goal, the leaders of labor, finance, industry, and government can combine their collective wisdom with the analytic skills of economists and our enormously sophisticated computer systems to devise means to restrain the upward spiral of wages and prices without violating the basic freedom and flexibility in our economic system. We urge that this kind of major effort be made to develop, test, and perfect regulations and administrative structures that can effectively control inflationary pressures by some means other than rising unemployment. Planning and controls—voluntary or mandatory—may be necessary, but these possibilities and others need to be studied carefully and without prejudice. The brief, inconsistent, and half-hearted attempt at wage and price controls during the Nixon years was not a fair trial of what restraints on inflation could be developed with commitment and imagination.

Full employment cannot be achieved so long as the federal government gives highest priority to inflation control or policy makers choose to control inflation primarily by letting unemployment rise. Making changes in this balance of policy will not be easy, but they must be attempted. From the viewpoint of children and their families, price stability should not be given higher priority than full employment as a national goal.

Full employment means a continuous nationwide demand for labor. But even when this demand exists in most regions, there are bound to be local problems as plants move or close up and the demand for one kind of service dwindles while buyers flock to another. Whenever there is a serious local shortage of labor—of engineers, let us say, for a large electronics firm—there is tremendous pressure for employers to raise wages to attract workers from other parts of the country or away from other jobs in the same locality. As a result, keeping to a standard of full employment will demand careful planning, private as well as national, to hold inflationary pressures down. We may sometimes need to use federal subsidies to offset the costs of relocating or training workers. Sometimes the government may have to subsidize employers to hire and train less skilled workers who might otherwise not find jobs. Companies will need to be doing better planning, just as the government will. Without the luxury of the perennial long lines of applicants for jobs, private industries will have to plan what their needs are going to be next year, which changes in technology will reduce certain job categories, and where surpluses of workers are likely to be found. Since it is in the best interests of employers to act on sound information about where the job market is going, one of the great national aims of a full-employment plan must be dependable and accurate information to enable employers to act in their own best interests and the public's, without the need for extensive federal regulations and compulsion.

What will all this cost? In one very meaningful sense, there is no cost—it is all gain when an unemployed and willing person is put to work doing something useful so that his or her children can enjoy the self-respect and stability that this brings to the family. Moreover, tax revenues generally increase by a healthy margin when unemployment drops. For instance, if unemployment goes from 8 percent to 4 percent, this 4-percent gain can produce something like a 12-percent increase in the gross national product and as much as 20 percent more tax revenue.

But there are some social and economic costs to reducing unemployment. The first, as we have discussed, could be a higher rate of inflation. A full commitment to children and families should not violate the national concern with those who live on fixed incomes, particularly retired workers. This concern is already built into social security payments, which rise with the price index. Economists have found additional feasible plans to give the same kind of guarantee to savings and other assets in order to keep investment high and lending rates down in any inflationary economy.[3]

Another cost will be the higher relative prices for particular goods or services that are now cheap because they are produced on substandard wages. We must expect the price of freshly laundered and ironed shirts, hand-picked fruit, and the twice-a-week house cleaning to go up as the workers who now produce them at substandard wages are given an alternative of steady work at minimum wage levels. But this shift in relative prices will happen only once; even then it is unlikely to make a major cut in anyone's living standard, and it will increase the standard of workers holding these jobs.

A third cost, specific to employers, will be that of finding new workers for job openings in a "tight" labor market. This will doubtless require a change in personnel recruiting and management, which may be regarded as a great imposition by some employers. But it is possible for firms to adjust to such conditions. We did it in World War II. With the help of trade associations and labor unions, employers and potential employees should be able to find one another.

Finally, with the federal government guaranteeing jobs at minimum wages to all those family heads who cannot find employment otherwise, the program will at times cost the taxpayers money. But quite apart from the fact that this program would be likely to produce better transportation systems, revived cities, cleaner parks, and needed goods and services not available now, creating jobs for the unemployed will save the taxpayers money as well. In 1975, there were approximately 3.3 million heads of households unemployed and looking for work. That year, state, local, and federal programs were paying $6.9 billion in unemployment insurance and also were paying over $4.6 billion in food stamps [4]—costs that will be dramatically reduced when many of these people are employed. If the government's tax or spending policies have put enough money into circulation, a great many of the jobs for these people will come from the private not the public sector. With more people at work than there are today, unemployment insurance would function as a temporary income support for workers in transition rather than as the covert welfare program it has lately become.

Who Gets the Jobs?

For far too long we have applied to the job problem the same old solution—uplift and reform the individual—that has proven so difficult to achieve in other realms. We have regularly responded to pressures for reducing unemployment by training workers, not creating jobs. But in this field as in others, the reality does not lie in individual failings. It lies in what opportunities are open to the individual. When the need for workers is high—as it has been in wartime—there has been very little talk of the need for job training; workers simply learn new jobs while they are doing them.

Unemployment is by no means distributed equally throughout the population or even that part of the population known as the labor force. For many years, the black unemployment rate has been double that of whites.[5] In 1976, the unemployment rate for inner-city black youths was 39 percent [6]—over one-third of those who wanted to work. And women are unemployed at a higher rate than men,[7] accounting for much of the high rate of poverty among families headed by women.

The disparity continues right into the ranks of parents who *can* find jobs. Throughout the history of this nation, castelike minorities —blacks, Mexican-Americans, Native Americans and, more recently, Puerto Ricans—have been massively underrepresented in the best paying jobs, whether blue-collar, white-collar, professional, or managerial, and, conversely, overrepresented in the lowest paying, most menial jobs.* One researcher has concluded that 90 percent of the income gap between blacks and whites is the result not of higher levels of unemployment for blacks but of lower pay for blacks with comparable levels of education and experience.[8] Similarly, working women have been confined primarily to domestic work, sales, and clerical positions. The Department of Commerce found that in 1974 the average earnings of women working full time were only 57.2 percent of what men employed full time earned.[9] Men are earning substantially more than women in all occupational groups and at all levels of educational attainment.[10]

The difference in earnings is not caused by a lower level of education and skills for women and minorities; if it were, more education and skill training would be enough to produce equal and fair employment and therefore close the earnings gap. But they are not enough, and any policies for equalizing employment opportunity that have tried to deal with the problem through education and training have had small success.

The major employment problems confronting women and members of racial minorities are employment barriers and job ceilings. That is, women and nonwhites, solely because of their sex and minority status, have traditionally not been hired for jobs in the most desirable occupations or have not been permitted to obtain their fair representation in such occupations. Minority group members remain

* The disabled represent another important disadvantaged group. The 15 or 20 million individuals with a work disability stemming from a health condition have unemployment rates roughly double those in the general population, and of course the disabled have significantly lower labor force participation than the able-bodied. But we cannot explore this issue here because the problems of the handicapped are not precisely parallel to the job ceilings suffered by minorities and women. It is difficult to separate the effects of discrimination —which alone cause a great many of the employment problems for the disabled —from the lower productivity of certain disabled workers in certain kinds of occupations. In absolute terms the numbers of children directly affected are relatively small; perhaps half a million to a million families with children are headed by a disabled breadwinner. But the difficulties in finding rewarding work that disabled adults suffer are a major factor that forecloses the future for handicapped children.

underrepresented even in such white-collar jobs as sales and clerical positions, although these jobs often require less training than blue-collar positions, where minority representation is higher. The problem is not that nonwhites and women lack ability. Rather, it is an informal system that makes it more difficult for most nonwhites and women to get any jobs in the first place, to gain entry into occupations that offer prestige and good salaries, and to be promoted to positions of greater authority and reward once they are employed.[11]

The nation already has many of the implements needed, in theory at least, to break down the job ceilings that constrict these groups. Title VII of the Civil Rights Act of 1964 and Executive Order 11246 together provide the basis for widespread action in favor of fair employment. But enforcement of these laws has been spotty, and the legal principles developed by courts under fair employment laws are not well suited to root out deeply ingrained discriminatory practices. Specific abuses can be fought under the law—although it may take years—and we take up this strategy next. In the long run, however, far subtler and deeper reaching structural problems are what need most of our attention.

Fair Employment Laws: Improving Enforcement

In 1972 Congress passed amendments to Title VII of the Civil Rights Act of 1964 that took the authority to institute discrimination suits against private employers away from the Department of Justice, which was concerned only with broadly based principles, and gave it instead to the Equal Employment Opportunity Commission (EEOC), which also has the responsibility of investigating complaints by individuals. Although it may have made sense on paper, this change substantially weakened the enforcement of Title VII by the federal government.

Before the amendments, the Attorney General could institute a suit anywhere he had reason to believe a "pattern or practice" of discrimination, as defined in Title VII, existed. Now this job falls to the EEOC, which cannot file suit until (1) a charge has been received, usually from an individual claiming to be aggrieved, (2) it has been formally designated as a "pattern or practice" charge, as distinct from an individual complaint, (3) the respondent accused of discrimination is notified of the charge, (4) EEOC has deferred to a state agency, where appropriate, (5) the charge has been investigated by the General Counsel, who handles the enforcement litigation, (6) the EEOC determines there is reasonable cause to believe that the employer is engaged in a pattern or practice of unlawful discrimination, (7) efforts have been made by the General Counsel "to eliminate the alleged unlawful employment practices by informal methods of conference, conciliation and persuasion," and (8) the authorization for litigation has been granted by both the General Counsel and the Commission.[12] Clearly the burden in these proceedings is not on the party accused of discriminatory hiring practices.

By tying the authority to bring suit to receipt of a charge of discrimination, the Title VII amendments require that suits focus on individual grievances, often at the expense of broad-based challenges to discriminatory practices. Although theoretically the EEOC can institute its own charges on broader-based issues, it operates on a limited budget and is inundated with the individual cases (its current backlog is over 100,000 charges) that the law requires it to investigate, so it is bound to devote almost all of its resources to these cases. Yet it has been well documented that there is little connection between individual complaints of discrimination and systemic discriminatory practices. Employees are likely to file charges of discrimination when they feel that they, individually, have been treated differently from other employees. These cases typically involve alleged departures from established policies, not shortcomings of the policies themselves.

Since systemic discrimination takes the form not of outright or open exclusion of women or minorities but rather of apparently neutral practices like the credentials "required" for a job, those who suffer from discrimination more often than not do not even realize that they are victims; only work-force statistics or other objective data will reveal it. Responsibility for challenging allegedly discriminatory, established employment policies on a plantwide, company-wide, or industrywide basis should be separated from the very different function of resolving individual claims of unfair treatment. The deeply rooted patterns of job discrimination in this country will not be changed by attacking them case by case. We believe that the authority to institute broad-based charges of employment discrimination must be vested in a separate division or agency with a separate budget that will not be drained by investigating individual complaints.

Another problem under the existing law is delay in the courts. Recognizing the importance of prompt judicial response to suits filed under Title VII, the 1972 amendments established special assignment practices designed to speed the process. But these requirements, unlike similar congressional requirements with respect to the prompt disposition of criminal cases in the federal courts, have been almost totally ignored. In fact, it is now common for Title VII cases to be delayed for five to ten years, during which the challenged practices continue. Certainly Title VII cases are complicated and federal court dockets are overcrowded, but this situation is intolerable. The courts should be required and enabled to treat these cases promptly.

One other broad instrument for changing job discrimination exists. President Johnson's Executive Order 11246, issued in 1965 and amended since then, is the most recent of a series of executive orders prohibiting the award of government contracts to employers who discriminate on the grounds of race or sex. The order is basically aimed at getting minorities and women into jobs where their present employment representation is poor. And under the order, the government's authority to require "affirmative action" by its contractors apparently even exceeds the reach of Title VII's prohibition against "discrimination in employment." [13] In short, affirmative action as called for under the executive order does not merely require the elimination of practices that can be proved discriminatory; it calls on employers, employment agencies, and organized labor to take positive steps to seek out qualified women and minorities for desirable jobs.

Executive Order 11246 has great potential for reducing job discrimination because of the affirmative action principle and because virtually every large employer in the United States is a government contractor. But unfortunately, the order has not even begun to achieve its potential. By early 1977, not one contractor had actually been barred from government contracts, and the very few proceedings to cut off contracts that have been undertaken have proceeded at an intolerably slow pace.

The problem appears to be the all-or-nothing character of the order. Either a contractor has all its government contracts cut off, or no remedy can be imposed. Even though in extreme cases this rule may make sense as a matter of justice, the effect of so catastrophic a remedy is that government administrators are unwilling to invoke it. By now their reluctance is so well established that the threat of the ultimate remedy has lost its power to persuade companies that are not complying with the order. The government enforcement agency should have a full range of powers to tailor the remedy to the particular discriminatory practice and, in general, judicial remedies should be pursued, not fund cutoffs.

The principle of affirmative action, which we endorse, has sometimes been interpreted by those who oppose it to mean preferential treatment for women and minorities. In fact there may be legal and political obstacles to giving preference to women and minorities as a means of fighting employment discrimination. After all, the ethic of individual merit is deeply ingrained in the national consciousness, even if it has been applied only intermittently to certain groups. But other changes that are consistent with the merit ethic would go far toward eliminating the basic causes of underemployment for minorities and women: the law should be appropriately amended to change standard practices of recruiting for jobs and of establishing job qualifications.

Most cases raising claims of hiring discrimination turn on the court's analysis of whether minority or female applicants have been treated fairly. This approach overlooks the crucial question of employment practices that effectively keep the pool of applicants from including a proportionate number of women or minorities. Where jobs have been traditionally closed to women or minorities, the impression—correct or incorrect—is fostered that they are not welcome in the job. Moreover, members of groups who have been excluded are denied a familiar role model to follow into a particular line of work. The effects of this are established early in childhood, and lessons learned this early do not generally yield to exhortation or propaganda later. Unless girls and minority group children see from experience that ability, education, and hard work will actually get them high status and rewarding jobs, they are obviously less likely to pursue education or training even if it is available.

Another important factor is that word-of-mouth recruitment, one of the most common ways to fill jobs, tends to reinforce existing employment patterns. When employees at a particular job learn of a vacancy, they tell their friends or relatives who are looking for work. The friends or relatives of whites are likely to be white, so when an incumbent work force is largely or totally white, word-of-mouth recruiting produces a disproportionately white group of applicants. The effect of this practice—even when the employer has no direct hand in encouraging it—cannot be underestimated because vast numbers of job openings are filled by people referred to the employer by other people who already work for the same or similar firms.

A remedy for this situation would be a statutory or regulatory requirement that major employers give formal notice of job vacancies, and an opportunity to apply, before jobs are filled.* Classified advertisements announcing the opening and a specific application period would serve this purpose for many jobs. If special skills or education were required, notification of requirements could be directed locally at the particular group from which eligible candidates are likely to emerge, such as college seniors or licensed craftsmen. These measures would both offset the inhibiting effect of past discrimination and give women and minorities more equal access to information about job opportunities.

Another major obstacle to the elimination of job discrimination is job qualifications that have very little bearing on how people will do on the job itself. People without established qualifications have often moved in and performed jobs perfectly well. Women working in airplane manufacture during World War II provide a classic example. Without in any way undermining real and valid qualifications, and without undertaking preferential treatment, very important progress can be made by eliminating unnecessary job qualifications.

The courts, interpreting Title VII, have made some progress in this direction. In *Griggs* v. *Duke Power Company* (1971) the Supreme Court held that it is the consequences of employer practice,

---

* This requirement, with respect to new hiring, would be similar to the requirement now imposed by many courts that all employees be given notice of vacancies in upper-level jobs, and an opportunity to apply, before the jobs are filled.

not the intent, that matters. If an employment test or educational requirement disproportionately serves to disqualify blacks for employment, it must be shown to be job-related. While not challenging the validity of merit per se as a criterion for employment, courts have ruled tha⁺ merit must be job-related. Thus, in the Griggs case, the court ruled that blacks could not be prevented from transferring from low-paying jobs to higher-paying jobs in coal handling simply because of poor performance on IQ tests that measured the ability to distinguish the meanings of "adopt," "adapt," and "adept" but bore no relation to the ability to handle coal.

No employment criterion perfectly separates those who can do a job from those who cannot. Yet by and large the courts have seemed willing to uphold a job-skills requirement that is just barely successful in predicting how well an applicant will do the work. If applicants for a secretarial post were given a French test and it could be shown that, although the job required no knowledge of French, 46 percent of those who passed did well in the job, as opposed to 42 percent of those who failed, this could be construed as a "positive" correlation. Even assuming the data is accurate, this kind of evidence does not address the question of whether other selection devices such as a work sample or an interview might be just as good or better at predicting success on the job, and with less discriminatory results. In fact, nothing correlates with job performance better than a work sample—that is, rather than an IQ test, a page of typing for a typist and a course of bricks for a bricklayer.

Title VII and Executive Order 11246 should be amended to require the employer to prove, in addition to the predictive validity of its existing criteria, that there are no other selection mechanisms available that will serve as well or better to predict job performance, and with less discriminatory effects. By regulation, a listing of appropriate alternatives for particular types of employers could be developed. The emphasis should be on work samples, performance in training, and other standards that do not measure differences in background or education that may not relate to work performance.

For many jobs, the major obstacle to the entry of women or minorities is a requirement for prior experience or training that goes beyond the actual demands of the job. Frequently, these "requirements" have not been applied to white men performing the same jobs. Often, too, the qualifications are inflated, and in fact the job can be quickly learned and competently performed by people who do not "qualify." The tendency of employers to exaggerate the skills required for particular jobs must be challenged wherever it adversely affects minority or women applicants. Moreover, even when a particular job truly requires certain skills—such as knowledge of the operation of a particular machine—but these skills can be readily learned through on-the-job training, an employer who has failed to hire significant numbers of minorities or women should be required to provide the necessary on-the-job training, rather than reject otherwise qualified minority or women applicants. In short, if the requirement is something that can be learned in a few days, it should not be treated as a qualification but as part of the familiarization with the job, just as learning the layout of the office is. The careful pruning of job qualification standards to the actual demands of jobs and a requirement of on-the-job training for skills that can readily be acquired would be major steps toward the goal of fair employment.

In sum, the employment of minorities and women can be increased, without preferential treatment, by measures designed to ensure minority and female applications, by the elimination of unnecessary requirements, and by requiring an employer who has not traditionally employed minorities or women in particular job categories to make training opportunities available. Necessary changes in the law should be made to achieve these ends.

Finally, we should note the relationship between full employment and fair employment. Historically, the periods when the gap between the wages of nonwhites and whites has closed most rapidly have been periods of low unemployment, generally associated with the manpower demands of a wartime economy. Similarly, women's entry into the labor force and access to more desirable jobs has been markedly increased by wartime manpower needs. Under pressure, blacks, Spanish-speaking Americans, and women previously considered "unqualified" for jobs were suddenly found fit and able. Conversely, nonwhites and women are likely to suffer most in times of high unemployment. The severe economic recession of the mid-1970's reversed an earlier trend toward the equalization of the wages of blacks and whites, undoing the gains made during the 1960's. Partly because nonwhites are the last to be hired, a firing system based on seniority means they are the first to be fired, providing a kind of cushion for whites' jobs. None of this means that full employment is a precondition for fair employment. But in the long run, we believe that the achievement of a more just system of hiring and promotion will be facilitated by national commitment to the full-employment economy that we have proposed.

We do not wish to minimize the technical or political difficulties that our recommendation of full and fair employment poses, but we are convinced that the United States will not offer real opportunity to all its children until it faces and overcomes those difficulties. While we cannot be certain of success, it is imperative that we try it. There is no way this Council can contemplate an acceptable future for children in a context of chronically or periodically unemployed parents. It is critically important to employ all parents who want to work.

But now we turn to the second major aspect of our jobs and income proposal, for it is equally important to consider whether parents have any viable choice—specifically, whether at least one parent in a family with young children can afford to choose the "work" * of rearing the children as a full-time alternative to being in the labor force.

Income Supports

The employment strategies we have discussed would give every American family with a member able to work outside the home the chance to support itself through a job. But even in a full-employment economy, some people will be temporarily unable to find work or earn enough to meet minimally adequate standards; other people, particularly single parents with young children, should be able to care for their own children full time if they want to. Other industrialized countries have developed conscious and coherent policies to support such families, and this country has ample resources to do so as well.

We believe that the best way to ensure that no family has to live at a standard much below half of the national median income is for the federal government to provide direct income supports, both to supplement low wages and to support adequately those who cannot or should not work. The program we propose rests on the assumption that the government is already doing all that it can to promote full employment.

Not that the United States currently has no income-support policies whatsoever. In fact, we have many different policies, each answering a different need, each built on different assumptions, each passed as law in a different era. Most of them have grown up in times of crisis or heightened public interest in a special problem. By now, this patchwork of support programs is almost impossible for potential recipients to decipher in order to discover what they are entitled to. The programs are expensive to administer. And by and large they do not offer coverage to one of the most vulnerable groups—the working poor, people working hard to earn incomes that are very low but just high enough to disqualify them for most public benefits.

Between 1965 and 1972, the United States doubled its overall spending on social welfare benefits—that is, on services and transfer payments. The increase, however, had little if any effect on the children of poor to near-poor families, and subsequent developments have made no significant changes. Most of the increased government spending that puts cash into the pockets of the poor has gone to groups other than families with children, in particular to the aged. The result, as we have said, is that the families of over a quarter of American children are left without the chance to provide a decent home environment. Other beneficiaries certainly merit the help they

* Child rearing, despite its pleasures and rewards, is a real job, perhaps the most important one for a vigorous society, but it does not provide a salary when carried out by parents, yields no pension rights, and is not even counted in the GNP.

receive, but policies that so neglect children and their families reflect a distorted sense of national priorities.

The programs that do pay something that benefits children in poor families are these:

Social security pays a stipend to widows or widowers and their dependent children if the deceased spouse worked in a job covered by social security (90 percent of current jobs are), or to the relatively few children dependent on retired or disabled people.

Unemployment insurance and *workmen's compensation* give important protection against the loss of income to many families with children. These programs pay rich and poor alike without an income test. Their function is extremely important for those they reach, but the families they do not reach tend to be precisely those families dependent on wage earners who are least successful in the job market. Moreover, because benefits typically are keyed to past earnings, children whose parents earned the least get the least protection against a substandard level of living.

Veterans' programs that pay for disability, survivors' benefits, and pensions also help families, but they too cover only a fraction of them and tend to miss the most vulnerable.

Aid to Families with Dependent Children (AFDC). Still other programs are designed specifically for the most vulnerable sector of the population, but they also have serious flaws. The public assistance programs generally known as "welfare" were launched by the Social Security Act to augment the income of specific kinds of citizens in need. The category that bears directly on children and gives them the most coverage is known as Aid to Families with Dependent Children.* The states share the cost of this program and the "need" of recipients is determined locally, sometimes individually, with large attendant costs in administration. Efforts to weed out the "chiselers" inevitably involve hiring auditors and checkers, which increases costs further and violates the privacy of many recipients.

AFDC is the program most people are thinking of when they complain about skyrocketing welfare costs. In fact, it represents only 5 percent of all federal, state, and local spending on cash assistance (social security and veterans' benefits are many times greater) and only 3.3 percent of all social welfare spending. From the beginning,

AFDC has had the explicit objective of protecting children (it is our only program with this specific aim), but it reaches less than half of those living below the scanty standard of half the median,** and those who do receive it often do not get enough even to reach the official poverty line, much less a level of minimum decency. Payments vary irrationally from state to state (for example, an average of $50 per month per family in Mississippi versus $346 in New York). Despite reforms, AFDC still usually pays more to a family

abandoned by the father than it does to one whose father persists in trying to support it—a situation which, of course, creates an incentive for fathers of families in desperate financial circumstances to move out.

AFDC also discourages parents from working, since even if they work at very low wage levels they lose most of their benefits. This feature creates what is in effect an extremely high tax rate (economists call it an implicit tax rate). A family with children, trying to support itself on earnings of $4,000 a year, for example, is eligible in most states to receive some help from AFDC. If they get a chance to increase those earnings to $5,000 a year, the benefits are likely to be cut dramatically—say by $600. In this case, then, the family's net gain would be only $400 a year, which means an implicit tax rate on the additional $1,000 of 60 percent—a tax bracket that would make even corporate executives shudder. Other combinations of AFDC policies imply tax rates well above 100 percent for some ranges of income, and rates close to that are not uncommon. The most discouraging case of all in our current structure is the abrupt cutoff or "notch" where a raise in wages of one dollar a year can mean the loss of several hundreds of dollars of benefits.[14] It is hardly accurate to call a program that works to break up families and discourage employment a "welfare" program.

* Other, so-called adult categories of public assistance, including the blind, permanently and totally disabled, and indigent aged, were consolidated into the SSI (Supplemental Security Income) program on a fully federal basis in 1972. This has provided generally increased and uniform benefits for these groups but has a relatively minor effect on poor children.

** In 1974, there were 7.9 million child beneficiaries, while 18 to 20 million children were living below half the median income.

Food stamps, inaugurated in 1961, is one of our better designed aid programs, since recent modifications give significant assistance on a sliding scale to families with incomes above the official poverty line. Most of the families we have counted as being below minimum standards are eligible for food stamps, although it appears that substantial numbers of people who are eligible do not participate. Since it applies only to food, the program is, of course, limited in what it can do to boost low incomes to an adequate level, but as the only program currently helping the working poor and near-poor, it helps to correct the shortcomings of AFDC. For those who advocate a reform such as the negative income tax or the credit income tax described below, food stamps stand as a functioning nationwide prototype of a program that is universal, provides a minimum floor, and does not cut off abruptly when income rises above an arbitrary notch but rather tapers off gradually.

Medicaid, like others programs in this patchwork, has been a mixed blessing. While it undoubtedly provides better health coverage to many families than they got before it was enacted, it has uncritically funded many kinds of care that are inappropriately elaborate, and has helped to push up health-care costs at an alarming rate, to the detriment of families that are not covered and even many that are. Nor has Medicaid gone very far toward promoting adequate child and maternal health programs—a fact reflected in the number of children who do not receive even basic immunizations and who do not visit a doctor or a dentist even once a year. (For a discussion of proposed reforms in the system that ministers to children's health, see Chapter 8.)

Finally, *housing subsidies* for low-income families also exist in one form or another in most states.

In the next few pages, we outline the second aspect of our proposal for a fresh effort to promote more equality in the economic standing of American families. A comprehensive system of income

supports, linked with policies to promote full employment so that no family in the nation could fall below half the median income, would render much of the present patchwork obsolete. An adequate income clearly minimizes the need for most specialized subsidies. Moreover, basic income supports would eliminate much of the cumbersome bureaucracy, with its potential for meddling in individual liberties, and many of the dozens of current programs intended to benefit families, children, veterans, the aged, and others. Supports of the kind we have in mind would eliminate the grossly unfair discrepancy between the working poor who receive no benefits from current transfer programs and often pay taxes besides, and those who receive almost as much from welfare.

Most important, living-standard supports that families could spend as they wished would increase a family's choices without dictating which services they should receive or interfering in their lives. They place a trust in each family's capacity to make basic decisions about how they lead their lives and how they bring up their children, giving the poor some of the basic freedom that the rest of the population enjoys. Thus living-standard supports directly increase the freedom of millions of American families with small children where the need of the second parent (or of one parent in a single-parent family) to work may go against the wish of one of the parents to care full time for children during their early years.

Principles for Income Supports

We have said that planning government initiatives to create full employment is a difficult task that has not yet received anything like the attention it demands. In contrast, although experts may differ on which formula is the best one, better income-support mechanisms have been well studied. It is clear that we need no new knowledge, no new institutions, and no prolonged period of experimentation in order to guarantee a minimal standard of living to all Americans. Income supports can be built right into a revamped tax system, or they could conceivably be based on the expansion to the whole population of the principles of universality and fair implicit tax rates embedded in a few of our current transfer programs. The point is for the nation to consider that each individual in the country is entitled to live at a level of decency. For every child, the opportunity should exist regardless of how and where the family chooses to live.

However it is implemented, any income-support plan should adhere to certain basic principles:

1) It should provide strong incentives to work. Maximum benefits obviously will have to go to families with no income. But when an individual goes to work, we urge that the program benefits be reduced gradually by a constant fraction of earnings so that taking a job will mean that one's income goes up significantly. However high the income, no person should have to face losing more than 50 percent of a raise through taxes or lost benefits.

2) It should contain adequate safeguards to prevent abuse. Adults capable of work who are not actively seeking a job or taking care of dependents should not be eligible.

3) For a family of four that satisfies the above requirements, it should guarantee an income floor equal to 40 percent of the median for families of that size, with appropriate adjustments in the guarantee for families of other sizes and types.*

4) It should—in combination with good employment opportunities—give the parent with primary child-rearing responsibilities a legitimate choice of whether to work or stay at home, without creating strong incentives or penalties on either side to influence the choice.

A Sample Support System: The Credit Income Tax

Income guarantees that meet these four standards would be possible to create in many forms, but before we discuss the standards in any detail, it may be useful to illustrate the basic idea with a simplified version of one of the most appealing designs, a credit income tax. We should emphasize that we do not wish these proposals to stand or fall on the basis of whether a credit income tax system is feasible in the near future. The principles we have listed here are what we believe are important, and we would endorse any plan, radical or gradual, that adheres to them.

The credit tax is an easily administered and straightforward plan that makes it possible to see how reforms affect income at different levels. It replaces most present transfer systems with a revised version of the income tax system, one part of the federal government that is usually considered to be efficiently run.

---

* Together with a guaranteed job, this level of income floor would raise virtually all families above half the median income. Only a small fraction of children would be living in families at the floor of 40 percent. A floor higher than 40 percent would create an unnecessarily large tax burden (also see p. 109).

As things stand now, of course, the tax system is no more comprehensible than the tangle of benefit programs we have described. Although originally intended to tax the well-to-do more heavily than those at low incomes, in fact the many deductions and exemptions it allows—for such things as home mortgage interest, property taxes, capital gains, and municipal bonds—mean that most people who are not in the top or bottom 5 percent range of income actually give the government about the same percentage of their pay in taxes. The share of their income that goes to taxes is virtually the same whether they earn $9,000 or $30,000.[15]

Furthermore, in the existing tax structure, exemptions, deductions, and tax shelters systematically discriminate against the children of the poor. Our present system of deductions represents a government subsidy to the rich that actually increases with income. Our federal tax system supposedly gives all parents a break by allowing a deduction of $750 for each dependent child. But a deduction is not the same as cash; it is only worth a percentage of $750 depending on the family's tax bracket. To a rich family, paying taxes at a top rate of 50 percent, two children are "worth" half the $1,500 deduction—$750 in tax credits. For a poorer family in the $10,000 range with two children, paying at a top rate of 20 percent, the children's deduction is worth only $300. For families too poor to pay any taxes at all, the children's deduction is worthless. These children's deductions cost the federal government between $5 billion and $6 billion a year and constitute in effect a regressive system of financial bonuses to the very rich.

In a credit income tax system, virtually all deductions, exemptions, and shelters would be eliminated. All earnings and property income would be subject to a fixed tax rate—that is, everyone would pay a flat percent (the same regardless of income). But every man, woman, and child in the country would be entitled to a tax credit, money they would receive if they had no other source of support. For the poor, this would be a tax in reverse—a payment made to them instead of taken from them. Since tax credits would offset taxes at low income levels, the effective rate of tax in the overall tax structure would increase as a family's income got larger.

All current social benefit programs that are keyed to income—primarily the welfare system and food stamps—would, along with the present unwieldy federal tax structure, be replaced by the unified credit tax program. Other current benefits that are not keyed to income, like veterans' benefits and disability insurance, would remain in force, but the benefits they pay would be counted as income when determining the appropriate tax or benefit level so that families in these categories did not get paid double. The tax would be levied on all forms of income except private transfers, such as gifts and child-support payments. The only deductions permitted would be for the direct costs of earning income, such as tools and union dues, for the

105

costs of child care necessary to enable a parent to work, and for charitable contributions.

In a credit tax scheme,[16] tax rates are set at a level to support the credits. Suppose in this case that the tax credit is set at $6,000 for all families of four with two adults and one younger and one older child. (The $6,000 figure is roughly equal to 40 percent of the median and is chosen advisedly. We have structured this whole example to demonstrate a decent minimum living standard for all.) Different size families obviously require different levels of support; the question is how to establish a scale for the variation. We are inclined to favor one based on the ages of the people in the family rather than one based on economies of scale for larger families. Using the four-person family with two parents as a base, we recommend raising the stipend by 33 percent, say, for another adult in the home, 20 percent for each child aged twelve through seventeen (who cost more to maintain than younger children), and 14 percent for each child under twelve; or, if there are fewer than four in the home, we recommend lowering payments by those amounts. For this example, we have divided this $6,000 family credit into individual credits of $1,980 for every person eighteen or older ($1,980 each for the mother and father), $1,200 for a child twelve through seventeen, and $840 for a child up through the age of eleven. This is guaranteed as an income for each one in the absence of any other source of support. The level of support, it will be noted, is slightly below half the median. In combination with a job guarantee, it assures any family with at least one member who can work an income above half the median.

The tax rate to be matched against the credit in this example is set at 50 percent,* so the individual adult's theoretical tax liability is half his or her total earned income. In practice, if income is low and the credit is larger than the tax liability, the individual receives money from the government rather than pays it. When earnings for an individual supporting no dependents rise to $3,960, or twice the credit level, the 50-percent tax rate produces a break-even situation, the tax owed equals the credit, and no money changes hands. As earnings go higher, the tax rate would still remain 50 percent. Thus a single person earning $6,000 a year would have a tax liability of $3,000 and a credit of $1,980, and would therefore actually pay a net tax of $1,020—an effective tax of 17 percent of his or her income. A single person earning $40,000, with the same credit of $1,980 and in this case a tax liability of $20,000, would wind up owing $18,020, an effective rate of 45 percent. Since the liability is always 50 percent

---

* The credit level is the important feature of this system, and the tax rate will have to be worked out in order to finance it. It would take detailed and careful calculations with up-to-date figures and projections to establish the rate exactly, but rough calculation suggests that it will be between 40 and 50 percent, and probably closer to 50.

and every adult always has the $1,980 credit, however high income climbs, the actual tax rate on earnings would never quite reach 50 percent. This means that no one, at whatever level, would be discouraged by "notches" in the tax rate from working harder to earn more. A four-person family with earnings of $10,000—who paid a federal income tax and social security of approximately $1,290 in 1974—would actually receive an additional $1,000 income from the government under this credit income tax.

Who Benefits?

Table 3 shows how this scheme would work at varying income levels for a family of two parents, an older, and a younger child.

Table 3	Illustrative Credit Income Tax for Family of Four			
1 Initial Income	2 Tax liability (50% of col. 1)	3 Net credit or income tax ($6,000 minus col. 2)	4 Final income (col. 1 plus credit or minus tax)	5 Effective tax rate
$ 0	$ 0	$ 6,000 Credit	$ 6,000	—
$ 3,000	$ 1,500	$ 4,500 Credit	$ 7,500	—
$ 6,000	$ 3,000	$ 3,000 Credit	$ 9,000	—
$ 9,000	$ 4,500	$ 1,500 Credit	$10,500	—
$12,000	$ 6,000	$ 0	$12,000	0
$15,000	$ 7,500	$ 1,500 Tax	$13,500	10%
$21,000	$10,500	$ 4,500 Tax	$16,500	21.4%
$30,000	$15,000	$ 9,000 Tax	$21,000	30%
$50,000	$25,000	$19,000 Tax	$31,000	38%

It is apparent that all families of this kind earning up to $12,000 would receive income supplements, so that this program, unlike current welfare payments, would benefit not simply the unemployed and the very poor but the working poor as well. Because of lower tax rates at middle levels than in the present system, the program would also benefit many families above the median income, in a percentage diminishing as income increased.

Table 4 shows a range of family types and incomes under the credit tax.

To figure out how much money any family has to spend in a year, one has only to combine the income with that particular fam-

Table 4	Benefits and Taxes for Selected Family Types under a Credit Income Tax (Net benefits are written as positive numbers, net taxes as negative ones)				
	Benefit or Tax				
Income (earnings before tax)	(1) 4-person; children 9, 14	(2) 3-person; fem. head; * children 9, 14	(3) 6-person; children 4, 6, 8, 10	(4) 2-person; adult couple	(5) 6-person; children 12, 14, 16, 18
$ 0	$ 6,000	$ 4,020	$ 7,320	$ 3,960	$ 9,540
3,000	4,500	2,520	5,820	2,460	8,040
6,000	3,000	1,020	4,320	960	6,540
9,000	1,500	−480	2,820	−540	5,040
12,000	0	−1,980	1,320	−2,040	3,540
15,000	−1,500	−3,480	−180	−3,540	2,040
18,000	−3,000	−4,980	−1,680	−5,040	540
20,000	−4,000	−5,980	−2,680	−6,040	−460
30,000	−9,000	−10,980	−7,680	−11,040	−5,460
50,000	−19,000	−20,980	−17,680	−21,040	−15,460

* The supplementary child support program described on page 114 would assure an additional income of $1,200 for this family at whatever level of income.

ily's credit or tax liability.* A little time with the figures shows how income supports done on this basis do not discourage working. If a father supporting a wife and two children (column 1) were earning $6,000, he would still receive credits of $3,000 and thus wind up with a net income of $9,000. The six-person family (column 3) with earnings of $6,000 would have $10,320 to spend. Both these families, in short, would do considerably better with their breadwinner working than otherwise. Remember that the income supports or credits would not be available to people not holding a job or at least looking for one, and that with guaranteed jobs for heads of households, every family with two parents would be able to earn at least half the average industrial wage—that is, by 1974 dollars, $4,800 or more per year. Add to that minimum annual income the help from income supports, and no family of four with a breadwinner working full time would have an income lower than $8,400. In a full-employment economy, in fact, most breadwinners would probably find work at better wages than those provided by the guaranteed jobs. So while some families might drop to the income-floor level—having to depend entirely on the tax credit to live—for short periods such as when changing jobs or during periods of illness, their typical level would be above the minimum standard of half the median.

The credit tax not only does not discourage working, it also does not discourage working harder, for a family or individual will always keep a full 50 percent of any increase. If a $20,000-a-year engineer gets a whopping raise to $30,000, his family will have $5,000 extra to spend next year.

In one-parent families without an absent spouse paying child support, the guaranteed credit would of course be the entire source of family income in the case when the parent decided to remain at home; for this category, the credit would not reach the minimum level. Hence we propose an additional limited system of supplementary child support explained in detail below (see page 114). A single woman with two children, such as the family shown in column 2, would receive at least $1,200 a year in addition to the credits, for a total income of $5,220. This level is above the most generous AFDC levels currently prevailing and is 30 percent higher than the current official poverty threshold for such families.

It should also be clear from Table 4 how the allowable deductions under a credit tax, such as the deductions for child care, would benefit families at all income levels equally. With a 50-percent tax rate, only half of such deductible costs are borne by the family; the other half is made up in either lower taxes or a higher benefit. Similarly, families at all levels would get equal benefits for their children. The difference between any two columns in Table 4 is the

---

* Some local options might have to be built in to adjust for regional variations in the cost of basic economic needs. These are not reflected in the chart.

same in each row: this implies that if the effect of having four young children as compared to none is to make benefits larger by $3,360 a year at an income of $6,000, then taxes will be lowered by the same amount for better-off families at income levels of $20,000 or $50,000.

To give an idea of which families would benefit through a revised tax system such as the credit tax, Table 5 shows the existing federal income tax and social security taxes (employee contributions only) for the same array of family types and income levels as in Table 4. The figures are incomplete because they do not include

Table 5

Comparative Schedule Showing 1975 Federal Income Taxes and Social Insurance Contributions for Selected Family Types

Income (earnings before tax)	(1) 4-person; 9, 14	(2) 3-person; fem. head; children 9, 14	(3) 6-person; children 4, 6, 8, 10	(4) 2-person; adult couple	(5) 6-person; children 12, 14, 16, 18
$ 0	$ 0	$ 0	$ 0	$ 0	$ 0
3,000	124.50 *	124.50 *	124.50 *	−175.50	124.50 *
6,000	−182	−393	−151	−673	−151
9,000	−1,040	−1,319	−736	−1,394	−736
12,000	−1,783	−2,050	−1,438	−2,145	−1,438
15,000**	−2,432	−2,781	−2,042	−2,862	−2,042
18,000	−2,995	−3,409	−2,601	−3,430	−2,601
20,000	−3,415	−3,869	−2,980	−3,850	−2,980
30,000	−5,798	−6,577	−5,249	−6,329	−5,249
50,000	−12,395	−13,867	−11,660	−13,140	−11,660

* Under the current tax structure, the federal government has just instituted a token credit for families with children. So the principle—now called Earned Income Credit—is there already, even though the maximum net payment any family can possibly receive under the EIC is $400 a year.

** For incomes of $15,000 and higher, tax calculation assumes itemized deductions of 16 percent of earnings.

either current income benefits such as AFDC and food stamps (which are highly variable from place to place and case to case) or income reductions by state and local income taxes. At higher incomes the actual tax paid under our present tax system may vary a great deal depending on whether deductions are itemized and, if so, how large the deductions are. The calculations for Table 5 assume a straight 16-percent deduction, although the average deduction is probably greater than that and taxes correspondingly lower.

As comparisons of Tables 4 and 5 show, four-person families would be better off under the credit tax scheme up to an income of $18,000, and families with four older children (column 5) would fare better up to $30,000. The single-parent family would benefit until the adult earned an income of around $17,000.

Comparisons of the two highest income rows suggest the added burden a credit tax would place on upper-income groups. The four-person family at $30,000 would end up with an income after taxes that is 13 percent lower than at present, and at the $50,000 level would feel a theoretical reduction of 17 percent. These calculated reductions would be lower in practice; they are exaggerated by the fact that state and local taxes are not included, and they may be further exaggerated by the level of credits and the tax chosen for the illustration. Both were chosen for their feasibility, but they were not based on a thorough analysis of the likely state of affairs in a future full-employment economy. A full-employment economy would probably allow larger credits and/or a lower tax rate which would, of course, leave all families with more money to spend.

Work Requirements

We have discussed how "notches" and high implicit tax rates in the current welfare system discourage work. That so many recipients of AFDC and other benefits keep working at all and trying to find better jobs as well is a testimony to the deep-running and almost universal desire to work. The federally funded experiment with income maintenance in New Jersey from 1968 to 1972 showed that an income guarantee (a low one, to be sure) did very little to discourage the men who participated from working to support their families. Other studies also indicate that the welfare poor do want to work.[17] Most poor Americans who are not working simply cannot find work that pays enough to make working worth their while. This is why we have made our recommendations for full employment and job guarantees for heads of households the first plank in our proposed family policy.

Still, an income-support program cannot assume that everyone in the nation would choose to work if he or she could draw a minimal living income without working. Although we believe the inclination toward abuse is far smaller than popularly believed, the working public is justifiably outraged by the idea of anyone at all drawing

111

support he is not entitled to, and has shown through voting patterns and pressure that it is actually willing to spend several times the cost of uncontrolled "shirking" in order to prevent shirking. To be feasible politically and economically, it is clear that income supports will have to have some kind of work requirement as a prerequisite to receiving support.

"Work tests" in the past have themselves been the subject of great abuse, being used by bureaucracies to force those who need public support to take substandard and exploitive jobs, or to deny benefits to those who cannot work but are put into the "employable" category anyway. We do not believe this needs to be the case with every form of work test.

First, it is important for any program to recognize that unpaid child rearing is at least as demanding and socially productive as paid work outside the home. Staying home to raise children is not cheating or chiseling. Second, it must be recognized that full employment is a critical part of an effective work requirement. If there are employment opportunities and guaranteed jobs for family heads at non-exploitive wages, it makes sense to expect capable adults to work. The same requirement results in pointless harassment when there is substantial unemployment. Finally, the best assurance against abuse of an active work requirement is to apply it to every adult in the country rather than just to those who are receiving supports. No one should receive personal tax advantages such as a personal deduction without fulfilling the work requirement, and this should apply to the wealthy as well as the poor.

In a full-employment economy, it should be possible to design a work requirement that does not abuse either recipients or the public purse. Whether we are able to institute a support system as broad and fair as the credit income tax or whether we take smaller steps toward the same goal, we should require that adults work full time or be registered with the employment service and actively seeking work before they become eligible for benefits.* Full-time work should be considered to include the unsalaried job of managing a household with children in it.** Of course certain categories of citizens—including children under eighteen, the elderly, and some of the severely disabled—would be exempted from the work requirement and still remain eligible for standard exemptions, credits, or supports, depending on their family's income. People wealthy enough to choose not to work would, when subjected to the work test, simply lose their tax credit or personal exemption. Just as with the present

* Special and somewhat intricate provisions will be required to provide equitable treatment for self-employed categories and at the same time prevent abuse.

** This will need to be defined more carefully but could be construed to mean one child under three, two under nine, three or four teen-agers or adult workers, for example, or a half-time paid job plus a household with an eleven year old.

programs under which a single mother's welfare payments drop when her children grow up and leave home, the prosperous businessman's wife with no job would also lose eligibility as a dependent on her husband's tax return when her children mature.

An Adequate Level of Support

Our proposals assure that almost all families with two parents can, in a full-employment economy with guaranteed jobs for heads of households, have at least one parent working to support the family. Assistance for families who are working but not earning enough to live decently is a prime goal of an income-support policy. No such policy can be considered adequate if it does not give substantial help to this group of American families.

But a support policy must, of course, carry a bottom line—a floor for those families who have no other means of support either temporarily or because no one in the family is able to work for wages. We are proposing that for a family of four the income floor be set every year at 40 percent of median family income for families of that size or level, which is still hardly generous but can cover basic necessities for a short time. In 1974, 40 percent of the median wages for heads of four-member households was $5,900 *—18 per-cent more than the official poverty line that year. (Families with a breadwinner would bring in more.) It is not a royal living, nor would it be available if the work requirements were not being fulfilled.

Although this base would create an adequate floor under the general range of the population, two special groups of children will remain at high risk unless special provisions are made for them. The first group includes children of single parents. We believe that some standardized means must be designed to assure that absent parents support their children to the best of their ability—for example, by

* This figure was rounded out to $6,000 in the credit tax example.

making a minimum contribution to the support of one's children a prerequisite for the receipt of income supports or personal exemptions, unless the parent is specifically excused from that requirement by a court order. Without child support, even the income supports we are proposing would not bring a household of three young children living with their mother (or father) up to the level of minimum decency if she chooses, as we believe she should be free to do, to stay at home and raise her children herself. We propose that when child support and other child entitlements such as survivor benefits are inadequate or are not paid at all, the federal goverment should guarantee support in addition to the tax credit, at levels as shown in Table 6 below. This figure would simply be added to the single-parent family's tax credit.

Table 6	**Supplementary Child Support Schedule**	
Number of children in family with absent parent(s)	**Benefit as fraction of 4-person guarantee under credit tax**	**Approximate dollar amount per year (at 1974 levels)**
1 or 2	20%	$1,200
3	25%	1,500
4	30%	1,800
5	33%	2,000

In many cases, the government would have to pay only a small fraction of these amounts to make up the same total, for most single parents would already be receiving at least some help in the form of federal survivor benefits or child support from the absent spouse.

The second group of children at particularly high risk are those whose exceptional needs cause their families, at whatever income level, exceptional financial strain: the handicapped. For a child who is blind or deaf, confined to a wheelchair or afflicted with cerebral palsy, the difficulties in leading a normal childhood are gravely imperiled not only by the deep-seated social attitudes toward handicap in our society,[18] but by the often prohibitive cost of the training, equipment, transportation, and counseling that it takes to give such a child simply an even chance. For these children's families, the cost of necessary medical or psychiatric services that can be covered by even a generous health insurance plan is only part of a far larger picture. The average house or apartment must be modified in many ways (for example, wider doorways, special cooking and bathroom facilities) to make it possible for a child in a wheelchair to move around as easily as his able-bodied siblings. A child with a chronic disease or a child confined to a wheelchair makes unusually heavy and costly demands on parents for transportation simply in order to lead a normally active life.

It is possible that some—perhaps even many—of the special needs of a family with a handicapped child could be met through better family services such as we discuss in Chapter 7. Yet parents would still need help that no service could really provide. One possible solution worth serious debate is for the federal government to establish an insurance policy for all families with disabled children. The insurance would function like social security, with all families contributing against the possibility of disability occurring in any child.

We are not suggesting that such insurance duplicate the frequently large settlements made in courts to plaintiffs who have been disabled; it would simply recognize that it costs more to raise a disabled child and indemnify accordingly.

Nor are we talking about medical insurance, for we believe that all families should have access to medical care, whatever their health needs, under a national health-insurance plan (see Chapter 8). Childhood disability insurance (CDI) would begin where a national health-insurance plan leaves off. Just as the aim of a national health-insurance plan is to allow every family to cope equally well with health problems, the purpose of CDI would be to give every family with a handicapped child the additional support it needs to keep the family together with a minimum of strain. Of course, the stresses a disabled child causes his or her family are not exclusively financial. But easing the financial tensions helps keep the family intact. CDI would help relieve families of some of their present dependence on institutions to care of their disabled children. Most children grow up in families; the disabled child should not be discriminated against in this regard.

Our only hesitation in recommending this insurance is that it might relieve some of the pressure that needs to be brought on the government to provide a rational, extensive family service system to meet the many diverse needs that families have for help in raising their children. The solution that is settled on, whether services, insurance, or a combination of these, must be considered carefully, for handicapped children and their families will suffer unnecessary burdens until they get more help than they are getting now.

Other Ways to Get There

There are substantial advantages in a unified structure like the credit tax—in equity, administrative simplicity, and ease of comprehension—but the files of Congress hold hundreds of proposed reforms that have gone into oblivion almost unremarked, so it would be naive not to acknowledge what a Herculean labor it will be to reform the welfare and tax systems at the same time.* If the task proves impossible in the immediate future, it is still possible to achieve a reasonable approximation of the kind of income supports reflected in Table 4 through some combination of piecemeal and incremental reforms in the present structure. The administrative cost would be higher and the result more confusing for families who would have to apply to a number of different programs to receive their full benefits, but if this kind of reform is possible before a thorough overhaul can be done, we would endorse it. The principle of support is more important than the vehicle used to secure it.

The recent establishment of Supplemental Security Income (SSI) replaces the adult categories of state and locally administered public assistance (for the elderly and disabled) with a fully federal program. This provides one model for similar reform of AFDC. SSI provides an income floor for these categories that is nationally uniform, and it has a fractional tax rate—that is, it does not penalize earned income with abrupt reductions in benefits. If food stamps and housing subsidies to families passing a test to prove their lack of means were also combined with a universal SSI-type program, it would be possible to realize a close approximation to the positive-benefit part of Table 4. Other income-related programs could then be reevaluated for their continued relevance. It would also be possible to secure our objectives by introducing a "children's allowance"—a payment made every month for every child in the country, as is done in France— along with a reform of the tax structure.

---

* It should be noted that the complexity of both tax and welfare laws require substantial labor for administration, enforcement, and compliance. Among the political realities is the fact that a drastic simplification (which is feasible) would amount to the abolition of many jobs—what some have described as a "public employment program for semiprofessionals."

Whatever incremental solution might be chosen, because of the problem of overlapping and "pyramiding" implicit tax rates from various programs now in effect, substantial coordination will be needed to keep the consolidated implicit rates of taxation below 50 percent, so no one at any level has to suffer the loss of more than half of any improvement in earned income. In particular, the individual income tax and social security contributions would have to be considered as part of the structure.

There are many further reforms that would improve the fairness and increase the base of the income tax.[19] This kind of reform is immensely important to improving family incomes because the willingness of higher income groups to pay for family benefits depends in no small measure on their belief that the tax system is fair—that others like them are paying as much, and that those who have more are paying more. The present tax system does not enjoy this kind of reputation and does not deserve it. In the end, we are doubtful that our objective for children can be achieved without a major overhaul of the federal income tax.

The Cost

What is the likely cost of this program of income support? Can the nation afford it?

For one thing, in a program of redistribution of income within a full-employment economy, there is no "cost" in its ordinary meaning to the private sector of the economy. Establishing a network of highways or maintaining a defense system, by contrast, does have costs in the sense that resources that could otherwise be devoted to private uses are instead devoted to public ones (with many private benefits, such as jobs). But there is no denying that some people—the group of families most at risk—would be retaining more of their income than they have before, or actually receiving net benefits, while others would be paying more in taxes than they do now. Although it may be appealing to think that the income-support program can be entirely paid out of the pockets of yachtsmen and world travelers, it cannot. In all likelihood it will come, at graduated rates, out of the pockets of people throughout the upper 25 to 30 percent of the current American income distribution, and the total needed from these people will be something in the range of $40 to $50 billion more than the current tax system collects from them.

It is worth repeating just how unevenly income and wealth are now distributed in the United States. The top fifth of families receives 41 percent of all income. The bottom fifth receives only 5.4 percent. In other words, the typical family in the top fifth receives eight times what the family in the bottom fifth receives, even after current welfare payments. If one looks at wealth alone (as distinct from income)—that is, the total assets of families including savings, stock holdings, and real estate—the discrepancy is even more glaring.

117

The top 2 percent of families holds over 37 percent of total wealth. The top fifth holds over 60 percent. The typical family in the bottom fifth has no net worth.[20] We believe this condition to be patently unjust. It alone is a compelling reason to change the overall distribution of material well-being. And it also means that families in the top quarter to third, who should bear the burden of costs of any plan to improve the well-being of poor families, can afford to do so.

Traditionally, American efforts to eliminate poverty and increase economic equality have dealt with everything but the fact of economic inequality and the economic system that allows and perpetuates it. All of these efforts have been unsuccessful: relative poverty has not decreased in over a century [21] in America. As long as our economic system permits millions to live in poverty and as long as our political system is not committed to the elimination of poverty, no programs of personal reform, moral uplift, blame, therapy, philanthropy, or early education can hope to eliminate the enormous harm to the next generation that poverty causes.

This is not to say that improving the economic status of low-income families is going to solve all the problems of children. It will not obviate the need to improve health care for children and pregnant mothers; it will not eliminate the need for a well-financed, responsive child-care network or solve the problems of unwanted children; it will not put an end to the psychological and social pressures of our high-powered, urban, industrialized, corporation-based society which place extraordinary strains on families. Nor will it end the virulent racial discrimination that remains the ugliest blemish on our society. But the evidence indicates overwhelmingly that improving the economic status of low-income families is the most crucial step for bringing American social practice into line with American ideals.

6. Family Work and Wage Work

GUY BILLOUT

"The timing of work" and "the organization of work" sound like terms that belong in corporate planning offices, but the meaning of these two phrases comes in the door of most American households five days a week. Families are connected to the work their members do in ways far beyond income alone. If a middle-management father's job moves from Detroit to Baltimore, so does his family. If a mother has to meet a crisis deadline at the office, she will probably have to miss the

school play. If a pregnant woman works at a job where the strain or the environment can damage the fetus, her child may feel the effects for a lifetime. Yet the work world itself, and national policies affecting work, take almost no account of family needs.

A child's fear of going to the dentist is not written into employment contracts as a valid reason for a parent to take the morning off. The intangible benefits that might come to a four-year-old girl from spending a few unhurried hours at midday with her father, however important he may feel it to be, may seem almost frivolous, dangerously self-indulgent, and unbusinesslike to his supervisors. Who can weigh the balance between the family's need for a parent's wages and the children's need to have more of that parent's warmth, attention, and energy than they may get? Why should women have to lose pay and benefits (not to mention promotions) when they take time out to bear and begin raising children? Why should fathers who wish to help raise their children be denied a significant part in the process because of too heavy a work load?

Parents in their new role as family coordinators may have little power in the face of the professionals they have to deal with regarding their children; ironically, they may have even less power in the very place where they themselves are professionals: that is, trying to hold out for family interests in the face of their paid work. The inevitable conflicts that arise between the demands of a job and the needs of a family are almost always settled in favor of the job.

Is there no other way for that job to be designed? In a conflict, does the family always have to be the one that gives? We do not believe so. It should no longer be assumed that families are not the business of employers or public officials. Corporate and government policies that influence work structure already have a deep influence on the supposedly self-reliant, self-sufficient, independent family unit.*

Our society can and should move toward balancing the competing demands of wage work and child rearing so that children's needs are taken more seriously. There are many ways to give both parents more satisfactory choices: through flexible work hours or carefully arranged part-time work, through improved ways of arranging time off for pregnancy and childhood emergencies, and through new ways to encourage several years' time out for child rearing.

In recommending changes in work practices, we do not suggest that they are a panacea for the problems of balancing work and family life. In fact, to have any impact, all of our work-practices recommendations depend on progress toward full employment, fairer

* There has been very little serious research done on critical details of this link between the customs and policies of work and what goes on in the home. See *Growing Up American,* a report of the Carnegie Council on Children by Joan Costello and Phyllis LaFarge. New York: Harcourt Brace Jovanovich, 1978.

treatment of women in the labor market, an income-support policy, and child-care and other supportive services for families with working parents.

In the short run, the greatest urgency must be given to providing all heads of households that contain children with full-year, full-time jobs. But it is also important to accommodate the desire of many parents, especially mothers, for flexible hours in full-time jobs, for part-time jobs, or even for "part-career" employment * so that they are not forced to leave their children in the care of others when they would rather not, and so that men, too, can genuinely share the work of child rearing.

Our proposals for full employment coupled with income supports would restore some measure of choice to low-income parents with primary child-rearing responsibility who are now either forced into the labor market by the pressure of desperate economic need, or forced to stay at home because they cannot get a job. A credit tax or any other basic income-support system would somewhat reduce one of the most disastrous consequences of the separation of work and family: the financial pressure to work outside the home when the parent feels that staying with the children, especially preschool children, is far more important.

But even with modest income support available for the parent with primary responsibilities for small children, one or both parents in almost all two-parent households and many single parents as well will still need or want to work. Apart from the income work is bound to bring, work has its own intrinsic pleasures and rewards. Even if all our proposals were implemented tomorrow, we would not expect —or wish—to see a dramatic reversal of the steady growth in the proportion of mothers who work. And so the problem of juggling the responsibilities of parenthood and jobs will remain, and changes in the timing and structure of work are essential to reduce the conflicts.

Flexible Scheduling

The typical American work week has shrunk considerably without losses in pay since the time when six days on the job was considered normal and seven not unusual in many industries.[1] In all likelihood the working hours needed to earn a full salary will go on shrinking. For the time being, however, for most families shorter hours are impractical because they mean less income. In addition, many adults enjoy work that requires long hours or intense commitment.[2] While flexibility is no substitute for shorter hours, it

---

* It is possible that eventually greater flexibility in the allocation of work time will involve not only the reorganization of daily, weekly, and annual work schedules but more widespread use of work patterns now used by only a few: life-cycle patterns that permit years of time taken out without great damage to a career.

does help parents balance the competing demands of home and work responsibilities. To be sure, some of the self-employed—independent craftsmen, for example—can set their own work hours. But barring a dramatic reversal in the trend that decreased the proportion of self-employed workers in the labor force from 20 percent in 1940 to about 8 percent in 1970, changes in the working conditions of the 92 percent who work for others will have the greatest impact.

A form of scheduling with special advantages for family life is "flexible hours" or "flexitime," in which employees decide a great deal about their own working hours. The term "flexible hours" is sometimes misleadingly used for other unconventional work arrangements, such as "4/40" (in which employees work four ten-hour days and get three-day weekends) and staggered hours (in which employees arrive and leave at different set times on overlapping schedules). Under truly flexible hours, employees can determine the number of hours they will work on any given day so long as the weekly hours add up to a required total in any given one- or two-week period. In some firms, this flexibility is modified by requiring all workers to be present during a core period but permitting them to arrive and leave at will before or after that.[3] The Metropolitan Life Insurance Company in New York, for example, gives employees the choice of coming in to work any time between 7:30 A.M. and 10 A.M., requiring only that they work a full eight-hour day once they have arrived. Such schedules allow parents to organize their work days to coincide more nearly with their children's schedules—to care for sick children, avoid the rush hour, run errands, or take a child to the doctor. Furthermore, the worker who can make adjustments in work schedules if the need arises has the psychological satisfaction of being able to control her or his own time.

The idea of flexible hours was first promoted by a German economist and management consultant, Christel Kaemmerev, in 1956.[4] Put into operation on a large scale in West Germany in 1967, the idea has since spread throughout Europe, Japan, and Canada. Today in West Germany over 3,000 companies use some form of flexible hours, directly involving over one million employees; in Great Britain, eighty companies and 500,000 civil servants are on flexible hours. In the United States, by 1973 twenty-four firms had converted to flexitime, including Hewlett-Packard, Scott Paper, Sun Oil, Nestle's division in White Plains, New York, and Lufthansa German Airlines.

Early evaluation has shown that when flexible working hours are adopted with genuine management support, productivity and morale improve and turnover, absenteeism, and overtime decline.[5] Obviously, this kind of plan can be as beneficial for employers as for employees. Flexible hours eliminate time lost through lateness and early departure, or through time taken off during the day, or sick leaves used for needs unconnected with illness. Although there

124

are some problems for employers—most notably, added costs of administration, and perhaps keeping plants open longer hours—many employers find these costs are outweighed by the benefits to management. Some problems can occur for employees, too: voluntary flexibility can become forced, and pay for voluntary overtime can be jeopardized. In all the schemes where there has been careful planning with good employee participation, these problems have been avoided. The applicability of flexible hours varies with the type of work and whether a firm faces regular hours of peak demand. Flexitime clearly is more possible in banks and insurance offices, less possible on assembly lines where work cannot go on unless workers are all on hand at once to perform each specialized function, but even in industrial situations some experiments are now under way.

One "flexible" innovation that does *not* seem promising to us involves the various kinds of "compressed" work weeks currently operating in the United States. The most common of these is "4/40," an arrangement that began primarily as a management idea for achieving high utilization of equipment, not as the employee's answer to the strains of combining home and family life. In fact, problems faced by working mothers are a disadvantage mentioned frequently by management. Ten-hour working days tend to heighten rather than alleviate conflicts between family responsibilities and work demands. Time off during a work day is all but unattainable under 4/40, and fatigue is a significant problem.[6] Children's needs are immediate; they cannot wait until Friday. This is not the kind of flexibility families need.

What interests us in the structuring of work time is not only that employers be convinced of added benefits to management in giving their employees more freedom to schedule their hours, but also that employers and employees begin to recognize more fully what a tremendous impact work patterns have on children. Some are beginning to. One vice president of Data Control Corporation, asked about his firm's new flexible program, said, "Flexible hours make better mothers and fathers of our employees."[7]

Part-Time Jobs

Parents' needs for more flexible schedules can also be met through the establishment of permanent part-time jobs.

At present, part-time jobs are rarely a satisfactory alternative for most Americans. Part-time work is usually found in the least skilled and lowest paying occupations, and it tends to be temporary and highly precarious. Most part-time employees are not unionized; many are excluded from health insurance and other benefits. In return for flexibility, many people who want part-time work have to take a job far below their skill levels and accept the fact that they may be out of even that job in a few months.*

Part-time workers, moreover, may get pushed around and have less control over their jobs than full-time workers. According to a survey at the University of Michigan Hospital, part-time nurses felt that they were less valued than full-time nurses; they also felt that their positions were less stable.[8] Most employers assume that since part-time workers are not present the whole time, they cannot be entrusted with supervisory functions. In firms where promotion means a management post with responsibility or supervisory functions, part-time workers are automatically excluded from moving up. The fact that in so many ways part-time work usually does not "pay" helps explain why so many parents who are primarily responsible for raising children also work on a full-time job.

The life of many families would improve with the restructuring of part-time jobs as full-time jobs in miniature. Part-time employees need the same rights on the job as their full-time counterparts. They need guarantees of job security and weekly hours, equal wages for equal work, and benefits such as paid vacations, holidays, paid leave for jury duty, and sick leave computed on a prorated basis according to the number of hours worked. For other benefits, both full- and part-time employees would profit from being offered the chance to choose a prorated benefit package they themselves selected from such offerings as health insurance, additional vacation time, life insurance, and so on.

To minimize costs to employers innovations in management and scheduling are important. For example, to overcome problems when one employee takes over from another, some firms have tried split-level arrangements, where part-time employees of different levels, such as secretaries and executives, are paired together half-time and work the same hours.

The government can help to upgrade part-time jobs by including them under workmen's compensation and minimum wage laws. Although the National Labor Relations Board covers part-time workers, in most factories and offices there is a presumption that they do not have to be included in regular bargaining units. Also, a number of laws specifically bar part-time workers from unionization in certain job sectors, such as state and municipal employment.

* In this discussion of part-time work, we are referring exclusively to "sunlighters"—that is, people whose part-time jobs are their only paid work—not "moonlighters," who are doing a second job for extra money.

One way of creating part-time work is job sharing or splitting, whereby two people share one job, each working half time. This approach has been tried in the New York school system, in the Roxbury Welfare Department, and on the production line at the Volvo plant in Sweden.

Work sharing by married couples was tried experimentally in Norway in 1971, with job schedules arranged so that each parent worked between sixteen and twenty-eight hours per week. The decision about how to split their time was worked out by each couple according to their particular needs.[9] Some couples split the day evenly, with one parent working in the morning and one in the afternoon; others chose to work the same half-day hours while their children attended a day-care center. Most parents involved expressed satisfaction with the work-sharing plan, particularly because of the greater time they were able to spend with their children.*

We support legislative proposals to require federal and state governments in the United States to set an example by creating more part-time jobs.

None of these strategies to upgrade and expand part-time work has much chance of succeeding unless we have full employment. In periods of economic recession, part-time workers can be among the first to go. Full employment is essential to forestall such layoffs; a high general demand for workers would also increase the demand for more part-time employees and help overcome the fear some unions have expressed that part-time jobs will be created at the expense of full-time jobs.

Time Out for Children

The one flexibility for families that has existed in American work schedules for some time is maternity leave for pregnancy and childbirth. This immensely important principle has historically been put into effect, however, at the expense of women's status on the job. Leave may have been available or even compulsory, but along with it came a loss in seniority and in promotion possibilities, and sometimes loss of all pay for the entire period of absence.

In the United States, paid maternity leave, for those few women who receive it, has been financed through disability insurance. Under its provisions, women have been eligible for paid compensation only as long as they were technically "disabled," usually two to four weeks. This approach does not begin to meet their needs or those of their children. In particular, current practice rarely takes into account the need for time off before the baby's birth.

Other nations provide greater support and protection for pregnant women and women with newborn children. In 1952, the Inter-

---

* It should be noted that part-time work for two parents is only feasible in families earning gross salaries over $8,000 a year. Below this level, two combined part-time salaries would not be adequate to support a family.

national Labor Organization fixed minimal standards governing maternity benefits, which included six weeks' compulsory leave after childbirth, six weeks' optional leave before the expected date of birth, security of tenure for pregnant women, and payment of allowances during their leave. In France, women are entitled to six weeks' prenatal leave, eight weeks' postnatal leave, and an allowance of 50 percent of earnings plus continuing employer contributions to social insurance programs. Likewise, in Western Germany women are entitled to six weeks' leave before and six weeks after childbirth and to partial social security benefits.[10]

We believe American employers should be required to support future children by granting their mothers a twelve-week leave of absence to be used before and after the birth of the baby in any proportion the mother chooses. The leave should not cause her to lose seniority, advancement privileges, or job security. To pay for these leaves, the disability system is workable, given an expanded definition of "disability" which would include psychological needs as well as physical incapacity and, to some extent, babies' needs for a mother's time. Clearly there is a need for longer leaves of absence in particular situations. Here, other funding mechanisms deserve further study, including employee compensation by employers for more prolonged childbearing leaves, perhaps at a reduced percentage of normal earnings, or an extension of unemployment compensation to cover maternity leaves financed through matching contributions by all workers, the employers, and the government. As an employer, the government could lead the way by establishing this kind of maternity leave in all its departments and services. Furthermore, we believe that one option the government and later all other employers should explore is combining such maternity leave with leave for the father from his job to care for the new child.*

Another area related to childbirth is protection of the health and safety of the unborn child while the mother is still on the job. If the woman is in a dangerous job, we support the right to change to a safer, less tiring job with the same employer during pregnancy without loss of pay or seniority, the right to rest breaks and reasonable working hours, and the right to a healthful and supportive environment with a minimum of tension and stress, as well as the right to stop working several months before childbirth without loss of pay (see Chapter 9).

Many mothers do not return to work immediately after the birth of a child but quit their jobs in order to stay home for a few years. That decision has always been a career liability: their seniority rights are lost and their skills can become rusty. The potential risks of child rearing to a career discourage many parents—and we

---

* Sweden recently adopted measures that give a couple seven months of paid leave for a new child. The man and woman are free to split this time according to their needs.

explicitly include fathers—from taking time off when their children could benefit from it. If we believe that parents should be able to take time out that they need for child care, we must enable them to get decent jobs when they choose to return to work.

Existing policies that enable parents to take time out for childbirth without penalty should be expanded to let them take more time off—as much as several years—and then return to work without having lost their former status. One model is wartime policy which required employers to hold a position open, including seniority rights, for workers drafted into the armed services. Perhaps it is unrealistic to expect a guarantee of the same job after an interval of many years, since the worker may have forgotten as much as the job has changed, but in that case at the very least industries and government should have programs to facilitate return to work.

Such policies could have a strong effect on the work patterns of both fathers and mothers, with tremendous benefits to their children. It could encourage women and men to approach their education and early jobs with a firm conviction that they would be free to return to interesting work after an interval away. We would like to see a broad effort to improve counseling and information that would encourage young men and women to consider the possibility that they may wish to intersperse wage work and family work throughout their lives. We also support services that encourage and assist mature women who want to return to work. For parents reentering the job market with rusty skills or obsolete credentials, schools and colleges fortunately are beginning to accommodate adults at night or at odd hours.

Part-time education for those who still have active home responsibilities should receive more scholarships and other support, such as child care for parents attending. More schools should offer refresher and updating courses, and more adult classes should be scheduled at times when young children are in school.

Making "reentry" easier may seem to have little to do with children, but our proposals are based on our belief that parents will feel freer to take time off to raise their children when they know that decent jobs will be open to them afterward. Needless to say, a national policy of full employment is once again the prerequisite to making this possible. As with counseling and training programs for teen-agers, all the reentry programs in the world will be pointless if jobs are not waiting at the end of the line.

There are many rearrangements and precautions that would tangibly reduce the present conflict between being a good parent and being a productive worker. The essential first step toward bringing work practices into line with families' and children's needs is a commitment to do so on the part of policy makers in business, labor, and private groups, including families themselves. A task force report on work in the United States [11] has illustrated how great a part of our nation's crime and delinquency, mental and physical health problems, and manpower and welfare dilemmas have their genesis in the world of work.

7. Services Families Need

As Mr. and Mrs. Henderson
pull into their driveway, three
people await them and their new
baby girl. Two are the Hendersons'
older children; the other, a
serious woman dressed in white,
is the nurse the Hendersons
have hired to help them care
for the infant for the first two
weeks she is home. The
Hendersons live in a large
house, and on Tuesdays and

Fridays a woman comes in to do the heavy cleaning. Mrs. Henderson is usually there when her children come home from school in mid-afternoon, but on days when she has to be away, she arranges for baby-sitting with a high school senior down the block or with Mrs. Murphy, an elderly neighbor. She also relies on these two to baby-sit on evenings when she and her husband go out.

The Hendersons consider themselves concerned parents. One of them usually goes to PTA meetings, and Mrs. Henderson regularly consults with their pediatrician, who sees the children several times a year for checkups, immunizations, and routine care. The Hendersons have asked their attorney to set up a trust fund so that a college education for their children will be assured.

The Hendersons are normal middle-class members of their community whom their friends and neighbors consider independent, upstanding citizens. Are these the kind of people who need the help of social services in raising their children or keeping their family intact? When we think about providing services to families, does a picture of the Hendersons come to mind? Probably not. The word "services" in this country has come to be associated with public charity and government intervention in the lives of families considered too poor, too unstable, or too incompetent to manage to raise their children themselves.

This is a myth. People like the Hendersons, whom no one regards as poor, unstable, or incompetent, have plenty of help in raising their children—much of it in services they need and use as much as do families on welfare or families where both parents work but earn low incomes. Of course the *names* of those services—by which we signal whether we find them stigmatizing and distasteful or perfectly normal and acceptable—are often radically different. When the Hendersons had their first child, the live-in nurse they had at home for two weeks not only fed, bathed, changed, and kept watch over the baby but gave Mrs. Henderson helpful suggestions on caring for him. If this same advice had been provided as a service to a poor mother, it would have been called "parent training" —a not-so-subtle label that implies the parent would be inadequate without the training. For a poor family, Mrs. Henderson's cleaning woman would be referred to as providing "homemaker services." Nursery school would be "developmental day care" or Head Start. Afternoon baby-sitting would be "after-school child care." Calling the pediatrician would mean "finding medical services," and for poor children, most routine visits to the doctor would be termed "screening, diagnosis, and treatment." The equivalent of the Hendersons' attorney would be found at a local legal services program, although this lawyer would more likely be engaged in tenant-landlord disputes than setting up a college trust fund.

Are a cleaning woman, nursery school, advice from the nurse, baby-sitting, and the annual eye exam the signs of a failing family?

Of course not. Are a need for homemaker services, child care, early education, parent training, and health services signs of parental inadequacy? Of course not. As we have said throughout this book, it is a natural feature of family life that parents today need the help of various other hands in raising their children.*

The difference between the services the Hendersons receive and those that poor families currently get is more than a matter of labels; it is also a matter of quality. For example, the publicly paid legal services lawyer simply does not have the time in his over-crowded day to give his clients anything like the kind of attention that the Hendersons' lawyer gives them. The quality of legal services for the poor rarely approaches what the more prosperous can afford to buy, and this difference holds true across the board. Mrs. Henderson seldom has to spend more than forty minutes with one of her children at the pediatrician's office. But if she were relying on a public clinic where no appointments are possible, she and her child might spend as long as five hours waiting to see a doctor whom they never met before and could expect never to see again.

Why should human services be most available to those well-off enough to buy them, when all families need them? In most communities, we have a model of one very expensive service that most parents use without having to "buy"—namely, public school. The same impulses that led us to create one school system for rich and poor alike should extend to other social services that families need in order to bring up their children.

"Services" is the catchall term for many of the kinds of help that parents use now that life is not the simple family affair it was on eighteenth-century farms. When we say "services," we mean the help provided families on an ordinary day by teachers, nurses, bus drivers, pediatricians, nutritionists, or social workers. At times, families may also need the help of employment counselors for unemployed parents or their teen-age children, housing or real estate agents to find a place for the family to live, a homemaker while the mother is sick, a psychologist to diagnose a child's learning problem, a lawyer if a child is unjustly expelled from school, and

* This chapter focuses on the needs of families because for the over-whelming majority of children the family is the unit which will care for children's growth and development. In the momentum to deliver services to families, however, we must not overlook the pressing needs of the 150,000 children who are not in homes of relatives and the additional 95,000 children who have no families whatsoever, the institutionalized children. While these children do not make up a large percentage of the population, their problems are so grave, they are so hidden from public view, and they so lack the advocacy that parents would provide if their children suffered abuses, that they are an extraordinarily vulnerable group. It is critical that we develop the procedures and public checkpoints to ensure that no child who can be placed in a family remains in an institution and that for those relatively few children for whom institutionalization is appropriate, an adequate level of service is provided to guarantee fair and humane treatment. (See Chapter 9.)

people who can make referrals to all of these. Families with unusual and more serious problems, whether a severely handicapped child or a parent who physically abuses a child, need help even more urgently. Some of these families and others as well may be unable to care for their children, so at the extreme end of the range of services we must include in our list the people and places that deal with children who are separated from their families: institutions for the delinquent and the severely handicapped, and foster care and adoption.

We do not believe that government can provide services to fill all the needs of all the families in the country. Instead, the long-term goal should be to enable families themselves to choose and pay for the services they want. But government does have a positive and active role to play. This chapter examines what is wrong with the family services currently provided at public expense and describes the characteristics we would like to see embodied in a new system. Chapter 8 looks at the special case of health care, the service on which we now spend over 8 percent of our gross national product.

We believe that families should have access to services without stigma or barriers based on race or class. We also believe that services should be provided as an integrated network, so that instead of isolated programs for children, we have coordinated national and local systems to support families, giving them maximum choice of which services will best strengthen their ability to cope with the problems of living. Parents should participate in planning and running services; services should make full use of parents and others as paraprofessionals and volunteers. Finally, as we will discuss in Chapter 9 on legal protection, we believe this country is currently spending a great deal of money on repair rather than on prevention. This emphasis should be reversed and every measure taken to save families before they reach the breaking point. A decent system of child care relieves some of the problems of child abuse and makes foster care a less frequent necessity; good family planning makes some health services superfluous; counseling, homemaking, and other services can sometimes make the difference that is needed to forestall removing children from a troubled family. An ounce of prevention often costs less than a later "cure."

If all families need help in raising their children, how are the families with very low incomes to find it and pay for it? Two broad strategies are possible.

The first is enabling parents to purchase the services they need on the open market. The goal of this strategy is to increase the purchasing power of families by ensuring work at a decent wage, by income supplements, or by social insurance that provides extra financial support in times of crisis or special need.

The second possible strategy is for the government to organize, provide, and pay for services for those who need them. The public school system exemplifies this approach, as do the direct (and usually free) services provided by welfare and health departments to their clients.

Our emphasis in earlier chapters on the overriding importance of full, fair, and flexible employment and of income supports indicates our preference for providing American families with the wherewithal for choosing and paying for the services they need. This strategy leaves in the hands of parents, rather than the government, crucial choices about whose help they want, where they go for help, and how much they want to pay. It is consistent with the high value we place on giving parents the maximum possible control over how they raise their children.

But providing the wherewithal to parents is not always enough. Although full and fair employment, income supports, and childhood disability insurance would take us a long way toward ensuring that all families have the help they need, a free market by itself will not produce the full range of family services or get them to all families who need them.

Some crucial needs of society require government initiative, action, and regulation to support and protect individual family choices. Services like fluoridation or inoculation against epidemics, for example, should be provided to whole populations, not left entirely to individual choice on a free-market basis. Orphans, victims of child abuse, and juvenile offenders require services that no one in their families can or will pay for. Certain geographic areas have trouble attracting the services they need; for example, we do not have an overall shortage of doctors in this country, but there are precious few licensed physicians in rural areas or inner cities. Research and development in the service field is unlikely to be done adequately by private providers alone. Nor will the cost of services remain low or the quality high without some government support for monitoring. Professional judgments about the need for services—a stay in a mental institution, removal of a child from a family, an appendectomy—are hard for parents to question, especially in the middle of a crisis. Given this widespread control of both demand and supply by professional providers in many services, some public assurance of control over cost and quality is necessary, either through regulation or through the provision of less costly or better quality services.

Government has a critical role to play in helping create and support some services, maintaining the quality of services, public or private, and keeping their costs within reasonable and affordable limits. We do not advocate government monopoly of services, much less dispensing services to American families on a take-it-or-leave-it basis. Our goal throughout is to enlarge the range of choices that parents have.

Services We Have Now

The present array of publicly supported services for families and children has developed over decades of emphasis on particular problems, such as the need to fund foster homes for children whose families cannot care for them, or to immunize children against diphtheria or polio. Some of these services are funded and operated entirely at the local or state level; others are managed at the state level with large federal subsidies in the form of revenue sharing or block grant funds (which basically provide money without dictating forms); a few, such as Head Start and Title I, are funded by the federal government. One survey of federal programs in 1972 showed 280 specifically designed to help families and children, administered by twenty different federal agencies. All but twenty-five of these programs provided services as their major function.[1]

Contrary to popular belief, many of these federally supported programs are not directed only toward poor children and their families. Some programs, such as school lunches, are available to all, but those who can afford to are required to pay some or all of the cost. Still other services focus on particular human needs without regard for ability to pay, including education for the handicapped, childhood lead-paint-poisoning control, centers for runaway youths, and programs for the prevention of drug and alcohol abuse.

Other programs, though nominally aimed at the disadvantaged, define "disadvantaged" very broadly. For example, the Appalachian Child Development Program helps all children in a disadvantaged region of the country; Title I of the Elementary and Secondary Education Act helps low-achieving children living in an economically deprived area whatever their family's income.* In fact, over three-quarters of the federal programs for families and children listed in 1972 were not intended primarily for the poor, and 35.6 percent of these were completely unrestricted, meant to benefit all comers, including middle-class children like the Hendersons' if they needed them.[2]

Despite the number of direct service programs to help families cope with their needs, the federal investment in these services is a small proportion of the federal budget. In 1976, the entire budget for family services (as opposed to tax exemptions, deductions, and cash transfers) amounted to about $30 billion; of this amount, $4 billion went to the public school system and $16.3 billion went for such health expenditures as Medicaid, much of it, of course, spent on adult family members. Nutrition programs, including food stamps (not a service proper) and the national school lunch program, accounted for $5.6 billion.[3]

However important these programs are in specific cases, the problems that have accompanied their piecemeal development are well known: as a nation, we have an inadequate, uncoordinated, and incomplete patchwork of family support services. Services provided at public expense are failing to support families in a number of ways:

Services are unavailable to many who need them. Children entering school are eligible to be screened and treated for physical and emotional problems (basically, what the Hendersons' children get at a checkup with the pediatrician) under the government's Early and Periodic Screening, Diagnosis and Treatment program. In the first nine years of the program, however, fewer than one-quarter of those eligible had actually been screened. Some states have actually screened as few as 1 percent; the most active state annually screens only 39 percent of eligible children. Furthermore, of the approximately 2.2 million screened children who proved to need treatment, only about 50 percent ever received it.[4]

---

* Grants for the Education of the Disadvantaged (Title I of the Elementary and Secondary Education Act) are a useful example of how a program can be targeted toward the needs of the poorest children without making the program exclusively for the poor. The federal funds are distributed among states and, within each state, among school districts in proportion to the number of low-income students who reside there. Within a school district, individual target schools are selected, based on either the number or the proportion of low-income children who reside in the schools' attendance areas. But within a target school, individual children are selected for Title I programs without regard to income but rather by their relative need for educational supplementation.

Since 1968, federal Vocational Education Amendments have required that at least 10 percent of vocational education funds be spent on handicapped and retarded children. But since these funds are expended through the public schools, some 128,000 children who are in state-run institutions do not benefit from them.[5]

A federal program supports special educational services for poor children. Some states and school districts have used these funds to pay for health services related to learning such as diagnostic testing, eyeglasses, and hearing aids. But poor children must be in special classes to be eligible for these health services. If a low-income family had five nearsighted children, only two of whom were in special classes, only those two would be eligible for eyeglasses.[6]

Services are fragmented. A young mother on welfare who becomes pregnant can seek prenatal care from her local health department clinic, but when it is time for the birth, she will be transferred (theoretically with her records but most likely without them) to a public hospital, where she will encounter entirely new faces and a new set of documents. The pediatrician who examines the new baby there will never see the child again. Instead, the young mother now has to take her baby to a "well-child" clinic—but not the same place where she got prenatal care. The well-child clinic unfortunately will not take care of a sick child, so when the baby falls ill she must take the infant to a private physician, whose fee will be paid by the welfare department, or to a hospital emergency room. If the child is found to have a handicapping condition, the child will be eligible for crippled children's services, but these will often be provided at still another place, and paid for with public health funds, which require a whole new set of eligibility determinations. This process, all too typical, would discourage almost any parent from getting that baby the medical care it is entitled to.[7]

Services do not encourage families to stay together. For many years, in order to get welfare, poor families had to prove that the father was absent from the house, which encouraged many poor families to separate or lie. Recognizing this, the federal government in 1972 passed an "unemployed fathers" provision which gave states the option of giving AFDC assistance to families with two parents. But, as of mid-1976, almost half the states had not adopted this provision.[8]

Families with temporary problems such as the illness of a parent may need help caring for their children. Child care during the day in another home or a center is the remedy that disrupts the family least; temporary foster care is more disruptive; placing children in institutions is the most traumatic of all. Yet close relatives who take a child in at times of family stress do not qualify for the payments most welfare programs give to unrelated foster parents; so when money to support the child is a major factor, this federal service policy encourages parents to place their children with strangers or in an institution.*

Most services are designed only to treat problems, not prevent them. The Child Lead-Based Paint Poisoning Control Program was enacted to help communities combat the poisoning that each year kills between 300 and 400 children and irreversibly damages the brains of 6,000 more. But program funds can be used only to remove lead paint from apartments where children have already been found poisoned.[12]

Medicaid programs in twenty-one states deny prenatal care to first-time mothers, even though studies have indicated that, compared with those who do get care, mothers who receive no prenatal care are three times more likely to give birth to infants with low birth weights, a condition associated with almost half of all infant deaths and with birth defects.[13]

Services are underfunded. The 1976 appropriation for federal child welfare expenditures (which is not AFDC but funds to help state and local welfare agencies provide protective services meant to prevent public dependency and neglect) was more than $200 million short of the authorization enacted by Congress.[14] The appropriations for Title I of the Elementary and Secondary Education Act have never matched the authorizations; in fiscal 1977, the appropriations covered the equivalent of an estimated 39 percent of those children judged to be in need in that year.[15]

Recognizing that educating handicapped children can place an extra financial burden on public schools, the federal government enacted the Education for All Handicapped Act in 1972. But the total

---

* The least disruptive solution is also the least expensive to society. Foster care costs approximately twice as much as care in a child's own family, and institutional care costs at least twice as much as foster care.[9] Yet in 1976, 73 percent of federal child welfare service expenditures were for services to children in foster homes, and less than 10 percent could be identified for day-care services.[10] Average monthly payments for AFDC foster care in five sample states in April, 1976, were, respectively, $91, $137, $141, $155, and $180; by contrast, average monthly payments for child-care institutions in these same states were $709, $1,015, $1,032, $1,165, and $992.[11]

amount of money authorized for this purpose for fiscal 1978 will amount to only about $17.50 for every handicapped child in the nation.[16]

Services stigmatize. Overall, the second-class nature of services for the poor is the biggest stigma of all. Specific instances add insult to injury: children who need services but receive them because a court judges them to be "persons in need of supervision" or "children in need of services" may later find that the stigma of their court records outweighs the benefits of any services they get. For example, in forty-seven states truants from school may get services by being institutionalized; but their records may later close job opportunities even if they go back to school.[17]

When the federal government required Head Start programs to make at least 10 percent of their enrollment handicapped children, many programs merely labeled as handicapped 10 percent of the children already enrolled, in order to receive federal funds.[18]

Principles for Change

Given these problems, it is small wonder that publicly provided social services have received a bad name among both taxpayers and recipients. Yet these problems are not inevitable. The way we provide services to families in this country could be very different if we started from different principles.

1) *Universal Access* As long as we care about the growth and development of this nation's children, services for all who need them must be the first principle. This means services that are open to everyone—whatever race they are, whatever income they have, wherever they live, and whatever languages they speak. The public has an interest in seeing that everyone has services available and that these meet federal standards of fairness and quality, even if they are privately provided. When the public decides that a service is essential and will be publicly financed for all users, as with education, then everyone should have equal access and get equal benefits. We believe that health care should fall into this category, as we explore at length in Chapter 8.

Whenever services are in short supply, we believe that priority should be given to families where the well-being of the child and the integrity of the family are in greatest jeopardy for lack of services. For example, if daytime child-care places are in short supply, children with special developmental, emotional, and educational needs should have a high priority. If homemaker services are scarce, families that require these services to prevent placing their children outside the home should have first claims. In practice, we believe this will mean that priority will most often be given to families at the lower end of the income scale, to families who cannot afford to seek the service from private providers.

The same principles—the well-being of the child and the integrity of the family—should determine priorities for the creation of new services when these are needed. And the community itself should determine its own local priorities, within broad federal guidelines, since the unmet service needs of Harlem are likely to be quite different from those of rural Nebraska.

2) *Racial and Economic Integration* Services should foster, as much as possible, the racial, class, and cultural integration of different families. Having black and white, middle-class and poor children in the same program not only teaches children about diversity but also builds the breadth of political support that is necessary to sustain adequate support for most services. Integration will be fostered most by making service programs universally available, regardless of family income. In addition, this goal will be helped by better consolidation and coordination of services. Community service centers, for example, ought to be organized to serve families with battered children, children who do not speak English, or children who may need special help to prepare for school—all problems that cut across the lines of race and class.

3) *Convenience and Coordination* In order to use a service, many families need "secondary support services" such as transportation, baby-sitting, someone who will answer their questions on the telephone, interpreters for those who do not speak English, and public information to let them know what is available. Most current service programs use all their funds for their own basic functions, with nothing left over to provide other kinds of help that will enable families to make use of the services. Secondary support services make other family services accessible and contribute to their efficacy well out of proportion to their cost. Therefore, there should be one place where families can go to find out about the available services they may need, to get proper referrals to the correct services, to make appointments, and to get needed transportation or baby sitters. To provide this, a referral-and-appointment center should exist in every town, county, or neighborhood, depending on the size of the area and the population involved.

Where possible, clusters of related services should be located together or close by each other—on the model of the county courthouse—so that families can go to one location for a variety of related services. When new services are added, they should build on existing service systems that are well accepted. Schools, for example, might also be used for providing health and early screening services.

Coordination should also take place at the federal level, and the government should review the standards it has already set for programs, eliminating discrepancies and conflicting regulations for similar services provided by several agencies.

4) *Maximum Choice* Service systems should strive to provide families with the widest possible range of options so that they can choose which services will help them most and which provider will suit them

best. An illness of one parent may require a visiting nurse, a home-maker, or temporary day care, but families should not be forced to put their children into day care because nurses or homemakers are not available. If they do choose day care, various types should be available: family, group, or center care.

5) *Parent Participation* Obviously, a good program for migrant-worker families would not be identical to a good program for middle-class suburbanites. The ethnic and cultural traditions of families and communities should be taken into account when organizing and delivering family services. In order to ensure that differences in child rearing and other family patterns are reflected accurately and sensitively in social programs, and to check remote bureaucracies, services should require inclusion of families in policy making, monitoring, and helping run the day-to-day program.

6) *Paraprofessionals and Volunteers* While good professionals—doctors, teachers, social workers, and the like—are important in diagnosing problems and providing services of all kinds, services should also draw on a range of paraprofessionals and volunteer help. The United States has enormous resources in parents, youths, and senior citizens. Using them as volunteers and paid paraprofessionals should be encouraged—and, in federally supported programs, mandated—in order to keep costs down, open up career options for the unemployed or those who choose to work in human services, and make service programs familiar and politically popular in the communities that use them.

7) *Prevention and Keeping Families Intact* A rational and unified system of services should put the prime stress on preventive services and those that disrupt family life the least. It should be as easy for families to go to a clinic for diagnosis and treatment of a mild problem as to the emergency room after the problem has become a serious condition. It should be more attractive for overburdened parents to use day-care and counseling services before they reach the point of harming their child than court-mandated services after the fact. As we spell out further in Chapter 9, the courts that deal with children should be empowered to order services for families in trouble before things have gotten so bad that a child must be placed in some form of nonfamily care.

Accountability: Increasing Parents' Control

These principles we have sketched out are essentially standards of fairness and quality that we would like to see applied to all service programs, not only those that are government run.[19] Just as restaurants have to meet minimum standards of public health and are not allowed to discriminate against racial minorities, so private service programs should not be allowed to fall below uniform levels. Federally determined standards for all services, some of which we will outline below, should be put into effect nationwide through legislation, where appropriate, and through agency regulations and executive orders as well.

Traditionally, people who provide services, at least those publicly funded, have had to account to their bosses, not their clients, for how well they are doing their job. This means that a father has very little say in how his daughter's day-care center is run, even though he may know more about the center's shortcomings and successes than the bureaucrat to whom they are supposedly being reported. We believe that the traditional enforcement of standards by administrative fiat must be balanced by giving authority and responsibility to the level where the service works. This is why there should be parent representation—which also serves the other purposes outlined above—as well as federal supervision. And parents should be involved in assessing more than just how programs are performing the job they set out to do.

At present, many agencies that operate services do some self-monitoring. Schools, hospitals, and counseling centers, for example, may undertake surveys of the number of people who need their service; they may plan whether to have one center or six; they may count how many of the people who need the service are getting it; they may try to survey how much the service is helping its clients. But in essence this is similar to a business auditing its own books, a practice long outlawed because of the obvious conflicts of interest. To reduce such ethical conflicts, in recent years some service programs supported with public funds have been required to hire outside evaluators. The trouble is that most such evaluators are profit-making consulting firms who know that if they deliver an evaluation of "poor" this year, next year the agency may give its evaluation business to someone else. The result is evaluations that all too often play things safe.

We propose that federal regulations take away from service operators such planning and assessment functions as overall coordination with other similar services, needs surveys, coverage surveys, and evaluations, and require communities to set up "consumers' councils" with heavy representation of parents to perform these auditing jobs. The councils should receive enough federal support to purchase technical assistance such as surveys. Their responsibility should extend to an area no greater than an efficient service "basin," that is, an area about the size of a school district. These councils will have to be independent of any organization that itself provides services. Also, they should be concerned with different services and different approaches to the same service, so they do not in effect become advocates for any single kind of solution of service needs. Since experience shows that getting parents and clients in general to participate effectively is far from simple, experimental versions of these councils should be tested.

Consumers' councils would first of all assess the need for services in their area of responsibility; second, survey how well programs are reaching people with those needs; and third, evaluate how well programs are actually alleviating the problems they were set up to solve, and whether they meet federal standards. Although the councils would not have the staff to do evaluations themselves, they should have the responsibility of choosing the contractor for every program assessment.

The fact that this kind of quality auditing is a yet undeveloped field, with none of the familiar devices that by now make the auditing of double-entry bookkeeping routine, should not be a barrier to beginning. However rudimentary the beginning standards that are developed, the benefits of auditing quality on a regular basis will be well worth the difficulty in creating the systems to do it.

The most important tool for making programs accountable for quality is accurate data open to those who evaluate the service and to individuals or groups who wish to challenge a provider of services. Within the bounds of respecting privacy, federal standards should open for public scrutiny the internal information necessary to evaluate how effectively each service program plans and how well it is performing.

At the national level as well, data on the conditions and needs of American families and children must be improved. Most of the major national data-collection systems, such as the National Bureau of the Census and Bureau of Labor Statistics, ask questions about problems, which at least begins to define what services are needed. But these data systems make no effort to connect the conditions for which they gather data to the coverage provided by federal programs to find out whether existing programs are even in place and trying to help.[20]

For example, the National Health Examination Survey (the single major source of national estimates on health conditions among children) produces a dozen or more reports every year on a wide and growing range of specific illnesses and symptoms.[21] But when it surveyed school-age children for vision deficiencies and asked whether they had corrective lenses, it did not ask why children who needed them did not have them, nor did it ask how recently the children had received a vision examination at school. Similarly, a special Health and Nutrition Examination Survey (HANES) series which determined the incidence of nutritional deficiencies among children and young adults did not ask whether the children received school lunches.[22] The Bureau of Labor Statistics in its national survey of employment and earnings asks whether an unemployed family head sought work in the last month but not whether federal programs are supplying assistance to the family or, if so, what programs or in what amount.[23]

While these data-collection systems should not be deflected from their primary mission of collecting information on national conditions regardless of what programs are in operation, adding a few questions to the existing forms could greatly improve the information available to people who design and monitor child and family services. The data should be presented in reports that emphasize the impact that programs have on children. Regular state-of-the-family and state-of-the-children reports should become routine.

Furthermore, everyone—from administrators of federal programs to members of Congress—will have a far clearer view of service needs and coverage, as well as the impact that services are having, once consumers' councils are able, under federal standards, to hold programs responsible for keeping up-to-date, accurate, and complete internal management records about the operation and effectiveness of service programs.

We believe that the responsibility for watching over standards and performance belongs primarily in two places: at the federal level where the federal intent was formulated, and at the level where the program functions—namely, with the programs' clients who serve on the consumers' council. Neither of these alone can do an effective job of monitoring because federal officials often have no idea of local needs and preferences, and consumers' councils may ignore federal standards and thereby neglect some of the local populations.*

What about state and local governments, where there are many agencies with responsibility for services? Unfortunately, many problems with current federally funded services originate with state or local governments, whose officials are not necessarily interested in

---

* The reason the federal government must perform this function has to do with the tension between collective and individual interests. Individual interests are well served by local town governments, which are politically responsible to the balance between tax costs and individual benefits. Essential to that balancing is the competition among towns to lower tax costs and to concentrate benefits solely on their own residents. Thus many towns do not spend much for education, hoping that those citizens who want it will go to school in a neighboring town. But the collective interests of society as a whole are ill served by such competition among towns, and we have always shaped our national policy to reflect this fact. Thus we do not let towns "compete" in providing for national defense, since we are quite certain that almost every town would substantially underinvest in order to lower tax rates. Similarly, we should not force local competition among towns in the provision of essential human services since that, too, leads inevitably to underinvestment.

147

either the programs or the principles but may instead be using the services for political ends or may simply want the federal money to use for something else. Block grants made to states with no strings attached often fall under the administration of state or local government, and with poor results, for recent history shows that local or state government control does not always produce the programs that Congress intended when it voted the funds.[24]

There are some hard conflicts between providing local control and assuring that federal standards are met. An example of this is the way that local interests dominated by sectionalism, provincialism, and outright bias and discrimination have often resisted federal enforcement of antidiscrimination requirements and other attempts to strike a fairer balance between the haves and the have-nots. Federal revenue sharing may be a convenient way to provide financial relief to hard-pressed local governments, but it can seriously undercut the enforcement of federal discrimination provisions. It also makes it easier for special interest groups with political strength to dictate how the money will be spent, while those who need services but have no political clout go wanting. For example, between the start of the federal revenue-sharing program in 1972 and early 1975, municipalities spent 44 percent of their revenue-sharing funds on public safety, 15 percent on public transportation, and 13 percent on environmental protection but only 15 percent on health and a mere 1 percent on social services for the poor and aged.[25] In many cases, communities elected to drop services that were once provided with federal money as soon as revenue sharing with local control gave them the choice.* A recent study of thirty-seven cities reported that only seven used any revenue-sharing funds to replace any terminating federal programs.[26] In essence, local governments decided to supplant local with federal funds to hold down local taxes instead of providing services.

Changes can be made at the state level, however, that will improve the delivery of services. In recent years, many major federal service programs have begun requiring states to submit a permanent or annual plan for providing and coordinating certain services. Such plans are required for Title XX of the Social Security Act, Aid for the Education of Handicapped Children, Vocational Education, the

---

* We do not advocate the retention of every current categorical aid program in its present form. On the contrary, consolidation of related programs and the integration of program functions (such as auditing, impact evaluation, needs assessment, and case monitoring) across programs and providers are both highly desirable administrative reforms. What is essential is that the consolidated programs also gain the kind of administrative mechanisms that will keep their efforts focused on the needs their original categorical versions were meant to fill in the first place. Unless both administrative reforms are installed simultaneously, consolidation of programs will mean only the stultification of national purpose in a morass of local interests. The needed administrative mechanisms are discussed later in this chapter.

delinquency prevention services funded under the Law Enforcement Assistance Administration, and a host of other laws. In some instances, state plans are the only part of an entire program that has to measure up to any specific standards about the substance of the program. Thus, the standards that the states have to meet in preparing their plans are virtually the only tool federal agencies have for keeping accountable the people who spend billions of federal dollars.

In practice, state plan mechanisms have unfailingly broken down. Part of the problem is that in the early years of a new program, the federal agency does not yet have the experience to set up any but formalistic criteria for measuring the adequacy of a state plan. For example, since 1974, the regulations for Title XX have required states to determine which services families need, but as of 1976 the federal government had no specific standards for how the states should go about determining this.

A more basic problem is that when a state plan is submitted, public comment often is allowed only during a brief period, usually ninety days. There is no requirement for hearings, and no requirement that any public comments be evaluated by the federal agency that gives the state its funds. Even if public groups or groups of beneficiaries had a decent forum, there is never funding or technical support for them to prepare careful analysis of the state plans that are proposed. Even if they had staff, time, and money, there is no requirement that the state give the public access to the data and information it used in the planning process. The result is that public participation is reduced to a charade in which individuals and community groups knowledgeable about their local areas but without access to resources, information, or a neutral forum helplessly try to out-argue a statewide bureaucracy.

We endorse the process of requiring state service plans, but urge that it be strengthened. The federal government should insist that state plans include all of the following elements, only a few of which are now required even in the best plans:

1) assessments of what services are needed in the state, where, and who actually is being served;

2) an identification of agencies and groups that could provide the service in question;

3) an internal system for reporting on the management of the program operations;

4) plans for how the program is to be evaluated;

5) mechanisms that allow the agency involved to follow the cases of individual children or families and be held responsible for their continued treatment.

6) Most important, each state plan should spell out ways services can be monitored by outsiders and clients, including ways for citizens

to participate in planning; grievance and complaint mechanisms for people who use the service; and various forms of technical assistance for agencies providing services run by parents and community organizations, so they can compete for contracts and funds with more experienced governmental and private providers.

Our proposals for firm accountability reflect a conservative view of the role of government. Government, we believe, should enable the simplest units possible—individuals and families—to make their own choices and control the shape of their own lives. In seeking to

ensure that federal law is enforced on behalf of families and children, we are essentially recommending family empowerment. Moreover, poor enforcement and poor implementation of laws that are already on the books have contributed powerfully to current gaps in family services and to the widespread belief that government does not mean to do what it says. Firm accountability can help reverse this trend.

Limiting the Public Cost

Who should pay for family services and how is a key question for family members, taxpayers, and legislators. Even "free" services such as public education must ultimately be paid for. In the same way, publicly provided family services have to be paid for, either directly by the user or indirectly by users and nonusers through taxes. Furthermore, the public purse is not bottomless.

At present, most prosperous American families such as the Hendersons pay for almost all of the services they use from their own pockets. Those who live in or near poverty can sometimes call upon services provided by taxes or by private charity, although too often they simply go without the help they need. Those in the middle do the best they can with what they earn.

If the proposals put forward earlier for jobs, income supports, and childhood disability insurance are implemented, that will mean that all families of four in which one member is able to work will have an income above half the median—at least $8,400 per year in 1974 dollars (see page 109). Not just people at the guaranteed job level, but almost all families up to an income of about $18,000 will have more after-tax income than they do under our current system. Child-care costs will be fully deductible from taxable income, which —under the credit tax we offered as an example—means an indirect federal subsidy of 50 percent. Single parents will either receive support payments from the absent parent or an income supplement administered through the tax system. Flexible work practices will make it possible for parents to combine child rearing and work outside the home with less complicated and less expensive child-care provisions, and a reformed tax system will mean that those who choose this will not be paying prohibitive implicit tax rates. Childhood disability insurance will protect families against the financial catastrophe of rearing a disabled child, enabling them to pay for special services like transportation just as the family with health insurance now pays hospital bills. A national health system, proposed in the next chapter, will guarantee all American families, regardless of income, good health care.

These broad changes would reduce the cost of services to federal, state, and local budgets by enabling parents to pay the expenses of services from their own income or insurance.

We have repeatedly emphasized our preference for directly supporting families rather than bureaucracies. But as we have also emphasized, government has to play an assertive role in ensuring that parents have control over the services they use. Furthermore, no one but government can guarantee equity of treatment, access for those who need the service, and good quality. Government must also be largely responsible for planning and for seeing that new programs are designed and tried out. As far as the costs of services are concerned, this means several things:

1) Public funds are necessary to develop national, regional, and local surveys of families' and children's needs and to create appropriate plans for meeting those needs.

2) In many cases, government must provide the start-up costs, and the costs of training new workers, for family services that are needed but not available now. For example, public support will be important for creating information-and-referral centers; public monies should help train homemakers who can help families passing through special transitions, or child-care workers for day-care centers.

3) Public monies are needed to fund demonstration centers and to evaluate the effects of existing programs. In the continuing discussion of the most desirable forms of nonfamilial child care of very young children, for example, federally funded demonstration and evaluation studies should play a major role.

4) Public funds are needed for consumers' councils to monitor family services and ensure that they meet standards of quality and requirements about parent participation, that they are financially accountable, and that they adhere to general legal requirements.

151

5) Public support will be needed for some secondary support and access services such as transportation to get people to the services they need.

6) Public funds and enforcement action will be needed to ensure more equitable access to the services families need. For example, ensuring that rural, poor, and nonwhite families have access to needed services that are now maldistributed will require federal action and, in some cases, federal funds to pay construction, training, and start-up costs in underserved communities.

7) In the foreseeable future, there are bound to be some families who cannot pay the full cost of all the services they urgently need. In such cases, we advocate subsidizing a portion of the costs which the family cannot pay from earnings, income supplements, or insurance benefits. The method of payment adopted by community mental health centers, in particular, has much to recommend it. In such centers, a wide variety of mental health services are available to all who need them. Users who can afford it pay the full costs of the services they receive. For those of limited means, payments are adjusted according to the incomes and assets of the family, with the public subsidizing the remainder. Of course, unless the use of sliding-scale subsidies is carefully adjusted, it will create the very high implicit tax rates for certain users that are a feature of the present system we are eager to see left behind. For if a family will lose, say, $500-worth of several services when an earner in the family gets a $500 raise, they are, implicitly, paying a 100-percent tax on the raise.

We should emphasize that there are important choices to be made in the balance between public subsidies for family services and direct public support of family income. In the short run, we recognize the need for services with at least some of their ongoing operating costs paid from public funds. Until we have full employment and a strong system of income supports, families in need will have to rely on a complementary mix of earnings from work, transfer payments, and subsidized services.

In the long run, we believe the goal should be to enable families themselves to pay for the help they need in raising children, keeping subsidization of the operating costs of public services as limited as possible. Only in areas such as health care and education do we support the full payment of service costs from public revenues.

We have indicated that we believe government has a major role to play in the creation, evaluation, coordination, and planning of services. And government must always be ready and able to step in to help families afford necessary help that they cannot fully pay for. But the overriding long-term goal of family policy should be to put even more families in the position of the Hendersons, to give them the financial and political power to select and control the services they receive.

8. Children's Health

At its best, medical care in the United States is the finest in the world. Yet for all our wealth and expertise, our system is not only unbalanced but expensive, and it delivers second-rate care to many people, especially to mothers and children.

We spend a larger portion (over 8 percent) of our gross national product on medical care and other health services than do other Western industrialized

countries, but there are six countries in which women have a higher life expectancy, eighteen in which men live longer, and fourteen that have a lower infant mortality rate, one of the key signs of good national health.[1] As with other family services, we live with a double standard in health care, and the distinctions between good care and bad are felt even before a child is born. It is now generally accepted that prenatal care should begin during the first three months of a pregnancy in order to have the greatest success in preventing infant mortality or other problems with lifelong consequences for children. Prenatal care this early is achieved for 70 percent of all live births in this country, but for only one-half of births to nonwhite mothers.[2] * In 1975, the infant-mortality rate for whites was 14.4 per 1,000 live births—its lowest ever—but the rate for nonwhites was 22.9—the same rate that American whites showed in 1960.[3]

In other words, in this most basic index of overall health, American nonwhites in 1975 were fifteen years behind the white population. This gap has not substantially closed in the last fifty years, despite a steady decline in the overall death rate for both groups, and despite demonstration programs in poor areas showing that concerted efforts to provide high-quality health care could greatly reduce the remaining disparities if the nation chose to do so.[4] If the entire United States achieved the low infant-mortality rate among whites, our international standing would improve from fifteenth to eighth.

These statistics reveal how American health care functions on two tracks, one to serve the poor and minority groups, and another for those who are assumed able to pay their own way. The first track is predominantly public and institutionally based, operating through such facilities as the emergency rooms and outpatient departments of municipal or county hospitals and public health department clinics. The other is predominantly private, operating from the offices of private doctors working in solo practice or small group settings. Differences between the two tracks are least pronounced in the area of tertiary care (which is the most highly specialized and sophisticated treatment) because major medical centers usually provide for rich and poor alike when health problems have become critical or complex.

---

* Early prenatal care is obtained by even fewer unwed mothers (40 percent of both whites and nonwhites), who are a high-risk group due to their generally young age and low income. The effect of this and other differences in care and health can be clearly read in the statistics that show an excessive number of low birth-weight babies born to poor and nonwhite mothers. Low birth weight (under 2,500 grams) is perhaps the single best indicator of risk or damage to surviving infants. While only slightly over 6 percent of legitimate live births to white mothers and those with family incomes over $10,000 were low birth weight in 1972 (the latest figures available), almost 10 percent of such births were low-weight in families with incomes under $5,000; and among nonwhite families, almost 13 percent of births were low-weight.

It is outside the hospital setting that the system breaks down, especially for the poor, and most especially for children, whose contact with the health-care system comes chiefly through services that focus on primary care, the kind of care dealing with basic and general health problems. Between 20 percent and 25 percent of all children in this country receive whatever health care they get from the public sector, which is chronically underfunded and politically vulnerable. Many poor and minority children do see private physicians, but the care they get has little continuity and frequently is of questionable quality. About one-fifth of poor and minority children have not seen a doctor at all in two years.[5]

Such disparities in health care are a by-product of the traditional American preoccupation—in health care as elsewhere—with helping individuals. Our private health-care system sets the terms for publicly funded health care and is based on the model of a single doctor providing a specific service for a specific fee. In great part because of this model, we typically see health care as the treatment of severe disease and fail to concentrate on primary, preventive care and on building good health, approaches that can forestall many expensive medical crises.

Moreover, many of the most urgent health needs of the population do not fit the pattern of "fee for services" that characterizes our system of private medicine. Hence, it is not surprising that doctors, who get paid essentially on a piecework basis (so much for a shot, so much for an operation), often neglect services they cannot put a price on; and they *are* inclined to provide services on which they can put a higher price.

For example, many of the most pressing and unsolved child health problems—behavioral and mental health problems, teen-age pregnancy, child abuse—often take large amounts of time for work with patients, using a variety of supportive services and health workers. Item-by-item prices on the components of such care are difficult to arrive at conceptually and virtually impossible to reimburse under a fee-for-service system. Moreover, most private doctors and hospitals are set up to deal with individual patients who find their way into the system, not to provide for the general health of whole populations or to assure that all get some system of care. (Indeed, medical education itself prepares doctors for little beyond episodic, hospital-based services.) Publicly funded health care unfortunately follows that same basic model and consequently does little better than private health care in the prevention of predictable health crises.

Beyond that, in the American competition for health dollars, crisis medicine gets priority. It is easier to get adequate public financing and program support to install expensive neonatal intensive-care units for damaged or very premature infants than it is to get authority or funding for contraceptive services or for routine prenatal care and nutritional programs for pregnant women. And

157

precious little of the money we now spend on health goes to children in any case. In 1940, one out of every two federal dollars spent on health went to children. By 1970, as other groups pressed their needs, this ratio had fallen to one in seventeen.[6]

Americans have a national conviction that we should preserve the independence of doctors, a conviction the American Medical Association has lobbied to sustain. It is only now becoming clear that in the area of health care, free enterprise cannot do everything. Competition between doctors does not get them into the areas where they are needed: Chicago's South Side and other poverty areas in that city have a ratio of 26 physicians for every 100,000 persons, while affluent areas of the city have 210 physicians per 100,000 population, a variation of more than 800 percent.[7] Thousands of rural communities in this country lack even one doctor and do not have any system of transportation to medical care elsewhere.

Nor is it challenging or profitable for doctors to concentrate on routine dental care, complete immunizations, regular and accessible prenatal and primary care, emotional or behavioral problems, or accident prevention—the immediate health needs which are most often unmet in this country yet which repay the comparatively minor costs of meeting them many times over in savings.

It is even less likely that the medical profession will concentrate on our most neglected long-term health needs: chronic conditions, psychosocial and learning problems related to family stress, and—the most neglected needs of all—prevention of crippling and handicapping conditions and the development of more healthful environments and behavior patterns. This is not merely a choice of the profession, but is abetted by the social encouragement the profession receives.

Faced with what amounts to a complex nonsystem, American families have to organize their own health care, guessing which type of doctor to see if something is bothering them (there are fewer and fewer general practitioners), and wondering how much it will cost and whether insurance or the government will pay for it (often they will not). It is no wonder that many people delay attending to health needs until a crisis develops, especially since private health-insurance plans are more likely to cover the cost of hospitalization than the cost of a visit to the doctor's office.

Even national health insurance, proposed as a panacea for all the problems in the system, will not solve them by itself. Until we address the difficult issues of reorganizing our national health-care nonsystem, of redistributing health services both equitably and efficiently, and of setting up controls that make medical professionals accountable to the public for what they do, it will be too costly to provide health care for everyone at public expense. It is not enough simply to extend the current system. It would be an enormous and costly mistake to place even larger sums of money at the disposal of miscellaneous health-care providers and financers (including local public health departments) with no concomitant increase in government power over how those sums would be spent. If government cannot or will not intervene on behalf of the public in the organization of health care, we should not be using public money to pay for it.

Goals for Change

Without undertaking here a full analysis of either the American health-care system or the multitude of proposals for its change, we can offer five broad health-policy goals for children and families. Achieving them is essential for meeting the health needs of children in a way that fits the general criteria for the family-support services we previously outlined. These goals are:

1) to make attention to nonmedical influences on health an integral part of health services delivery and planning;
2) to remove barriers that keep children from receiving care because of their families' economic situation, race, or ethnic origin;
3) to organize the health-care delivery system for children in order to emphasize preventive care, primary care, and more humane care;
4) to create publicly accountable health agencies that will assure that services of high quality are available to every child as needed;
5) to increase and strengthen the capacity of communities, parents, and children to act on their own behalf as both health advocates and health caretakers.

We make no claim that these goals are brand new; variations of them have been proposed by both public and private commissions, study groups, and individuals for at least fifty years. They remain, however, unachieved and nationally unacknowledged as health goals.

Goal One: To make attention to nonmedical influences on health an integral part of health services delivery and planning.

Health in childhood as well as adulthood is a state of body and of mind which requires an ecological perspective to fully comprehend and support. It is a mistake, although one frequently made, to equate "health" only with the services that the health-care system provides. Healers, drugs, and special treatments are needed when illness strikes, but far more than these goes into staying healthy. For children and adults alike, poor health is caused by diet, poverty, stress, and industrial pollution, as well as by genes, microbes, and accidents. (Roughly half the children who die between the ages of one and four are the victims of accidents, including those involving motor vehicles.)

Reacting against the American overemphasis on established medical science, recent critiques of medical care have highlighted its limited value in such cases as unnecessary tonsillectomies and heart surgery, and have pointed out such medical dangers to health as cancer risk from X rays or the dangerous side effects of drugs.[8] These critiques are an important antidote to the conventional belief that doctors can and should cure everything, but we would express a note of caution here, too: if it is untrue that doctors and medical care can do everything, it is also untrue that they can do nothing of value. Personal health services are important and, when delivered properly, contribute to the health of both individuals and society. A wealthy and humane society can afford to offer care to the individual *and* health to the whole population.

What is necessary is a far more discriminating analysis of the actual effectiveness of all health-care practices, from routine physical examinations to coronary artery by-pass surgery; consideration of a far greater range of methods to achieve the same ends (so that for the purpose of reducing cancer deaths, smoking and industrial carcinogens receive at least as much attention as programs for treating cancer); and an opening up to informed public debate and accountability of the way health-care priorities are set.

One likely result of an "ecological" reappraisal of health priorities might be that environmentally raised problems would begin to be forestalled before they reached a doctor's office. The nation's health resources could then be focused more sensibly on high-risk groups. Victor Fuchs presents a relevant example in regard to reducing infant mortality:

> Medical care programs aimed at groups with particularly high risks—very young girls, women of low socio-economic status, and the like—have in recent years been able to show substantial reductions in neo-natal mortality. Therein may lie an important clue to the role of medical care. For very

160

risky pregnancies, the quantity and quality of care available may be critical; for pregnancies that present little risk (that is, among well-educated, well-fed mothers, neither very young nor very old) the quantity and quality of care may be of minor importance, except insofar as poor care can be worse than none at all.[9]

We are not asking doctors to drop their stethoscopes and take on every burden of society. We do envision the relationship of the health-care establishment to environmental concerns falling into four broad categories:

1) Responsibility for some health-support efforts should remain outside the health-care sector, but that sector should promote them far more aggressively than it does now. These include drives for good housing, full employment, income support, and broad environmental protection, all of which would improve conditions that are among the major long-run determinants of the population's physical and mental health.

2) Other health-supporting policies that do not usually involve direct patient-by-patient services should be major goals of the health-care system itself, promoted in cooperation with others. These policies include environmental and occupational health measures, good nutrition, health education, and a requirement that all public legislation and major corporate plans be accompanied by statements, like our current environmental impact statements, that indicate what effect the new measures would have on families and their health.

3) Those personal health services which require close collaboration with or incorporation of educational, social, or psychological services should be recognized as the new frontier of public health activity and receive appropriately greater attention, manpower, and financial support. These collaborative projects include reproductive services, mental health and family counseling, projects to deal with children's school problems or drug abuse, and the care of handicapped children.

4) The health-care system should design its own internal policies to support health. These policies include good jobs with career ladders, fair employment practices, freedom from occupational hazards, the elimination of racism in providing services, and the promotion of healthy life styles through better working conditions, child-rearing supports, and education.

Parents and communities should demand the active cooperation of the health-care system in working for these goals, should monitor compliance, and should develop better strategies for effective cooperation between professionals and community members in achieving them. As we reduce our expectations of modern medicine and shift resources away from some of its components, we must simultaneously change our personal and collective beliefs about medicine.

161

If medicine alone cannot keep us healthy, we must find ways to help do it ourselves. Sometimes individual responsibility and change will be necessary (for example, not smoking, exercising regularly, or eating better) if we want to live healthier lives (see Goal Five). But sometimes collective change and new responsibilities will be in order—using less plastic if its production causes cancer; reducing pollution by improving mass transit; rethinking the responsibility of private industry to society.

Goal Two: To remove barriers that keep children from receiving care because of their families' economic situation, race, or ethnic origin.

This is a rather old-fashioned goal to introduce in the 1970's. The 1960's was the decade of equity; now, it is frequently said, we must move beyond that to other concerns. We acknowledge that equal access to health services is not enough in itself to guarantee good health care, or good health, but until a significant degree of equal access has been achieved, even a health-care system reorganized according to our other goals would be unfair because services would not reach all those who need them.

Access to health care regardless of economic situation or race means simple things. It means being able to take your child to a doctor or hospital when you are worried about his or her health without also having to worry about whether you can afford it or whether the doctor will agree to see you. It means being able to choose a source of care or types of treatment on grounds other than their price or whether you meet their financial eligibility criteria. It means being able to make decisions about keeping a severely handicapped or retarded child at home on the basis of human factors—the best interests of the child and the family—instead of financial ones.

Access also means not being refused care or being provided with different care because of your color, your sex, the area where you came from, or where you now live. Although much overt racism has been eliminated from the health-care system in the last two decades, it is by no means completely eradicated and is now often masked by economic barriers. Poverty and minority group status are strongly correlated in our society. Many modes of care (public health department clinics, city and county hospitals, "Medicaid mills," etc.) operate chiefly for the poor, which means that black and Spanish-speaking populations are often the ones that must make do with these less desirable or less well-funded services.

We have mentioned the links between the economic status of families and the health care their children are likely to receive, and documented them in our book on social and economic inequality in the United States.[10] The medical and other expenses of a handicapped child, of course, can impoverish even a family that was previously

162

well-off. Despite ever increased public funding for health services, studies show that in 1970, poorer families spent a higher percentage of their income on health care than did the more affluent. Furthermore, those percentages for all income groups except the very poorest (under $2,000 a year) had not improved since the early sixties.[11]

Part of the explanation of this inequity is that the poor have substantially less health insurance coverage than others, and children have the least insurance coverage of any group in the nation. In 1970, the last year for which figures are available, 23 percent of the total population was not covered by hospital insurance (the most common kind).* While children up through the age of seventeen made up 36 percent of the total population, they made up 44 percent of this uninsured group.[12] Although visits to a doctor outside a hospital are more relevant to most children's health needs than hospitalization, only half of all children were covered by insurance for these visits; an even smaller share of poor children were covered.[13]

Although Medicaid (the federal-state medical payment assistance program) has reduced the discrepancies between the services and financial protection that the poor and nonpoor receive,[14] it remains seriously flawed and inadequate. It reaches only some of the families who cannot afford adequate medical care. It is still part of the welfare system with all the attendant indignities of that system. And Medicaid varies enormously from state to state in terms of who is eligible for care, what services are covered, and the number of physicians who are willing to participate. Because of the careful distinctions maintained between paying and nonpaying patients, and because of the multitude of possible payment sources, poor or near-poor patients today have more forms to fill out and fewer services fully paid for than other patients. Though many medical fees are too high, paradoxically, the limit on the fee that can be charged for serving poor people often is unrealistically low. This last factor, seemingly in the patient's favor, in practice is one of the reasons physicians and health institutions frequently are not eager to take Medicaid patients.

Other categorical federal health service programs directly provide free or low-cost care to the poor and medically underserved, such as neighborhood health centers, maternal and infant care projects, and children and youth projects. However, these programs have never reached more than a fraction of the potentially eligible families, because they are small-scale demonstration projects with inadequate, short-term funds. Head Start and Follow Through, although primarily compensatory education programs, also provide or pay for health services for certain poor children. But they, too, reach only a fraction

---

* Despite the persistence of inequalities between economic classes, insurance coverage in general has increased dramatically in the last forty years. In 1940 only 10 percent of the population had any health insurance at all.

of the target populations: 15 percent for Head Start, 2 percent for Follow Through.[15]

Together, these public programs have been unable to guarantee that every child has an equal chance for decent health care. Even Early and Periodic Screening, Diagnosis and Treatment (EPSDT) (the special Medicaid program for children up to the age of twenty-one which was designed to reach families not using health-care services regularly), has reached less than 20 percent of eligible children. It has provided only a fraction of the care potentially available under its auspices.[16]

This is not equal access. It is not equitable care. And these are not the signs of a health-care system doing everything possible to achieve those goals.

The simplest way to remove economic barriers to health care is to provide all Americans with what is already familiar to many people with private health insurance: a health insurance card that entitles them to all necessary care. The card would provide enrollment in a universal National Health Insurance Plan (NHI), which would pre-pay virtually all health services. We believe that establishing such a plan should become an immediate national priority.

Reasonable people will disagree over how much the insurance should cover and how the nation will pay for it, but there can be no reasonable disagreement that it is patently unfair in a democratic society to deny health care to any child because of his or her family's inability to pay for that care out of its own pocket. In some cases, such as emergency medical services or diagnosis for treatable cancers, access to health care is a matter of life and death. In many other cases, though death does not necessarily follow without care, the likelihood of death or severely damaged life is significantly increased without it (for example, prenatal care for high-risk mothers, early detection of handicap and chronic illness, help for child abuse and neglect, and the correction of poor nutrition).

In a society in which a very high value is placed on medical care, in which such care is purchased in great quantities by the middle class and the affluent—in such a society, the inability to obtain health care for whatever reasons must be regarded as a denial of a basic social right. We emphasize this point because there is extraordinary resistance to accepting it in this country. Our lack of a system for providing health care to the entire population is now almost unique among industrialized nations. Not only England but most Western European countries and Israel have such systems. Canada, a nation very similar to ours, has gradually instituted a full national health insurance program with, on balance, excellent results.[17] The effect on equity and enhanced access for the poor have been particularly notable.[18]

We believe that a national health insurance plan is the best way to remedy *some* of our system's most serious inequities. A variety of legislative plans are now under consideration in Congress.[19] But inaugurating a national health insurance plan without at the same time reorganizing the health-care system would be dangerous and a grave disappointment to the American people. Being able to pay does not guarantee that services are available, appropriate, psychologically attractive, or satisfying to a family. It does not mean that attention will be paid to the quality or the efficacy of the services that are paid for. Nor would all current proposals for NHI lead to great improvements for children. In short, an insurance plan, though necessary, is not sufficient to create an adequate national system of medical care, and, as we have already stated, medical care alone does not produce good health.

The general characteristics we consider essential if any NHI plan is to be in children's best interest are summarized below. We can scarcely improve on the clear, short list of six essential components which the Children's Defense Fund has proposed:

1) universal eligibility
2) comprehensive benefits for all services
3) no charges to patients for primary care services—i.e., checkups and other kinds of diagnosis and treatments a nurse or primary care physician gives
4) payment methods which include incentives to use the most suitable type of care and the most appropriate personnel so parents are not taking their children to an emergency room for checkups seeing specialists unnecessarily
5) subsidies to clinics, hospitals, group practices and other providers for necessary outreach and support services
6) technical assistance and start-up funds for new providers in areas with a shortage of services.[20]

To these we would add only one further component:

7. strong cost control and quality assurance provisions.

There is currently great debate over whether we as a nation can afford NHI. The fact is that the true long-run costs of NHI are unknown and to a large degree unknowable. More than $103 billion was spent on personal health services in 1975,[21] or over $475 per person, much of it paid directly by individuals for care or for the purchase of insurance.* If all this money were rechanneled through the federal budget, it would appear to cause an enormous increase but would actually only be a transfer of money from private to public accounts. Universal public health insurance would fill many current gaps in health coverage, and thus the total costs would probably exceed this transfer amount by amounts estimated at from $6 billion to $20 billion.

Yet contrary to some rhetoric, the costs would not be limitless nor necessarily set off runaway inflation. Among the significant findings of a ten-year study of child health services in Rochester, New York, was the discovery that demand for and use of child health services show a "ceiling effect." The authors write:

> It has been a common assumption that an increase in providers will increase services rendered, and that a reduction of financial barriers leads to an upsurge in demand. In our community from 1967 to 1971 more pediatricians became available, a neighborhood health center was started, and Medicaid was introduced, yet contacts per child with health care providers decreased. If the same holds in other communities, this decline should provide reassurance about current plans to implement national entitlement to medical care for children. For this age group, at least, we can predict that there will be no upsurge in demand.[22]

One reason behind the ceiling effect appears to be the relatively healthy nature of the childhood population: once basic services are provided, previously undetected problems taken care of, and parents reassured, there just is not that much medical care to be delivered. To the extent that good child health care is preventive, it also limits costs.**

Overall, many health costs can be better policed than they are at present by the accounting and monitoring systems we will describe below. But in the long run, costs will depend on how much society changes other components of the health-care system. Insurance for

---

* This per capita average is heavily weighted by the large medical expenditures of the elderly. While entirely trustworthy figures are unavailable, most estimates of per capita expenditures for children run about $150 a year.[23]

** We should note that the results from Rochester do not suggest that the health-care system itself became less accessible to children, although even Medicaid was unable to generate an increase in the percentage of poor families with a regular source of care.

problems becomes less costly if many problems are prevented in advance through such measures as environmental protection and accident prevention. Within medicine itself, costs can be held down by shifting our emphasis from providing expensive specialists in the last stages of emergencies to more moderately priced healers earlier on. In addition, several payment devices deserve exploration as a means of keeping health-care costs within reasonable limits. These include paying doctors a predetermined sum of money annually to provide all care for a child or a family (a system called "capitation" or prepayment) rather than paying by the number and kind of services they provide, and requiring sliding-scale payments geared to family income for discretionary services such as cosmetic plastic surgery.

Structuring a national health insurance system around the needs of children, as we propose below—perhaps even restricting NHI initially to children up through six years of age with yearly increases in the age range covered—in itself should serve as a cap on health expenditure trends. Starting with children would create new leverage on the entire system, pushing it in the desirable direction of what one expert has summarized as "a greater emphasis on prevention and health maintenance, of a payment system which would encourage the provision of a broad spectrum of services rendered in organized settings, and of the development of mechanisms to encourage easier and equitable access to appropriate services." [24]

Goal Three: To reorganize the health-care delivery system for children in order to emphasize preventive care, primary care, and more humane care.

Equity in child health requires the major changes in health care financing that would be achieved under a form of national health insurance. But we have learned that financing alone, without control, drives medical prices up without totally resolving inequities in access to health care. The nation also needs to make changes in what services are provided and paid for. Providing money to bring new clients into the system without balancing its one-sided emphasis on major surgery, technological sophistication, and life-saving heroics, and without reorganizing the way the system does business, will lead to too much money being spent for the wrong things.

Moreover, although general reform is important, it should begin with health for children. Indeed, we must oppose any general plan for reorganization that does not begin with the needs of children. This is not because we feel that children's health is in any way more important than that of adults.

It is, first, because there are greater returns, in terms of later problems prevented and costs saved, in promoting health for chidren before they become adults.

Second, the present health-care system traditionally pushes children's concerns to the end of the health line, and it is all too easy for that pattern to continue. We have a health-care system centered on hospitals, but children are rarely hospitalized. The killer diseases and outrageous total costs of health care routinely make headlines, but children after the first year of life have the lowest death rate of any group in the population and require proportionally fewer of the nation's health dollars. Yet the real health needs of children—reproductive services for parents, preventive services including services for detecting preventable childhood antecedents of adult diseases, services for handicapping conditions, nutrition, mental health, and family support services—are neglected. If one were to design a health-care system around the needs of today's adults and then adapt it to children, children would seem minor problems, but the system would not account for many of their potential needs and would not be designed to prevent the same health problems that afflict today's adults from damaging the next generation as well.

And third, we believe that beginning with children would have enormous benefits for all. A health-care system that served children more appropriately would, by its very shift to preventive and organizational issues, in fact serve most adults better as well.

Focusing on children and on the prenatal care their families receive requires paying fresh attention to simple things, to universal human and biological needs, and to ways of maintaining good health (which most mothers and children enjoy) rather than only treating illness. Because *all* children need to be assured of minimal services (prenatal care, good nutrition, preventive services, dental care, and simple acute care), decent care for children could create models for how the rest of the system could improve its equity, universal access, and population-based kinds of coverage. Because effective referral systems will be needed for high-risk pregnancies, for children with chronic diseases and handicaps, and for other children with episodes of serious illness or trauma, designing a sound children's health system would force closer attention to relationships among many parts of the health-care system, from the family doctor to the intensive-care unit to regional planning of services, and to new ways in which these disparate units can be mobilized on behalf of any patient.

Because children's health needs involve good nutrition, family counseling and guidance, coordinated work with day-care centers and schools, dental care, accident prevention, and freedom from harmful environmental factors, we would be forced to consider both an expanded definition of "health care" and a more comprehensive meaning for what planners call the "health-care team." Because the great proportion of care for most children can be provided with high quality by nurse practitioners or other midlevel professionals, we would be forced to shift away from traditional models of care delivery and control that are dominated by physicians. Because children's health needs are largely predictable, their illnesses over quickly, and their treatment not astronomically expensive, children's health programs underscore the value of such orderly methods of payment and organization as prepayment and group practice. Because children's health is influenced by so many things other than traditional medical care, we would be forced to look for major sources of care and health beyond the hospitals, medical centers, and individual physicians' offices, toward schools, community health centers, community environmental resources, and the family.*

Even those children with the kind of serious problems that our present health-care system has so specialized in treating would be far more easily identified and cared for within a truly comprehensive child-care system. Although the system knows how to cope with their problems once they arrive at the right hospital or treatment center, many "high-risk" children are never found. Until full-service programs for all children are in place, we cannot be sure we are reaching all high-risk children with the quality of care to which they are entitled.

Several variations on what such a child-focused health-care system might look like have been developed in recent years. The broad outlines of what we think such a system might look like and should do are clear.

We could begin with a program under which each new mother was visited first in the hospital and then during the first weeks at home by a public health nurse or other trained home health visitor. The purpose of the visit would be to discuss the role in health care of parents' child rearing practices and the models they set for diet and exercise, the importance of regular health-care checkups even for apparently well children, to find out if the family already had a satisfactory regular source of preventive and acute care and, if not, to describe available sources and arrange an appointment. At the same time, schools and other community institutions could be used to help families with school-related problems, with environmental con-

* It is interesting to note that current analyses of deficiencies in rural health and health-care delivery point toward very similar reforms. Karen Davis and Ray Marshall, in a draft report on rural health care in the South,[25] emphasize the need for community-sponsored health centers with teams of health workers, for emphasis of environmental health and preventive medicine, for changing the training of professionals, and for special attention to nutrition, home health care, and maternal and child health care.

ditions such as surroundings that invite accidents, and with family planning.

Once the health-care system had reached out to all children as early in their lives as possible, it would offer a full range of appropriate services. In addition to prenatal care, delivery, newborn care, and visits to well children stressing preventive services, this basic "package" would include assessments of how a child was developing and advice to the family on its role in caring for the child's health (see Goal Five). Also included would be care for acute illnesses; early diagnosis, treatment, and continuing services for children with handicaps and chronic conditions; nutrition services; dental maintenance; and family planning or reproductive services for the parents.

Basic child health services are as much common-sense advice as anything else: good care involves allaying the fears of new parents about minor upper respiratory infection, explaining the normal range of developmental milestones, or suggesting ways to get through teething or dealing with bed wetting or phobias. Where specialist or hospital care is needed, the system should concentrate on making referrals easily and quickly, on returning the child as soon as possible to his or her home and to the care of the family doctor or at least a facility in the child's own community, and on coordinating health services with nonmedical resources such as schools and day care.

Child health care demands outreach, active follow-up, and a deep awareness of how the context of care influences its effectiveness, all sadly neglected components of current health planning. The context of care, by which we mean its cultural and professional overtones, is doubly important in the case of children because health services need to be appropriate not only for the child but also for the parents, who obviously will not bring their children for care unless they feel positive about it. Clearly, more children are more likely to receive more health services if their parents can take them to a nearby health center or doctor's office that is welcoming and comfortable and that brings together several services (such as dental care, lab work, and counseling).

The way health care is financed can have a great deal to do with whether it is humane. Impersonal, assembly-line care is encouraged when a doctor earns more money the more patients he or she sees. Prepaid NHI would remove at least one factor that discourages doctors from taking the time to answer patients' questions fully. Because Americans persist in believing that good health is a product of medical care alone, we continue to think of the human side of medicine as a frill. In fact, it is essential to good child health care.

People often worry when they do not have access to health care, even if they do not need it immediately. This in itself is an important and valid reason why easy access to care—in settings designed to establish trust and relieve anxiety as well as identify health problems —must be central in any future health-care reforms. But ease of initial access or entry should not be confused with a totally laissez-faire attitude of permitting whatever health services either the family or physician wants. As we discuss further below, it is essential that we as a society always take a careful look at the effectiveness and necessity of even the most common medical procedures and expenditures.

Today we know very little about the best way to treat diseases of childhood (or adulthood). Universal financial access therefore does have some risk of overtreatment, inflation, and excessive demand on the system. A balance must be struck between guarantees of initial access that protect children from receiving too little care, and more systematic monitoring and evaluation of health services delivery to protect children against too much care from services of the wrong kinds. We believe that greater control on unnecessary or harmful medical care can go a long way toward releasing the resources and energy needed to expand currently underdeveloped services such as outreach and support services.[26]

Goal Four: To create publicly accountable health agencies that will assure that services of high quality are available to every child as needed.

Consider an analogy: what our public school system would be like if it were run in the same way as our current health-care system. Public schools would enroll only those students who chose to come in, and in fact no public school would be permitted to open unless a parent or group of parents could prove that there were no parochial or private schools in the area and that they did not have the money to pay for private tutors. The public school system would be under constant pressure to close its doors whenever the private schools charged that it was competing with them for students. However, it would be under equal pressure to take on all the "problem" students that private schools and tutors had given up on.

171

A child would not necessarily go to public school on a regular schedule, nor would classes always meet in the same place, at the same time, or with the same teachers. Very rarely would anyone take a careful look at the whole child or his or her overall educational progress. There would be no cumulative record of grades or courses taken; the math teacher would have no idea how much math her students had taken before or what other courses they were currently taking, or what students weren't getting any math at all. Parents would be responsible for finding out what classes were offered, what the requirements were for participation, and how to interest the teacher in their child. And, most important, there would be no organization such as the PTA, community school board, or even an elected board of education to whom parents could turn with requests or demands if the range of classes did not meet their needs or those of their children.

The point of this analogy is to emphasize how far we have to go to create anything remotely resembling a universal and publicly accountable health-care system for children. We do not mean to hold up public education as the perfect model. In fact, public education suffers from many of the same kinds of elites and public pressure groups as does the health-care system. It does not provide equity of access or uniformly high-quality instruction. Like medical care, public education is expected to do more than it is capable of. Yet the model of universal, free public education does embody certain values that are helpful in rethinking the health-care system. Without new models for making health-care providers focus their attention on the general health of a defined population of children as well as on the health of their own personal patients, it will be impossible to improve our children's health substantially. We are concerned with two interconnected problems: the large number of children who are now falling through the cracks of the system, and the lack of a rational way to plan our health-care system and allocate funds based on the population's needs.

Most providers in the American health-care system are concerned with those children who walk through their doors. The lack of home visitors to new mothers is just one sign of how little planning is done for finding those who never appear. Patients' records, such as they are, are basically private and uncoordinated: one doctor may have excellent records on his patients but no information about their treatment elsewhere; other doctors, centers, or programs treating the same patients for other aspects of their health do not know what the first doctor is doing for them; no one at all knows how many children altogether are being seen, how often, and for what. And if no one knows how many children are receiving care, we obviously do not know how many are not. Even a pediatrician who is eager to serve some children outside his or her own practice has no easy way to find them.

This incoherence works to the disadvantage even of those families able to buy care for their children. A family newly arrived in an unfamiliar town has almost no way to find care except through the classified telephone directory, the emergency room or outpatient department of a hospital, or—if they are lucky—an acquaintance who may know of someone who provides the kind of care they want. By contrast, a family on welfare or a family moving into a public housing project may come into contact with housing administrators or welfare department personnel whose jobs involve them with whole populations and who are therefore likely to know something about the range of health services available. If the family is lucky, those services may even include a comprehensive public care program right in their neighborhood.

A population-based approach to health and health services is the great undeveloped potential of the branch of medicine known as public health. A public health worker is likely to ask the question, "Have all the children in this community been fully immunized?" while a private physician or hospital director probably asks, "Did we do everything possible for that last patient?", or at most might ask, "Have all *my* patients been immunized?" Public health's concern, in short, is the community as a whole. Private doctors and hospitals may give excellent care to a subset of their community— the physicians' patients and the hospitals' users—yet for the health of all, someone must be held accountable for the answers to questions such as these: Has every newborn child received a complete examination and has every family been put in contact with a regular source of care? Are remediable problems and handicaps being detected early and corrected or ameliorated? Are community health resources being directed toward the most urgent needs? In other words, to achieve a significant improvement in health care in this nation, someone must be given the responsibility of worrying about whole populations.*

One might think that these concerns are being taken care of by state and local health departments and federal health programs. They should be. But none of these organizations has been able to do the job because they are set up in ways that mirror the imbalances

* Many health experts agree. *A Right to Health,* for example, says: "A key element in developing adequate access to primary medical care is the clear determination of who is responsible for organizing ambulatory medical care within a specific geographic area and of how coverage of every person in the defined population can be ensured. . . . Coverage of a defined population involves both assurance of financial entitlement to necessary services and an available source of care that is held responsible for providing comprehensive basic services. Entitlement alone, in the absence of other public interventions, will not achieve at tolerable cost the organizational and manpower arrangements necessary for an accessible, efficient, and effective organization of community ambuatory services. . . . Hence, consideration of the incentives necessary to organize these elements into a coherent system in which leadership and allocation of responsibility are clear is of high priority." [27]

of the private medical care system. They have never been given responsibility for the entire range of children's health services, and even in terms of the basic but important job of collecting data, their mandate scarcely extends beyond recording births, deaths, and cases of communicable disease.

It is ironic that legislation is now on the books at federal and state levels that does mandate broad public intervention in children's health care on a population basis. The mandate is not being carried out because of inadequate funding and because enforcement provisions are weak. An almost revolutionary first step on behalf of children's health would be to implement and fund adequately the existing provisions of Title V of the Public Health Services Act, the Community Health Services Act, Title XIX of the Social Security Act (Medicaid), an assortment of federal nutrition programs,* the Developmental Disabilities Act, and various state and local maternal and child health statutes.

While these programs embody a reasonable approximation of the type of service program we outlined in the previous goal, even if fully carried out they would not produce a comprehensive, publicly accountable system. Most of the programs make no provision for systematic community input or control, and they do not have the power to change the basic rules of the game. What these programs of good intentions need is a structure in which they can be expanded, modified, and made more secure as part of a comprehensive, population-based national health care policy.

Recently, still other approaches have been set up to address issues of public control of health care: comprehensive health planning agencies, mental health planning regions, Professional Services Review Organizations, and the regional health planning agencies established nationwide under recent legislation (P.L. 93-641). Usually these devices involve partial regulation by quasigovernmental bodies. Yet even these do not really take on the underlying problems of the incomplete private model on which health care is based, nor the fragmentation it encourages. Nor have they expanded the definition of health care to include all those elements essential to promoting good health for children.

What is needed is federal legislation to create a network of "consumer councils"—local, regional, and national community health authorities (CHAs). At the local level, a community health authority would be the equivalent of a local school board for child health. Every authority would have the following responsibilities and functions:

    1) to assure that every family is aware of the health and health-related services in the locality and of their special importance

---

* Most notably the Special Supplemental Food Program for Women, Infants and Children (WIC), National School Lunch Act, Child Nutrition Act of 1966, School Breakfast Program, and Child Care Food Program.

for pregnant women and young children;

2) to inform, educate, and persuade every family to take advantage of the care available, with emphasis on preventive and basic services; *

3) to assure that the services and resources provided are adequate but not excessive for the community's needs and reflect a balance of the community's and the nation's priorities;

4) to provide or support better referral and feedback procedures among all health service providers, including consistent record systems;

5) to maintain publicly accessible data of health services utilization, quality, and cost;

6) to provide a forum in public meetings for public discussion and monitoring of all health services;

7) to set long-range goals and establish mechanisms to implement them;

8) to carry out quality- and cost-control activities consistent with the preceding tasks.

We believe that public health departments, if required to build in more aggressive community participation and control, can be the basis for this CHA. We say this despite the rather dismal record of most such agencies either in general—as effective advocates, service providers, or enforcers—or in their specific and traditional role of providing maternal and child health services.[28] Many people argue that health departments themselves are responsible for the sad state of public health care programs today—that they are rigid, outdated bureaucracies filled with second-rate personnel, lacking experience with or commitment to providing direct service to individuals, afraid of their own shadows and kowtowing to medical societies and private hospitals. Furthermore, since current financing trends assign local governments increasing responsibility for providing public medical and health services, local health departments must compete with all local priorities for proper funding. In good part, we regret to say, these accusations are true. One recent study has shown that public accountability, aggressive outreach, or concern for the whole population at risk are not high priorities for state and local health agencies.[29]

And yet if we chose to by-pass them, a suspiciously familiar new body would have to be created, for one cannot operate or monitor a publicly financed and universally accessible system without public institutions. Certainly, trying to change an existing model is harder than creating one from scratch, but we now have a partial structure of public programs and public accountability. To have any hope of success, we are going to have to work with the agencies we have, enlarging their power and shifting their priorities.

* Children's and parents' rights to refuse treatment, of course, also need protection. See our discussion of these issues in Chapter 9.

The development of CHAs with the power to carry out the mandate outlined here is, in our opinion, the keystone of a better child health-care system and the most difficult goal of our five to achieve. It requires a thorough redefinition of the way we think about health care and a major shift in power and resources from private to public control. For in order to be able to guarantee that appropriate services are available to all families, the CHA must have the power to ensure the public accountability of all the doctors, nurses, pharmacists, hospitals, nursing homes, and other health-care providers, public and private, in its area; to monitor the services offered all patients, not just the poor; and to intervene if needed services are not provided equitably. The CHA cannot achieve equity or plan a more effective system if it can impose restrictions only on certain variables (hospital beds, for example, but not office practice) or for certain groups (the elderly in nursing homes, but not children).

At the regional or state level, state health departments, as well as the "Health Service Agencies" established under P.L. 93-641, provide a similarly flawed but yet practical base for CHAs. In fact, a recent document prepared by the Office of Child Health Affairs within the U.S. Department of Health Education and Welfare proposes a very similar five-year plan for a new federal role in maternal and child health,[30] centered around an expanded role for HSAs, and a transfer of Medicaid administration to the Public Health Service in HEW from the Medical Service Administration in the welfare division of HEW.

Three objections to such an active public program need to be taken particularly seriously: inflexible programming, questions of privacy and confidentiality, and impersonal care.

Most federal "master plans" are unworkable at the local level. We do not deny that confusion and jurisdictional overlaps may go on for years. These can be minimized, however, by aggressive legislation which does not leave major components of the health-care system outside the CHAs' jurisdiction. CHAs will also need predictable, substantial financing to do the job well. More serious among local problems is the danger that CHAs will not be sensitively tailored to local needs. We believe that several separate kinds of CHA will be necessary—for major urban areas, small towns, and rural areas—although lack of previous experience with such publicly accountable and broad-based programs makes it impossible to state with any certainty what the best population sizes will be.

What does seem certain is that clear and mandatory national standards must be matched with local flexibility in meeting them. It is also vital that local flexibility in achieving mandated outcomes be reinforced with federal, or regional, monitoring and realistic grievance and challenge mechanisms. As we have pointed out before, the harsh legacy of racism and the denial of services to minority groups demand that "local option" and "community control" not be permitted to become euphemisms for inequality and exclusion.

In some ways, our recommendations for greater public accountability and more accessibility conflict with growing concern over the misuse of medical and related records. Confidentiality is an important contributor to the candor that makes possible effective communication between doctors and patients, and it must be protected. Hence, we believe public data should be general or statistical in nature, with identification of specific individuals removed. Second, access to all public health records must not be linked to welfare, law enforcement, or such private industry areas as credit and insurance, except on the specific request of the individual (or parent) involved.[31]

Psychiatric records are a particularly thorny issue, as is the question of a parent's right to access to the health records of older children. But we believe that concerted efforts, adequately funded, can permit us the great benefits to be gained from publicly accessible community-based comprehensive child health data while protecting the rights of individual parents and children to guard their health records from misuse.

Past efforts to bring the private health-care system under public accountability and sponsorship have been thwarted not only by the sheer political and economic power of those with the most to lose—organized medicine, health insurance companies, hospitals, and drug companies [32]—but also by an understandable reluctance on the part of the public to take on such a responsibility for themselves. The American Medical Association has tried—with considerable success—to persuade the public that any attempt to remove the power from the private sector will result in a system of "socialized medicine," wherein no one can choose a doctor and the relationship between patient and doctor is reduced to a sterile assembly line of impersonal care.

There are some legitimate concerns about what a completely public health-care system would do to some of the strong advantages of the current pluralistic and market-based system. The possibility of depersonalized, slipshod, bureaucratic care is real. Waiting times might increase. The discontent of physicians would rise in many situations.

But human care is neither always possible under our current system nor impossible in public or community facilities. In our present system, free choice, a high degree of satisfaction for physicians and those patients able to buy any care they need, and the ability of doctors to live in well-supplied areas have been gained at the expense of less powerful and articulate patients and providers, namely poor and lower middle-class patients, and nurses, orderlies, and technicians. We believe that no scheme or program of reorganization is acceptable if it does not begin by addressing the issues of organization, public accountability for all parts of the system, and a population-based approach.

Goal Five: To increase and strengthen the capacity of communities, parents, and children to act on their own behalf as both health advocates and health caretakers.

Community participation must be built into every aspect of the health-care system or the system will continue to care more for itself than for its clients. To achieve communities that are capable of exercising this responsibility, we need not only CHAs or their equivalent but also a public that is well informed on the facts and issues, that has the power to influence decisions, and that assumes active shared responsibility for its own health as well.

We believe that community control of agencies responsible for health planning and allocation of health resources, including CHAs, can be started by requiring that 60 percent of the boards of these agencies be lay people. Indeed, all organized settings that provide health care should have similar provisions for client control. Real costs are associated with such procedures, such as providing training to new community representatives and publicity or election costs; special federal funds should support such costs.

But to be effective in using this power, individuals and communities need to know a lot more about the complicated health-care field than they do now. Incredible gaps in information now exist on even the most rudimentary variables of health-care delivery. We can

178

report accurately how many fighter planes or cans of deodorant were sold last year or how many people visited the White House, but we cannot tell how many American children in local communities received what kinds of health care, how much it cost, or with what resulting benefits to their health. Since for the most part our doctors are not accountable for information about what they do, we have no systematic source by which to judge our overall health needs. Thus, those who advocate reform do so from weak positions, particularly when numbers and hard data are highly regarded by legislators and policy makers.

The notion of giving more information to the public or even the individual is in itself a radical challenge to the current professional control of the system. Doctors have traditionally opposed lay control of any health agencies on the grounds that unwise or dangerous decisions will result because laymen do not know about the field. One answer is to give the public the knowledge it needs to make those decisions responsibly. We have seen that without public participation, the decisions made have not always been in the public interest. Could it be that the providers of health care do not have enough information to make well-informed decisions on behalf of the community and its children?

Information can also be a particularly powerful tool for individual parents as advocates for their own children. As we have mentioned before, even a parent who is able to purchase services is frequently unable to find out enough about services in the community to make intelligent choices among them. Doctors often complain about patients "shopping around," but at the moment, patients have almost no other way to assess the field. We believe families need to do *more* careful selecting. They also need access, as others have proposed as well,[33] to all their own medical and health-related records, with people at hand to provide training or help interpreting them. People are the best advocates when they know the most.

Doctors do not provide the bulk of health care for children; parents do. Much of childhood illness is minor and will go away without treatment; it can also be extremely uncomfortable for both parent and child. Acute illness often causes great anxiety for a parent who does not know how serious it is or what to do, and it sometimes carries great risk. Not knowing the meaning of symptoms or being uncertain of their ability to care for the child alone, most parents have no choice but to call in the person who does know. Yet numerous reports have now demonstrated ways to enable parents to become more responsible and appropriate users of the system, so they know when to call the doctor, when to take the child directly to the emergency room, or when chicken soup is all that is needed. In discussions with providers, in classes, or both, parents can be given more detailed instructions than they get now; they can be taught, for example, how to take throat cultures and use otoscopes (the instrument for ear examinations) before calling the doctor about suspected strep throat or middle-ear infection. A new category of health workers called "nurse practitioners" has proved even more effective and more interested than doctors in these educational and participatory practices.

Some mechanisms are startlingly simple. One, for example, is twenty-four-hour telephone access to someone who can answer questions. Parents can also improve their skills just by reading the increasing number of excellent parents' guides to health care which no longer emphasize always calling the doctor at the first sign of illness.* These resources, however, are not totally effective if the doctor or nurse does not respect the approach and still treats the mother of a sick child as a worrier or a nuisance.

Changes in this area will require substantial changes in the education and training of many health professionals. Involving patients is one of the most exciting areas of child health care, and indeed of health care in general. The almost total disregard of the patient (or his or her family) as an active participant and decision maker in medical education must and can be eliminated. Some pediatricians are knowledgeable in child development if not in nutrition and child care, but the majority of medical visits children make are to persons with inadequate or inappropriate training in these areas. And even the thoughtful pediatrician will rarely have observed the child outside the limited—and often biased—setting of an office or clinic. Parents themselves usually know far more about their children than physicians, who see most children only rarely. But parents frequently know very little about medicine or really sick children, or how to talk to a busy, brusque professional. Plain common sense would suggest that these gaps be bridged, and that parents and medical specialists can do best by the child by collaborating with each other. Interpersonal skills, team approaches that include the patient, and patient education techniques can be taught to health-care professionals as effectively as anatomy and pharmacology.

* For instance, Children's Hospital Medical Center and R. I. Feinbloom, *Child Health Encyclopedia: The Complete Guide for Parents.* New York: Delacorte Press/Seymour Lawrence, 1975; Boston Women's Health Book Collective, *Our Bodies, Ourselves.* New York: Simon & Schuster, 1973, for family planning and pregnancy; D. M. Vickery and J. F. Fries, *Take Care of Yourself.* Reading, Mass.: Addison-Wesley, 1976.

One of the most fascinating experiments in child health care we have come across is the work of Charles and Mary Ann Lewis in California called "child-initiated care." [34] This is an effort to find out how elementary-school children behave if given opportunities to make many of their own decisions about health matters. In this school, children can go to see the nurse practitioner whenever they want to. The nurse involves the child in describing his or her problem, figuring out what it is, and deciding what should be done. The experiment did not seem to encourage hypocondriacs and other chronic over-users of health services; such patterns turned up no more frequently among the children then they do among adults. More important, the findings clearly suggest that even very young children have a far greater capacity to understand health and illness and to make responsible choices than most adults imagine. (This approach has since been extended to other school systems.) Since lifelong health habits, including attitudes about the use of health services and one's personal responsibility for health, are established during childhood, stressing the child's potential independence and truly informed consent to the care he or she receives would have valuable effects over a lifetime.

In this chapter we have presented a quick overview of the current American health-care system as it affects children and families. We have seen that its vast and in many ways unique resources are still inequitably distributed and are not accountable to the populations they should serve. We have also argued that despite the current outcry over runaway medical care costs, the preventive and efficient model of universal, population-based primary child health services continues to receive a dangerously low priority. Our earlier theme of the American focus on individuals has reemerged as astounding neglect of environmental health and education as methods for promoting health, and as an extraordinary resistance to public health care and national health insurance. We believe our five broad, long-range child health goals are the antidotes to these trends. These goals work together as a unified plan, but each one can also stand alone if circumstances permit action on some but not on others. In the long run, however, all are essential, and achieving them all in a balanced way should produce much better health for more American children than any one or two of them pursued in isolation.

9. Protection of Children Under the Law

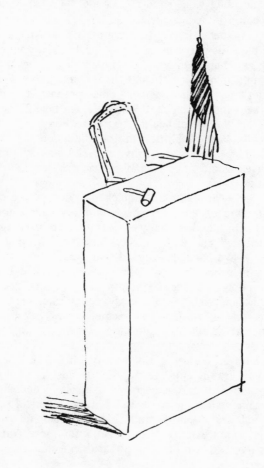

GUY BILLOUT

Changes in family life are bound to provoke changes in family law. When the family was the focal point of a child's life and enjoyed a virtual monopoly as the source of education, health services, employment potential, and recreational diversion, legal doctrine rested on an assumption that parents had a "natural" or "inalienable" right to raise their children as they saw fit. Although as far back as 1838 American courts proclaimed the state's right to protect children from neglect or corruption, the state rarely intervened in child rearing. In this century, however, as the family came to share the

familiar tasks of teaching, caring for, and disciplining children with such other social institutions as schools, welfare agencies, doctors, and clinics, new relationships between children and these other authorities developed. The law was forced to recognize these relationships because it often had to resolve conflicts between parents and social institutions as to who should have authority over the child. Out of such tensions have come Supreme Court decisions concerning such things as compulsory schooling and child labor laws.

Yet through most of these developments, children themselves went largely unacknowledged. No one had heard of children's rights. Historically, the law assumed that a parent or guardian—unless "unfit"—would represent the child's interests where they demanded legal intervention; in parental default, the state would undertake to do so.

The right of children to be viewed as legal "persons" capable of interests and deserving representation independent of their parents has emerged only recently, clearly inspired by many of the attitudes of the 1960's—erosion of faith in any authority, parents' included; the movements that view all consumers, including children, as having some right to determine what happens to them; and the generally increased awareness of civil rights and civil liberties. Furthermore, the new belief in children's rights may have been partly inspired by a general recognition of the capability, intelligence, and maturity of children at a young age to make decisions on their own. Whatever the cause, in recent years the legal trend has been decidedly in the direction of granting children greater legal rights and responsibilities both by statute and by court decisions.

It seems likely that the balance of legal power among parents, the state, and children will continue shifting, which is healthy; but we are concerned that too much if not most of the law affecting children has been hammered out on a case-by-case basis. Few if any jurisdictions have tried to take a comprehensive look at all the legal principles affecting children to see if they make sense in terms of our current knowledge, experience, and norms for families and children, and to enact an integrated, comprehensive children's code. This should be high-priority work for legislators, lawyers, parents, child advocates, people who work with children, and other interested groups in every one of our states. Some groups—notably the American Bar Association/Institute of Juvenile Justice Standards Project, on which we draw for many of the recommendations here—have made a commendable start.[1] The start must be carried through— expanded, evaluated, refined, and adapted throughout the country.

While we hope that laws and legal rights will always have a limited role in children's lives, they are necessary for the extreme cases where family life breaks down, where schools, parents, and children are in conflict, and where the state imposes controls on or denies needed services to a child.

We do not look to legal reform in children's rights as the primary source of a better life for children and families, but we do see it as a necessary foundation for determining the inevitable disputes that will arise in any set of relationships so complex as that of child, family, and state.

We propose to summarize most of the issues that a comprehensive look should encompass, illustrating the disrepair of some of our laws in critical areas of family life, and identifying favorable legal portents where they exist.

We have limited the brief review of this chapter to six broad areas:

1) children's rights in relation to the family in extreme situations, including (a) situations (defined on the books as child abuse and child neglect) where society intervenes in a family to protect the child from anticipated harm at the hands of the parents; (b) times when parents try to turn their child over to institutions; and (c) situations where parents feel that their authority over a child has broken down and they ask the state to take the child in hand (status offenses)

2) legal protection for children being raised in institutions rather than families

3) disagreements between children and parents about the children's health care, schooling, or work

4) legal protection of children in schools

5) rights of children against environmental and health hazards that our technological society forces upon them without their knowledge or consent (this is an area in which there are many legal unknowns)

6) who will represent children in their newly defined rights.

Children's Rights in Relation to the Family

Our broad goal as a Council is to sensitize and even mobilize society to support the family's authority and viability, so we believe our laws should be geared to maintaining the family's integrity and to offering help and services in crises. Only when the family fabric is so irretrievably rent as to actively endanger children's safety and health would we sanction the removal of a child to another place.

Present family law is too ready to break up families without providing them a chance to survive with help; at the same time children must be afforded increasing protection from needless abandonment by parents who are having trouble coping. In the past, the sanction for parental failure has been the child's consignment to an unnatural institutional environment; the sanction for the child's own misconduct has been precisely the same, and—incredibly enough—so has the sanction for a child with a handicap. To preserve for as many children as possible the integrity and identity of family life, the authority of both the state and the parents to remove a child from the family must be regulated and circumscribed by legal protection. Our laws as well as other social policy must push in the direction of keeping families together until the child is ready to live independently.

"Neglect" and "Abuse"

There is tension, of course, in the definition of danger to children, and who defines it. Every state has some kind of child-abuse or -neglect law that confers broad authority on public agencies and courts to intervene in family life in the interests of children who are threatened by neglect or abuse by their parents. Under these laws, parents can be criminally prosecuted for their conduct and children can be removed from their homes. Very often no clear standards are stated as to what constitutes "neglect" or even "abuse." The laws are intentionally vague to allow the local family judge to exercise broad discretion about what to do in individual family situations. Most laws allow the court or policemen or social workers to take the child away even before a court hearing if they believe his or her welfare is threatened. Very often, a judicial finding of neglect or abuse by parents, or even of their "unfitness," is sufficient to have a child removed without proof that the child has in fact been damaged.

Child-protection laws are necessary; society must have authorization and rules of law by which to proceed when parents neglect or abuse their children (or are accused of such misconduct). Although neglect and outright abuse of children by their parents appear to be different phenomena, in fact they have much in common.

Large numbers of American families frequently find themselves in economic and emotional distress. Whether they are victims of chronic fatigue or of a crisis ranging from unemployment, not enough money, and depressing living conditions to physical disabilities, alcoholism, or mental illness, most of these families could be significantly helped by very practical aids such as more money, better housing, homemaking assistance, employment counseling or training, or temporary respite from the children in day-care programs. Sometimes they may need family counseling or individual treatment of the parent. But the parents in these families are not necessarily unfit; they are often responding to tremendous pressures. All too often, an arrogant state legal apparatus invokes the doctrine that the parents are "neglecting" their children and removes the children without attempting to give the family the supportive help it needs—for example, the money to buy food, pay the rent, or pay the homemaker who could care temporarily for the children while the parent recuperates from illness or goes out to look for a job. Even conscientious social workers and court personnel often have no power to command the tangible resources that might help the family continue intact. All they have is the coarsest implement: removal of the child.

This means that well-intentioned and even not-so-well-intentioned courts and social workers, acting in the "best interests of the child," can impose their norms of morality and upbringing upon families. Families live differently from one another, they treat children differently, they expect different standards of behavior, and they punish differently. Most families accused of abuse and neglect are minority families with low incomes, often one-parent families. Judges and court personnel, on the other hand, generally come from quite another social, economic, and ideological world. Behavior that may be quite normal in another social milieu may be shocking to them in terms of their own, and as a result they can be too quick to condemn and not eager enough to invest time and attention in trying to help. Moreover, they can, ironically, be blind to the deficiencies in institutional alternatives to which they send children. Some juvenile judges have never visited the local orphanages, foundling homes, shelter homes, or detention facilities to which they consign children every week.

In 1976, there were some 100,000 children in America who had been removed from their homes under neglect laws. One study showed that in Los Angeles and San Francisco, the court felt compelled to order removal in 60 percent to 65 percent of the cases in which it assumed jurisdiction; in New York, the figure was 50 percent.[2]

In thirty states a finding of "neglect" can be based on the parent's inability to provide a child with necessities due to poverty. Here is a classic case of blaming the victim.

In many other cases, children are removed from their homes because of overliteral interpretations of what constitutes "moral danger." This might mean that their mother is sleeping with boyfriends, frequents bars, smokes marijuana, or throws wild parties. Mothers of illegitimate children are particularly vulnerable to such findings of neglect.

In some jurisdictions, handicapped children who need special and expensive special schooling or medical care must become wards of the state before they can obtain such services. There is no specific law under which their families can get support or services while the children remain in the home; only if the family gives the child up can the deeper pocket of the state be touched.

In too many of these cases, the state's intervention means that the child is going to be removed from home. This is a drastic and wrenching solution, yet the state too seldom uses any other formula that might help keep the family together. The separation is probably hardest on the children it is meant to protect.

The more fortunate of the removed children go to foster homes, the others to group homes or welfare institutions. Yet even for foster children, there is growing concern. In the words of one expert:

> Any child who is compelled for whatever reason to leave his own home and family to live in foster placements lives through an experience pregnant with pain and terror for him and potentially damaging to his personality and normal growth. It is abnormal in our society for a child to be separated for any continuing length of time from his own parents and no one knows this so well as the child himself. For him, placement is a shocking and bewildering calamity, the reasons for which he usually does not understand.[3]

Foster care is by definition temporary or transitional, whereas children crave continuity. Normally the fixed constellations in their chaotic universe are their parents, but foster care means that the child is subjected to the divided loyalties and authorities of his natural parents, his new surrogate parents, his social worker, and perhaps even the juvenile court judge. Foster parents are typically admonished not to encourage lasting loyalties or overaffectionate feelings in the child, since the foster parents theoretically fulfill only a transitional role between one home and the next and, in fact, most children in foster care move at least twice before any permanent placement. Yet in San Francisco the average time spent in foster care is nearly five years, and 62 percent of the children placed are expected to remain there—that is, out of their own homes—for their entire childhood. Only 15 percent to 25 percent of children placed in foster care return home. And the number who eventually get adopted is even lower—less than 15 percent. If a child remains in foster care for eighteen months, his chances of adoption or returning home are remote.[4] The roughly 40,000 children living in welfare institutions such as orphanages and shelter homes are undoubtedly worse off.

The irony is that when society removes children from their homes, it usually ends up paying more and doing less for the child than if money had been available to help the original family. So parental neglect—or a court finding that it exists—often becomes the trigger for community neglect.

Our laws concerning neglect are a legacy from an individualistic era when a family was assumed to be self-sufficient and able to care for its own. Neglect is too often still regarded as a willful act of uncaring parents (for which removal of the child is a just punishment), not as a failure stemming from immense social and economic pressures on families for which society must help pay. Our society, and our legal system, are not yet willing to be affirmative about families, to give them specialized, individualized, noncategorical help so they can provide decently for their children. Rather, society feels compelled to label and punish the parents—in the name of the child. The child's interests are superficially the focus of neglect proceedings, yet in reality the child is rarely consulted, nor is a reasonable choice made as to whether the child's future is best ensured by bolstering up the home or relegating him or her to the limbo of a state ward. Hence, families—and children—have no affirmative rights in our common or constitutional law for the minimum essentials they need to survive, grow, develop, or flourish in a family setting. The law affects families principally in a negative, punitive way; it reaches them chiefly when they are charged with doing wrong toward their children. Even then, the law usually claims no power or authority to order other social agencies to help; its power is too often limited to watching, monitoring, checking up, supervising, and ultimately taking children away. Only at that point is society willing to spend money on the child, in what is usually a futile effort to provide a substitute home.

We therefore endorse four principles of reform in the abuse and neglect laws:

1) Before any child is removed from his or her home for anything but the briefest emergency period (say, 72 hours), there must be a clear and convincing showing—in a due process hearing where the child as well as the parents have counsel—that the child is in imminent danger of serious physical harm or of extreme psychological or emotional harm.* Neglect and abuse laws should be redefined to allow intervention only (a) if the child has been abandoned or is very likely to suffer serious physical harm inflicted by a parent or parents intentionally or as a result of their failure to protect the child adequately; (b) if the child shows identifiable symptoms of mental distress traceable to parental actions and the parent(s) refuse to seek professional help; (c) if the child has been sexually abused by a parent.

2) There must be a strong presumption in favor of children remaining in their natural home or with relatives. Before a court removes a child from his or her nuclear or extended family, it must

---

* Acceptance of any kind of "emotional harm" as grounds for neglect or abuse is worrisome because of its inherent potential for subjective judgments discriminating against minority cultural norms. For instance, one state allows a court to take jurisdiction over any child "whose behavior indicates social or emotional maladjustment." Although the strictest standards should be used for "emotional harm," we are constrainted to admit that there are cases where a child is so psychologically abused by parents or guardians that intervention is justified.

be satisfied that no reasonable strategy of family crisis intervention can save the integrity of the home as a decent environment in which to bring up a child. Providing a daytime baby-sitter or an adequate day-care option may rehabilitate a neglectful mother far more successfully than taking her children away and punishing them for her sins. Courts should be required to decide at the earliest possible stage of any legal proceeding whether a salvage operation is possible, and from the time children are capable of expressing themselves, their own desires on whether to stay or go should be given great weight.

Furthermore:

When it intervenes, a court should pick the disposition which alleviates the immediate danger to the child, cures as best it can the damage already done, and aids the parents in avoiding future endangerment to the child.

When a child must be removed, every effort should be made to remedy the conditions in his or her own home so that he or she can be promptly returned. There must be a specific plan provided to the court about what services will be offered to the parents to make this return possible, and the child's situation should be reviewed at least every six months to monitor the progress of the return plan.

If there is not a reasonable prognosis for the child's return home at the end of a reasonable period (one year to eighteen months), parental rights to the child should be terminable if there is an adoption placement in the offing unless this would damage the child because of his or her ties to the parent; or if, in the case of an adolescent, the child objects.

When a child has formed a close relationship with foster parents and they are willing but financially unable to adopt him or her or become the legal guardian, subsidies should be provided for that purpose.*

3) Before any child is removed from home, the court must make a finding that the place to which he or she will be sent will be less damaging to the child's physical and emotional welfare than the home. This may require judges to visit and assess the child-care shelters and welfare institutions in their jurisdictions.

4) Courts must be given authority to order other public agencies to provide—on a priority basis—the services families and children need to stay intact. (This power should commence even before formal neglect and abuse proceedings are filed on a showing of need.) The families that come before the court for neglect and abuse

---

* Thirty-one states have adoption subsidies. These subsidies are of special benefit to minority children in need of placement, because they increase the possibility for adoption by minority families who have only modest means. In 1969, of 171,000 legal adoptions, only 19,000 involved minority children. There are, however, an estimated 80,000 nonwhite children in need of adoption.

—generally families in desperate need of help—can rarely afford these services themselves, and being put on a waiting list at a community mental clinic or a day-care center is small comfort in a crisis. If courts are considered capable of wielding the ultimate power of severing families, they must also be invested with the lesser power of making priority demands on social services to help floundering families. The court should not, of course, have the power to impose services upon a child or family against the family's will without a finding of neglect or abuse.

Child abuse, as distinct from child neglect, deserves special mention. Although reliable statistics are scarce, there is evidence that it is on the rise; there is also evidence that its incidence increases following unemployment and economic recession. Abuse and neglect are first cousins; they are most prevalent in the same groups of undereducated, overwhelmed, close-to-poverty families. Purposeful abuse of a child, however, is frightening and, to many of us, unfathomable. Every year some children are killed and maimed by their parents. In the light of this, society is certainly justified in taking intrusive steps into the private world of the family, such as mandatory reporting by doctors, nurses, teachers, and others of suspected child abusers; central registries of such reports; and emergency removal of children who appear to be seriously abused or endangered.

But even in this emotionally laden area, there are countervailing concerns.[5] Child-abuse laws ought to be specifically limited to serious physical or psychological abuses. Access to registries of complaints must be limited, the circumstances of emergency removal must be carefully delineated to prevent harassment and humiliation, and due process hearings following removals must be prompt. Even here, the abusive parent's typical isolation, frustration, and inability to cope must be viewed, at least initially, as a correctable condition if help, regular contact, and sympathy are extended. For almost anything would be better than the current solution of consigning the damaged children of abusive parents to the same institutional ware-housing and pillar-to-post temporary care arrangements as the rest of our discarded children. The law in its present stage promises them little more than the promise of stark survival, and many grow up to repeat the cycle by becoming child abusers themselves. Hence our four basic principles of reform apply to child abuse as well as to child neglect.

"Voluntary" Separations of Children and Parents

We have talked so far of society's right to break up families. Families however, often self-destruct, formally or informally. Any comprehensive look at child and family law must take into account the rights of both parents and children when the parents seek to disengage themselves from their children, either out of a sense of hopelessness in coping with special health, developmental, or emotional problems, or for less understandable reasons. In such unfortunate situations, the law has to provide some mechanism whereby inevitable separations will be recognized, but the damaging effects upon the children will be ameliorated, and familial separations which are not inevitable and which can be avoided are prevented by adroit outside help.

Some parents who would never dream of starving or beating their children simply give up on parenthood or become so ground down by the burdens of a handicapped or misbehaving offspring that they volunteer to turn the child over to a state agency, the juvenile court, or even a willing relative or friend. If an hysterical new mother, encouraged by a doctor, wants to institutionalize her deformed child immediately, should the choice be hers alone? When parents at their wits' end with an emotionally disturbed or developmentally disabled child commit him or her to a mental hospital or an institution for the "retarded," should the child's vehement protests be listened to? These altogether too common dilemmas raise profound questions about the legal as well as the moral responsibilities of parents, which society has never definitely resolved. Do children have a right to their natural parents, no matter how reluctant the parenthood? Do parents have a right to give up on their children because of the children's physical and mental handicaps, mental illness, or just plain disobedience and orneriness?

Our society has in the past been willing to accept for state custody any or all children that parents wanted to surrender. Assuming the children were in fact verifiably mentally ill or retarded, state institutions would take over their care, and even healthy children could be "put out" for adoption. The underlying assumption has been that an unwilling parent is not a good parent, or that parenthood is so natural and binding a tie that only the most unworthy or unfit parents would voluntarily undo it. These are no longer satisfactory assumptions, if they ever were. Indeed, in our complex, frag-mented, often overwhelming society, parents can be driven to institutionalize a child by the sheer lack of resources and support in coping with children who require specialized care, education, or training of a kind and intensity that a normal parent with limited resources cannot always give. The failure of most of our communi-ties to provide homemaking or baby-sitting services, respite care, special education, or daytime programs for handicapped children has been documented at length. The demands of an emotionally disturbed or physically or mentally handicapped child can drive a family to exhaustion, despair, and even dissolution if it is not given adequate advice and help. Parents of such children sometimes understandably decide to institutionalize the child. And state cus-todians or hospital gatekeepers are not generally equipped to pro-vide services that might reverse the decision.

What do institutions promise for the newly arrived child? The facts are tragic:

According to the Joint Commission on Mental Health of Chil-dren, one-fourth of the children committed to one state's mental hospital "can anticipate being permanently hospitalized for the next 50 years of their lives." [6]

Ninety percent of mentally retarded institutionalized residents are admitted as minors and stay an average of fifteen years.[7]

The Joint Commission on Mental Health of Children concluded that "instead of being helped, the vast majority [of institutionalized children] are the worse for the experience."

The National Association for Retarded Citizens reports that "most residential facilities for the retarded throughout the country are large, overcrowded, and impersonal." [8]

Studies consistently show that parents without knowledge or broad access to community-based services are more likely to insti-tutionalize their children. One study of 1,000 New York children whose families sought institutionalization showed that 72 percent had had no prior psychotherapy, 85 percent no prior evaluation, and 71 percent no special education.

Only recently has the "voluntary" placement of children in institutions been challenged in the courts; child advocates now claim that just as adult confinement for mental illness or handicap must be preceded by a due process hearing to show that it is necessary, so a child deserves to have it first proved that he or she cannot be ade-quately cared for at home or in the community.

It is by no means an easy issue. After all, parental love and dedication cannot be compelled by court order. But what can be explored in a court proceeding is how to provide help in the many borderline cases of parents who basically want to keep their children at home, but not at the cost of the sanity and health of the rest of the family.

Without such a necessary, albeit agonizing, review of the situation by an impartial tribunal, helpless families tend to block out and forget the absent and isolated child once he or she is institutionalized; often they formally terminate parental rights after a year or two. The child becomes multiply doomed—by the disability, by the institutionalization, by the lack of a family, and by the stigma attached to all of these.

We therefore endorse legislative or judicial reform that would:

1) Ensure a full due process hearing on the necessity for institutionalization of any child placed in a mental institution or specialized facility by his parents for more than a few weeks, and set up such a hearing immediately for any child so placed who is already a state ward.

2) Provide for periodic judicial review of all children in any kind of institution or substitute home to assure that they have not simply been forgotten, and to decide whether they are ready to return to normal home life again.

3) Insist that society provide the least restrictive kind of specialized care that a handicapped or mentally retarded child needs to keep that child functioning in the mainstream of community life. This might mean special education, individual or group outpatient therapy, day-care programs, periodic respite care to allow fatigued parents a reprieve, family counseling, or even placement in a group home in the community. State hospitals and large retardation institutions should be a placement of last resort, acceptable only for as brief a period as is necessary to treat or prepare children for a more normal life situation. Community-based, small, and homelike substitutes for these institutions should be developed, but these, too, must be subjected to intense scrutiny and accountability. To the extent that hospitals and institutions cannot be eliminated, supervision and resources should be provided to ensure that they are humane, decent, and responsive to what the children in them need.

Rebellious and Runaway Children

It is not only the physically or emotionally disabled child that parents give up on; another is the rebel in the family—the unruly, misbehaving child who causes parents to say, "I can't do anything with him—*you* take him!" Parents are often the ones who bring these children to the attention of the juvenile courts, where they generally are classified as Persons In Need of Supervision (PINS) or status offenders. Just as society, through its neglect laws, has too often imposed its own imperatives on families of varied backgrounds, so parents of varied backgrounds and generations, through the PINS laws, have too often tried to impose legally their norms on a new generation living in different times. And the basic paradox of our social policy is that we will not help the parents who want to keep their children, but we are quite willing to accept responsibility for children whose parents give up on them.

Although state laws differ, status offenses commonly cover some seven categories of behavior: (1) disobedience of "reasonable" orders of parents or custodians; (2) running away from home; (3) truancy; (4) disobedience of the "reasonable" orders of school authorities; (5) acts which are permissible for adults but are offenses when children commit them, such as possessing alcohol or tobacco, or frequenting pool halls or taverns; (6) sexual immorality, sometimes called leading a "lewd and immoral life," or being a "wayward child"; and (7) acting in a manner injurious to oneself or others. Other forbidden acts include "being in a disreputable place," "associating with bad companions," "keeping late hours," "begging alms," "being found in or about a railway yard or truck terminal," and "using profane language." The juvenile court has traditionally been allowed on a petition by parents, schools, or social agencies to take custody of status offenders and order them to obey their parents' injunctions, to stay away from bad companions, to go to school, and to keep curfews, along with a variety of other commands normally within the parents' discretion. If these children persist in being disobedient, they can be sent away to the same training schools as juvenile delinquents.

Jails,* detention homes, and training schools are filled with "rebellious" children whose only crime has been disobedience, and among the ranks of these rebels, girls appear more often than boys. What is worse, status offenders are held for longer periods than the more hardened juvenile offenders, because their parents are more reluctant to take them back. But of course prolonged confinement does not make them better behaved, more obedient, or less hostile to their parents. It is generally agreed that some revisions of these antiquated status-offender laws are overdue; the debate is over whether the juvenile court should have any jurisdiction over such children at all. One school of reform would limit the sanctions that the courts can levy on children, forbidding them to be placed in jails, detention homes, or training schools and focusing on family counsel-

---

* There are 100,000 youths placed in adult jails or police lockups every year. In New York State, one survey showed that 43 percent of children in jail were status offenders.[9]

ing, probation, and, if necessary, placement in a group home as more appropriate remedies. A more radical proposal is to abolish juvenile court jurisdiction over status offenders altogether and simply provide social services on a voluntary basis to help children and families at war with one another. But even if juvenile court jurisdiction is redefined to omit status offenses, on-the-spot decisions must still be made about whether society will relinquish all of its protective instincts on behalf of the child. Can society formulate new, more specific responses to save the youngster from the terrors of the night and physical dangers without getting into internal family conflicts or having to put its full force behind parents' authority when no violations of the law are involved?

These problems are being wrestled with by juvenile law reform groups. The excessively broad PINS laws seem destined for restriction, but new authority must be devised to allow police, teachers, doctors, parents, and perhaps even courts to exercise limited authority in situations where a child's welfare or life may be in danger. Such *ad hoc* remedies might include returning a child home, taking him to an overnight shelter, or subjecting him to emergency medical treatment. The limited range of these permissible actions will be frustrating because it will not permit an utimate solution for bad relations between parent and child, but in the long run, it will probably produce less damage than the needless incarceration of hundreds of thousands of rebellious children in sterile and often dangerous state institutions. And at some age short of legal majority when he or she is capable of living independently or with limited supervision in a hostel-like setting, a child may well be entitled to a ruling of incompatibility or emancipation from his or her parents.

Rights of Children Without Families

Children at highest risk are those who spend substantial parts of their childhood in institutions, without family life of any sort. In 1970, there were 255,000 children in welfare institutions, group homes, detention homes, shelters, training schools, mental hospitals, and schools for the handicapped; many of them remained permanent residents until they reached age eighteen or even longer.[10] Unfortunately, most such institutions are as far from homelike as imaginable.

They are big. They are usually far away from the community. They generally have large, impersonal staffs on rotated eight-hour shifts. Overcrowded, regimented, and sterile, very few of them have varied programming or an adequately trained staff, and most are dominated by an aggressive peer subculture.* The asylum mentality lingers on; somehow we insist on punishing children for the sins of their parents who would not care for them or did not bring them up right. There has been a overwhelming consensus for decades among academics and child-care workers that children need one-to-one relationships with caring adults in order to develop, that they need the stimulation of the outside world to grow and practice social skills, and that they must continually be acknowledged as separate and special individuals. But change in our treatment of children without families has still not taken place. Legislatures will not vote to close down big, outmoded institutions or to provide the money for small residences more troublesome to administer than big institutions. Most parents are too concerned about their own children to invest their time or support the investment of public funds in the children of "unfit" parents. Many Americans object to the possibility that such children might be housed in their neighborhood. Children institutionalized because they have been abandoned or abused fare little better and often worse than children institutionalized because they are delinquent, and large numbers of children move from the first category into the second. Some states even revert back to the ancient practice of banishment and deport their wards into distant states, away from all semblance of community ties, because they are not willing to create appropriate facilities at home.

What are the legal rights of such children? Until very recently, it would have been accurate to answer: None. The state, acting in place of the parents, did as it pleased with its wards. Only in the last several years has an embryonic legal doctrine evolved which would accord children without families the right to at least a minimum of what it takes to promote normal health and development. This doctrine has been variously labeled a "right to treatment" for mentally ill or defective children (drawing on an analogous medical-mental health model); a "right to rehabilitation" (for delinquent youths); a "right to protection from harm and deterioration" while in state custody; or a "right to a minimum acceptable standard of care and treatment" for juveniles. Whatever the name, the minimum has been held by various courts to include a nourishing diet, protection from assault by staff and fellow residents, some privacy in sleeping and bathing quarters, access to recreational opportunities and socialization with the opposite sex, adequate education and medical care and, in a few cases, the right not to be moved away from the home community

* This danger of peer exploitation is also present for children who live on the outside, but in their case the family can act as a counterforce or a sanctuary.

except in very special circumstances—unless the child cannot be adequately cared for there because he or she is dangerous or requires specialized care available only in distant locations. This is a fledgling doctrine not yet endorsed by the Supreme Court.

While judicial supervision is notoriously better at preventing harm than at advocating compassionate homelike environments for children without families, legal precedent nonetheless is a needed weapon for assuring a minimum threshold of decent care for institutionalized children, and we support it.

Hence we recommend that a state be held as accountable for neglect and abuse of the children in its care as parents are. Indeed, the state should be held to a higher standard, for it cannot plead ignorance and lack of resources.

1) State laws should explicitly recognize the rights of institutionalized children to the level of care and specialized services they need for healthy growth and development.

2) These laws should also include the right of institutionalized children to be housed and cared for in small, homelike settings in a community except when they require intensive and specialized services available only in a high-quality institution, or their behavior makes them too dangerous for community living. They should never be permitted to be placed in jails or adult prisons.

3) The civil rights of institutionalized children deserve express recognition. Although inside their homes all children are controlled to some degree as regards freedom of speech, movement, and association, state guardians must be held to a standard of reasonableness in imposing curbs on these rights.

Although these minimal legal rights can in no way compensate children raised without families, we believe that society owes them some guarantee of protection from the further deprivations they now suffer at the hands of callous state guardians.

Children's Rights to Make Decisions
About Health Care, School, and Jobs

Courts have traditionally shied away from becoming involved in conflicts over such family decisions as the proper school, the choice of medical care, or the rules of the home. A doctrine of parental autonomy has ruled, allowing parents authority to dictate for their children matters of education, work (within statutory limits), use of money, religion, recreation, standard of living, clothing, diet, housing arrangements, and discipline.

As the child matures, however, he or she and the parents may clash on critical matters such as whether the child should stay in school or go to work. Sometimes a child wants medical or psychiatric care and the family refuses to provide it, or the family wants the child to undergo surgery or psychiatric care and the child rebels.

Formerly, only a child whom the courts declared to be "emancipated" (usually sixteen or above) could legally withstand the parents' decision. The formula for emancipation is elusive: a child can be declared wholly or partially emancipated for a specific purpose. If a girl, for instance, is declared wholly emancipated, she gains the right to live where she pleases, earn and keep her own money, and take care of her own body and soul. Since total emancipation implies a severance of parental rights and responsibilities, courts have been reluctant to find it except in cases of marriage or enlistment in the armed forces, and they usually require parental consent to the act of emancipation itself. Partial emancipation means the child has the right to make decisions of his or her own in a particular area or areas only, such as keeping or spending wages.

Judicial emancipation, however, has proven too clumsy and inflexible a tool for introducing into certain areas of family decision making some rights of personal autonomy for the child. In the past few decades, the pace of adolescent economic and social independence has quickened, and it has become necessary for society to make some piecemeal accommodations in order to prevent parents from denying children certain privileges that society wants them to have. For instance, as a result of the escalation during the 1960's of youthful experimentation with alcohol, drugs, and sex, the vast majority of states have passed laws permitting minors (sometimes over twelve, sometimes of any age) to seek treatment on their own for venereal disease; a smaller number permit minors to seek help for alcohol or drug dependence, and to obtain birth control information or devices. In 1976, the Supreme Court ruled that a state could not make parents' approval a precondition for abortion in the first trimester, no matter what the age of the pregnant girl. A half dozen or so states now permit children above a certain age (fourteen to sixteen) to obtain other kinds of medical or psychiatric treatment of their own. Even these advances, however, leave a majority of states operating on the traditional premises that except in emergencies or for legally emancipated minors, whether and how a child receives medical care is at the parents' option.

While we are fully aware that access to good medical care is something most parents fervently want for their children and that it is most often denied children not by their parents but by society's unwillingness to provide it, there is nonetheless a need to formulate policies and sort out the conditions under which children should be able to obtain medical care themselves. The current statistics on unmarried teen-age mothers and fathers, teen-age suicides, alcoholism, and drug use leave little doubt that some families are so out of touch with their children's problems and needs that their younger members must be given access to medical care for survival.[11] For example, teenage mothers give birth each year to more than 600,000 children who have a higher than average risk of birth defects; one in twenty teen-agers has a "drinking problem"; suicide is the second leading cause of death of youngsters fifteen to twenty-four. The issue of independent access to medical services is less critical for children up to the age of nine, but it is certainly one which lawmakers must deal with in any comprehensive code for children of all ages. And indeed there are equally compelling legal issues affecting younger children that involve parental decisions to volunteer their children for "research" or to allow them to be used in radical, experimental, or surgical procedures.

Health care is only one example of an area in which children who continue to live—and who we wish to see living—in their own families may nonetheless need recognition of rights to make critical choices for themselves. There are many more, and almost all are controversial. In general, we believe it is the job of the legislature (and sometimes the courts) to decide in which areas and at what ages the risk of parental denial of necessary services or options carries with it so severe a lasting detriment to the child's health or future that he or she must have independent access to those services or options. The areas in which such independent power of decision is legitimized by the law should be reserved to those with important consequences for the child and quantitatively for society as a whole. We believe, however, that recognition of some such preserve of children's rights can aid rather than detract from family integrity. What it does is provide an alternative to formal severance proceedings such as "emancipation" or PINS proceedings at the same time that it empowers the child, who must increasingly deal with institutions outside the family, to legally demand services and have service-provider institutions respond to his or her needs.

We do not intend here to lay down all the areas or indicate the precise ages for such decisional power. We will, however, signify a few of our tentative predilections. Without attempting to design a legal health-care code for minors, we believe that revision of existing laws of access are necessary.

1) The age at which minors can seek medical treatment on their own, without subsequent notification of their parents, should be lowered from eighteen or twenty-one. The exact age will have to be debated, but children of any age caught in desperate situations because of drugs or pregnancy should be able to consult a doctor without fear of exposure. (Obviously, a good doctor would try to persuade children to involve their families.) The doctor's dilemma of when, if ever, a parent should be notified because of genuine fears for the child's health or safety is not easily soluble by any pat formula.

In general, the doctor's presumption should be in favor of confidentiality.

2) The question of a minor's legal right to medical care has usually been academic: even if he or she had a legal right to such

care, who would pay for it? A common-sense approach suggested in the Juvenile Justice Standards Project Report on the Legal Rights of Minors is that parents should pay for those services they endorse or those administered in emergencies; minors are responsible for those they are legally authorized to obtain on their own. However, if a minor is insured under a family's public or private health insurance policy, that policy should be legally required to allow a minor who by law is authorized to consent to medical services or treatments to file claims and receive benefits, regardless of whether the parent has consented to the treatment. And the public or private health insurer should not be allowed to inform a parent or policy holder that a minor has filed such a claim or received a benefit unless the physician or the child has done so already.

3) Finally, a code should deal with the thorny question of when a child may refuse the medical or psychiatric treatment his parents want him to receive. What is the age at which children give truly "informed" consent? At one extreme are frightening examples of parents unilaterally "volunteering" their children for psychosurgery, behavior-modification programs with aversive stimuli, electroshock, nontherapeutic medical experimentation, sterilization, and abortion. At the other extreme we readily acknowledge the absurdity of letting a needle-shy seven year old decide he does not want a measles shot, or a debilitated but frightened youngster refuse surgery to repair a heart defect.

Nothing is more basic to a child than his bodily integrity. "Research" or "donation" surgery or experiments not for his own benefit should be barred until the child can give informed consent for himself. Extreme therapies utilizing psychosurgery, electroshock, and aversive stimuli for behavior-modification should be subject to review and approval by a professional peer review group or interdisciplinary human rights committee that is independent of the parents. And, as courts have increasingly ruled, the competent adolescent child * should be able to say no to any unusual procedures, medical or psychological.

Drawing lines is difficult in this area. An avalanche of sophisticated medical techniques, chemotherapies, and psychological behav-

---

* A child incompetent for reasons other than his or her age should have a special nonfamily guardian for this purpose only, appointed by a court to give or withhold consent.

ior-modifying procedures in recent years has been followed by a disturbing number of studies raising doubts about the procedures' long-range effects on children's bodies and minds. Parents are in an uneven bargaining position with the proponents of such procedures. For this reason alone, we find merit in surrounding many severe therapies—physical and psychological—with precautions such as the necessity for independent consultations and an adolescent's right to refuse, for it is the child who will suffer if the gamble is lost.

Children and families may also come into conflict over the child's entry into the world of work or his or her departure from the world of education. Under the child labor laws, going to work generally requires parental consent for a child under age, and permission to leave school at age sixteen is similarly conditioned. In reality, most parents cannot force their wishes on a recalcitrant child.

While we are not in a position here to make specific recommendations on the liberalization of such laws, we do suggest that our laws must catch up with our sociology about what kind of institution the American family has become. Most functioning families do not need laws to govern their internal dynamics; malfunctioning families need some outer limits to protect vulnerable children from parental exploitation which falls short of abuse or neglect but which severely threatens their future functioning educationally or in the work place. A set of legal principles must begin to be fashioned around the awareness that in today's families, from puberty on, children are dealing almost as equals with adults in the outside world of health care, school, and work. At the same time, as long as the family unit can remain viable—with outside support if necessary—it must be protected from premature invasion and dissolution by state apparatus. We believe that both goals can be accommodated by selective legislative choices about adolescents', and in some few cases even younger children's, rights to challenge parental decisions.

Children's Rights in School

During the past decades, the struggles of students, with and without their parents' backing, against what they deemed the outrageous restrictions or actions of insensitive school authorities has created a new era of "school law," usually referred to as students' rights. Their confrontations with school authorities, often conceived in hostility and resolved in mutual suspicion, have produced a set of precedents as yet uncertain and unstable. Yet we find some of the directions taken deserving of support. We will set out here some of the directions which school law has taken of which we approve and some of the directions in which we think it must go forward.

1) We believe in compulsory education, but its timing and the sanctions for failure to go to school need radical reassessment. Society should continue to be responsible for offering education up to the high school level (or for twelve years) to any child who wants it. The

child, however, should have the opportunity to take it in several bites. There should be provision for older adolescents to drop out for a year and come back, if a satisfactory work or other out-of-school experience can be arranged. This right should continue at least up to age twenty-one.

2) Truancy, or failure to attend school, is currently punishable by referral to juvenile court, where a sentence of probation or even reform school can result. Some current proposals for changing this arrangement would remove truancy from the juvenile court's jurisdiction and insist that the schools deal with it themselves. Certainly such a path is better than removing children from their homes because they play hookey, but it does pose another danger. Many schools want to get rid of their poor learners and troublemakers and are passive partners in truancy; "pushouts" are as common as "dropouts." Thus attempts at reforming truancy laws should provide in their place some required mechanism by which the school must continue to check up on absent students, attempt to persuade them to return, meet with parents to work out underlying problems, and perhaps even resort to a court for enforcement of a plan for attendance—always with the understanding that the child will not be considered a delinquent or removed from home for not conforming with the plan. Schools must be forced to bear a responsibility for getting and keeping children in school; mere abandonment of truancy laws will not necessarily accomplish that aim.

3) The unilateral power of schools to suspend and expel, almost at will, for "disciplinary" reasons has been eroded by a series of court decisions in recent years. We applaud those decisions, which recognize the vital interest a student has in staying in school, if only for purposes of acquiring the credentials (degrees, course credits, certificates) needed for entry into many jobs, and which question the frequently arbitrary pattern of discipline. We agree with the courts that the degree of due process protection should increase as the possible sanction grows stiffer. For any serious suspension (over one school week), we would endorse a full panoply of due process rights: notice of the offense, the right to a hearing by an impartial hearing officer, the right to be represented by counsel or a lay advocate, the right to examine relevant school documents ahead of the hearing and to confront and cross-examine witnesses, and the right to appeal to a higher echelon in the system than the school involved.*

* The Children's Defense Fund's school suspension study [12] showed that among 24 million children surveyed, a million children were suspended during the 1972–73 school year. Usually school records were vague about the causes. One-third of the suspended children and parents interviewed said suspension was for "fighting"; two-thirds for nonviolent misbehavior; only 1.6 percent involved abuse of teachers. Nonattendance, tardiness, insubordination, and smoking were common causes. Minority children stood a higher chance of being suspended or expelled than their proportionate numbers in the school population would suggest.

203

We would also limit the causes for any suspension to serious misbehavior, normally limited to situations involving physical danger to others or intolerable disruption of the educational process, laid down in clear written rules disseminated to all students. And finally, in the belief that nothing a student does merits expulsion except an act that would compel a juvenile court to remove him or her from the community entirely, we would wipe out altogether the threat of permanent expulsion.*

4) A child's right to education should be a right to an appropriate education suited to any special needs or handicaps. This legal principle—that our public schools must have a "zero-reject" policy— has received support in the courts and in the 1975 Education of All Handicapped Children Law. Belatedly, public schools are now required to offer the physically and mentally handicapped child, the learning disabled, and the non-English-speaking child an opportunity to be educated. Adequate resources and programs for such individualized schooling of every child will depend on the political and economic priorities in each community and in each state, but whatever resources do exist should be shared equitably among and inside school districts. No students should be left out of the school system intentionally or unintentionally because they are denied the special help they need to travel in the educational mainstream.

5) We have been concerned with the way that schools often track students for life, and we know the solution to such a situation lies much deeper than changing laws. Still, extreme types of tracking do lend themselves to some legal controls. Thus the assignment of a student over the objections of parents to a special class for slow learners or for the "educable retarded" or for behavior problems should be legally challengeable; that is, it should be possible to force a hearing in which the school must prove that the child legitimately belongs in such a special category. Too often minority students, especially those who do not speak English, are assigned to special classes for reasons of prejudice or because teachers cannot cope with their culture, rather than for any justification based on their native abilities. Although some students genuinely need specialized help, others are too easily shunted off into special classes, and an insistence on due process and rights of challenge can help to protect them.

Students are also unnecessarily pigeonholed and stigmatized by their school records. Pupils' personal files containing informal comments, speculations, and opinions of all kinds, from a child's first day in first grade until graduation from high school, are often casually passed around. These records travel along with children from teacher to teacher and school to school; police, courts, and government agencies have ready access to them. The so-called Buckley Amend-

---

* There may, of course, be cases where a child who is continually molesting or endangering fellow students or teachers may have to be provided alternate education in a different setting.

ment (the Family Educational Rights and Privacy Act of 1974) has made a propitious start in controlling the inherent abuses of such record freewheeling; it allows parents (and children over eighteen) to inspect and ask for correction or supplementation of such records; it restricts access of outsiders and requires notification to parents when requests for such access are made of school officials. More basically, however, our laws need to sort out what kind of records about schoolchildren are really important to keep and to analyze whether many of the cumulative paper dossiers that schools keep do more harm than good for children in later life. Perhaps school records should be treated like the arrest records of children and destroyed after a period of time, except possibly for "objective" grades or test scores. Indeed, when children finish each grade, only the most essential material about their performance or needs should be retained and passed on.

6) In accordance with our general preference for the family as the primary decision maker for the child, the school should not assume noneducational, essentially family functions. Schools should promote sound routine health care, but they should not probe for intimate details of family life through psychological testing without parental consent; they should not seek to compel parents to put "hyperactive" children on drugs as a condition of staying in school; they should not play amateur psychologist in treating or even diagnosing children as normal, disturbed, emotionally unstable, or the like. Only if the child's educational achievement is suffering or if his or her behavior in school is markedly disruptive should the school involve itself with the child's psychological development. And any action in such situations (except perhaps that involving the diagnosis or treatment of adolescents of an age of consent by other professionals) should be initiated or approved by parents.

7) Last, because schools are often big and institutionalized, we believe each should have an "ombudsman," a designated person to whom a student can voluntarily confide intimate problems, such as drug involvement, sexual activities, and even family troubles, with absolute confidence that his disclosures will not be revealed to school officials, law enforcement officials, or even the student's own family except where their own lives or the lives of others may be in jeopardy. Schools should also have a bona fide grievance mechanism that is not loaded in favor of school personnel and in which the students themselves participate to vindicate the wrongs they feel they are suffering.

The one-room schoolhouse with the schoolmaster who knew every pupil by name and came to dinner monthly is no more; massive, often impersonal school bureaucracies exercise powerful control over children's present and future lives. There will inevitably be recurrent conflicts between the school on the one hand and parents or pupils on the other over the school's demands and actions toward its students.

In the past, parents and pupils have been awed by educational expertise and often unduly deferential to educators. We believe that parents and pupils must become more active in the educational process in voicing their demands and seeking redress for their grievances. If they are to do so, there must be rules of the game that all players know and respect. We support and urge thoughtful deliberations on a school code by parents, teachers, school officials, and the most affected group—pupils themselves.

Children's Rights in a Technological Society

There is one unexplored terrain in children's rights about which we want to comment briefly. This is the legal recourse children should have against society and its varied instrumentalities for the assaults on their bodies and minds perpetrated by technology: environmental pollutions, food adulterations, drugs marketed without adequate investigation into their side effects, nuclear "accidents," contamination from the parents' work place.

One forceful example is the case of a small factory in a town of 20,000 in Virginia. The factory manufactured Kepone, a highly toxic pesticide, for a period of sixteen months in the 1970's. Within a few years, 70 of the factory's approximately 130 workers had contracted serious and sometimes irreversible illnesses ranging from liver damage to severe neurological disabilities; 30 were hospitalized. The Environmental Protection Agency subsequently found traces of Kepone in the air sixteen miles away from the town, in river water forty miles away, and in shellfish taken from the James River sixty-four miles away. Six months after the plant was shut down, doctors still found traces of Kepone in the blood and liver of the workers' children. Experts are unsure how much of such absorbed Kepone is dangerous, how long it stays toxic, or what its health effects on the children of the workers will be ten or twenty years later.

Who was responsible? Two ex-employees of a major national chemical company started the Kepone factory in a converted gas station; the sole buyer of Kepone was the Allied Chemical Company, which had itself developed the pesticide. The improvised plant had no health or safety controls; employees did not know there were any dangers to their handling and breathing the chemical-laden dust. Even when the dust destroyed the bacteria in the town's sewage disposal system, when the neighbors complained about the continual dust clouds emanating from the plant, when the local air pollution gauge registered large particles of the substance, even when employees first developed the shakes, local, state, and federal regulatory agencies did not act. Belatedly, the workers who were affected sued the chemical company for damages to themselves and their families.

In another state, asbestos-plant workers sued their employer on the grounds they were never informed of the high risk of cancer not only to themselves but to their families from contamination by breathing fibers they brought home on their bodies and clothing. In still another case, children and spouses of the victims of drowning from a defective dam operated by a mining company obtained a favorable settlement based on the emotional agonies the experience caused them. Abroad, the deformed child victims of the drug thalidomide have also received money from the manufacturer.

But damage suits are an after-the-fact remedy and even then are usually successful only where it can be proved that the manufacturer (or perhaps a regulatory agency) acted negligently in not informing the consumer or worker of the dangers involved in use or exposure to a toxic substance. The manufacturer or regulator can often counter that there was not sufficient proof at the time to show any substantial dangers or that the consumer or worker knowingly chose to take the risk, just as smokers do. Sometimes, as in the nuclear breeder controversy, the risk of death or disease to some citizens, including children, has been assumed as a matter of public policy by the entire community or nation. In addition, substantial financial recoveries are, unfortunately, the exception rather than the rule due to the delays, uncertainties, and expenses of protracted litigation. And of course they do not begin to compensate the victims for the tragic physical and emotional losses they suffer.

Every day in the newspapers, parents read allegations of serious damage to children's health from chemicals in the work places of their parents, additives to baby food, pollutants in the air or water supply, chemicals found in mothers' milk, and prescription and nonprescription pediatric drugs. Many of the allegations prove to have a basis in fact. Perhaps the most crucial and dangerous cases concern the health of the unborn. The best case documented to date, by a study recently completed by the National Institute for Occupational Safety and Health, involves the reproductive problems of workers exposed regularly to waste anesthetic gases. The results showed that women employed as operating-room personnel had an increased risk of spontaneous miscarriages and congenital abnormalities in their children.[13] Babies born to operating-room nurses were three times as likely to be deformed as babies born to women in other jobs. Furthermore, there was shown to be an increased risk of birth defects for the children of male operating-room personnel, whose wives would not have been exposed to anesthetic gases.

Other substances which are known to have harmful effects on the fetus or the parents' reproductive functioning include benzene, carbon monoxide, carbon disulfide, hydrocarbons, lead, mercury, Kepone, and vinyl chloride. Occupational exposure to carbon disulfide [14] and diethylstilbestorol [15] have been linked to sexual impotence in men.

In addition to chemicals whose harmful effects are clearly documented, workers are also exposed to many substances which are "potentially toxic to reproductive functions" but whose effects have not been studied—textile workers, for example, more than 65 percent of whom are women, are exposed to dust, dyes, mothproofers and flame retardants.[16] Lab technicians—over 80 percent of them women —are exposed to radiation, carcinogenic chemicals, antibiotics, solvents, and bacteria. We know that diagnostic radiation during pregnancy has been associated with excess leukemia or cancer in children.[17] Radiation exposure also can cause abnormal sperm production.[18]

The Occupational Safety and Health Act (OSHA) of 1970 specifies that all workers must be guaranteed a safe and healthful work place. That law should be construed to cover, as well, effects on the workers' children, born or unborn. Lead is one toxic industrial substance whose harmful effects on reproduction have actually been taken into account in setting exposure standards. Exposure to high concentrations has been shown to cause chromosome aberrations that could affect future offspring; [19] lead exposure is also correlated with increased risk of spontaneous abortions in women [20] and with abnormal sperm production in men.[21] The OSHA standard on lead recognizes that lead can cross an exposed woman's placenta and enter the fetus's blood stream. Of the 500 standards in effect, this is the first even to mention reproductive problems.

We endorse this approach and believe it should be based on the needs of the most vulnerable—the fetus—when women of reproductive age are involved. The rapid development of the fetus in the first three months of pregnancy makes it extremely susceptible to toxic influences. The mother may not even know she is pregnant during this period, and by the time she discovers she is, toxic substances may have already passed to the fetus. Standards, therefore, should be strict enough to protect all fertile women. This would have the added benefit of also protecting men; substances that cause birth defects can also cause genetic mutations, affecting the fertility and reproductive functions of fathers as well as mothers.

We believe that protection of children from the fallout of technological progress deserves a far higher priority in our legal system (as well as in our political and moral hierarchy) than it now gets. The ways to establish meaningful children's rights to ensure adequate preventive and compensatory efforts by private manufacturers and public regulators are by no means clear. We can suggest only a few possibilities for others to explore:

1) Children's compensation laws, patterned after workman's compensation laws, might by-pass cumbersome lawsuits and provide an administrative mechanism for establishing the connection between industrial activity and the damage inflicted. They would provide compensation from a required fund carried as part of every industry's insurance package.

2) A special children's addendum to every environmental impact statement could be required by federal law, to highlight special dangers to children's health or welfare. (This idea has been explored by the nonprofit Family Impact Seminar at George Washington University.)

3) We could acknowledge in our laws that since children are not permitted to participate in political decisions about community risk, or even in parental decisions about consumption of risky products or work in risk-ridden environments, they are in no way prevented, as their parents might be, from suing the manufacturers, vendors, or employers for the damage they suffer as a result.

4) We could insist that our regulatory laws and policies for watchdog agencies such as the Food and Drug Administration and the Environmental Protection Agency put a legislative priority on children. This would involve higher standards for approval of products and operations where children's health is concerned and a lower tolerance for "reasonable risks" when they accrue to children, as well as insisting on wider publication of suspected dangers of products and operations to children at an earlier and less substantiated stage than now prevails for the general population.

5) Manufacturers of products aimed at a children's market

could be required to conform to the same standards that a reasonable parent would be held to toward his or her own children. Translated, this would mean a duty not to withhold or distort information that might make a parent refuse to buy the product or refusal to put a product on the market that presented a risk a reasonable parent would not allow his or her own child to take.[22]

These are incubator ideas at best. The critical point is to elevate and expand our national concept of children's protective services. Child protection should go far beyond the traditional model of social workers looking out for neglected or poorly fed children to embrace a federal children's consumer and environmental watchdog agency that screens the practices of private industry and government alike for their effects on children and communicates an early warning to parents and others who care for children about issues they should focus on. This is a difficult task to ask of any governmental agency, and there is no doubt that such an agency could be kept honest and safe from cooption only by private child advocates on the outside. Much thought would have to be given to how the agency could stay free of conflicting loyalties to other regulatory agencies and political offices and still have access to their secrets; to what its enforcement and investigatory powers should be; and to what its responsibilities should be for communicating information to the public. We make the suggestion humbly, aware of the poor track record of most bureaucracies in protecting the consumer. But no one inside the government now seems to be doing this job even nominally or acknowledging that it is worth doing. In the long run, nuclear power, disruption of the ozone layer, chemical additives, prescription and over-the-counter drugs, and industrial pollution may well present more pressing legal problems for whole generations of children than do a relatively small number of neglectful or abusive parents.

Who Will Fight for Children's Rights?

Laws and legal rights do not enforce themselves. The history of the juvenile court, designed as a benign nonadversary forum to determine the "best interests of the child," teaches the lesson that children need their own independent and skilled advocates to state their cases if they are not to be exploited. Until the Supreme Court's 1967 Gault decision and the appearance of Legal Services offices under the Office of Economic Opportunity (supplemented in some cities by Public Defender or Legal Aid offices), the notion of children's lawyers was virtually unheard of. Nearly all of the progress made so far in establishing children's legal rights has come in the past decade, largely as a result of these storefront lawyers and a few civil rights organizations who counsel children, inform them of their rights, defend them individually in court, and initiate class actions to protect them from social or institutionalized neglect or abuse.

Children's lawyers have always been scarce, and their lack of a financial base makes them an endangered species. The problem remains acute as to where enough adequately trained and decently paid lawyers will come from to operate a rational legal system that supports children's rights. Legal service lawyers are chronically overworked and underpaid. Other public-interest organizations are restricted in the amount of legislative advocacy they can do and still remain tax exempt. Few if any prepaid legal insurance plans provide for child advocates. And aside from the need for lawyers to represent children directly, there are glaring needs for truly independent ombudsmen not just in schools but in juvenile institutions and agencies of all kinds to call attention to outrages.

In a simpler world, parents were the only advocates children needed. This is no longer true. In a complex society where invisible decision makers affect children's lives profoundly, both children and parents need canny advocates. What if all parents made relatively small financial contributions to such a cause? It would provide a politically insulated fund for lawyers, ombudsmen, agency monitors, and even attempts at legislative reform. Alternatively, parental pressure for public funds must be exerted to provide these legal services for children, who cannot pay for it themselves.

10. Converting Commitment into Politics

The most pressing problems of families and children, it is now clear to us, are in fact the problems of society. We may yearn for the storybook picture of untroubled families in charge of their own destinies, but we now live with a reality very different from this. It is time for parents, citizens, private business, and public officials to face up to the many new shapes that are emerging for the old family and to bring our ideas and policies into line with reality.

When parents feel powerless, it is not because they really need

213

reform, therapy, or education, but because they *are* relatively power-less in today's society. Changing that fact requires not just individual change, family therapy, or childhood education, but social, economic, and political change. Most children's problems are also social problems. Change must be not just personal but also political.

When they blame themselves, American parents define their family problems as somehow rooted in themselves. They thereby neglect basic questions: how to give parents more power outside the family, how to make the distribution of rewards in our society more just, how to limit the risks of technology. Time and again, parents have asked what they themselves are doing wrong, not how the society is pressuring them. They have asked how to change the victims of our social order rather than how to change the forces that victimize. They have asked how to become informed consumers rather than how to exact real social responsibility from private and public institutions.

Now it is time for parents and, in fact, all who care about children to take on a new set of responsibilities. In addition to being in charge of the private facts of inner family life, parents now have little choice but to concern themselves as well with the public facts of the society that impinge on their families.[1] In addition to being private nurturers, responsible parents and all who care about children growing up must become public advocates for the children's interests, and that cause must be interpreted far more broadly than it ever has been before.

Public advocates for children should begin by asking unexpected questions about children. Whether in dinner-table discussions or national policy debates, they should ask not only about how to change—or help—individual families, but about measures to modify economic and social factors that affect families. Besides worrying about report cards and pediatricians and growing pains, they should worry about jobs, the structure of the labor market, and the degree of social justice in the nation. When they talk about a child falling behind in school, they should ask about more than the teacher: they should ask what kind of future that child can expect when schooling is over. Public advocates have to ask about tax reform, about reorganizing health care, about racism, about sexism, about energy—all for the sake of children.

Policies that address only the immediate needs of children, in short, generally miss the shaping social context that largely decides whether families will have space to develop and their children room to grow.

In addition to raising unexpected questions, people concerned with children need to become more used to taking political action. They can do so through the community service councils and community health agencies we recommend. They can also do so by encouraging organizations that are concerned with children, such as the local and national PTA or the Junior League, to keep pushing political issues that touch children.[2] Writing letters to Congress, supporting lobbying efforts, and preparing tough questions for campaigning political candidates about their views on children should be as much a part of child rearing as changing diapers or drying tears. Children need advocates in politics, and for the sake of the children, parents and all others whose interest is in children have to be among them.

That children are being harmed and need not be is reason enough to make changes. Americans cannot continue to think of themselves as moral citizens while they continue to tolerate the remediable anxieties, the endable harm, the foreseeable and harmful technological side effects of our society on so many of its citizens. Parents and children are today unnecessarily harmed—in ways that we might prevent. It is the simplest principle of morality that we cease to hurt others, especially those who, like children, have done us no wrong and bear little responsibility for their condition.

Change is also practical. Far more public money goes to support children in public institutions than it would cost to provide their families with the financial help that often makes institutionalization unnecessary. The United States spends countless billions of dollars in compensatory programs without seriously attacking the social problems whose impact on children we need to compensate for. The amounts we spend on our multitude of ill-coordinated and overlapping child-health programs would nearly suffice to create a unified, rational system that would guarantee good health care to all children. The list could be lengthened, but the point is clear. Our nonsystem is extraordinarily inefficient and costly in terms of attaining the results it achieves. Simply on grounds of the short-term efficiency of the dollars we already spend, we need a thorough revamping.

Our society needs the best adults we can make: adults who are caring, resourceful, moral, whole, and physically healthy. When we fail to support the development of the next generation and of the families that nurture them, we deprive ourselves and the nation of a part of our children's potential. Children who lose a sense of decent future are likely to become dispirited, angry, withdrawn, enraged. Above all, if they are excluded from the mainstream of society, they are rarely able to contribute to the well-being of society as adults. Indeed, it is from the ranks of such condemned children that a large share of tomorrow's public wards will be recruited: the criminals, the derelicts, the embittered, the vandals, the muggers. For those Americans who enjoy the privilege of relative affluence, failure to support a comprehensive child and family policy is like deferring a heavy tax to their children. For failure to change today will lay on the next generation heavy social costs with a high moral, social, and financial price tag. On the one hand, they are the costs of wasted human potential; on the other hand, they are the costs of trying to deal in the next generation with all of the problems of crime, deep disaffection, delinquency, and withdrawal that could have been prevented.

A Policy for Children and Families

Here in a brief review is the national program—the broad, integrated, explicit family policy—we believe public advocates should support for the sake of children:

1) Public advocates should support jobs for parents and a decent living standard for all families.

We need to adopt a new "decency standard" for thinking about poverty—a line based, in any given year, on 50 percent of the median income of a family of four. No children in the nation should have to live in a household with significantly less income than this. The means to achieve this are:

Full employment We need to reduce unemployment for heads of households to no more than 1 percent or 1½ percent, bringing the general unemployment rate down to between 3½ percent and 5 percent.

To do this, the government should consider a mixture of policies: increasing the amount of money in circulation for economic stimulus when the economy is operating far below capacity, giving business an incentive to hire more people, and providing incentives for industries to move into areas where there are high concentrations of unemployed persons.

As a back-up, the federal government should provide guaranteed work, at wages of at least half the average for industrial workers in that year, for at least one parent in every family that contains a child if the parent has been without employment for over three months.

In national economic planning, full employment should be considered as important as keeping prices stable. A major effort should be made to develop and perfect regulations and administrative structures that can effectively control inflation by some means other than allowing unemployment to rise.

Fair employment We must reduce job barriers and job ceilings for racial minorities and women. Everyone supporting children should have a chance at the best rewards for hard work and all children should have a decent future to look forward to.

Specific charges of job discrimination can be dealt with by improving the enforcement of our current laws and regulations, in particular by speeding cases through the courts and giving the government more flexible remedies than total cutoff of government contracts with employers who show evidence of job discrimination.

Deeper reaching job discrimination can be attacked through encouraging affrmative action. Furthermore, new legislation is needed to change the usual methods of recruiting employees and establishing job qualifications. New regulations are needed to give a government agency that is not already saddled with handling specific complaints the responsibility for instituting lawsuits wherever there is reason to believe that a broad-based pattern of discrimination exists.

A decent minimum income level for all The country should provide a back-up system to full employment that puts an income floor under every American family.

Such a system would incorporate or reform elements of the federal income tax system, welfare, food stamps, workmen's compensation, and veterans' benefits. It should maintain incentives to work by reducing its benefits gradually as income from work goes up. Such a system would support the working poor as well as the unemployed and very poor.

A parent with the primary responsibility for raising young children should be guaranteed a passable family income if she (or he) decides to stay at home. Adults should not be eligible for income supports, however, if they are capable of working and not actively seeking a job or taking care of young children; such a work test would apply to the wealthy as well as the poor. Neither should benefits go to absent parents with a source of income who do not make contributions to supporting their children.

A sample system of income supports worth considering is a credit income tax. Replacing the current system, it would tax virtually all income, allowing deductions only for the costs of earning income, including child-care expenses, and for charitable contributions. All taxpayers, whatever their income, would pay the same flat percentage and all would be entitled to a tax credit, in cash if they had no other source of support or in a credit applied against the taxes they owed if they did have income. The example shown in Chapter 5 would tax almost all four-person families with incomes under $18,000 less than the present system. If a credit tax is not immediately feasible, similar results might be obtained by modifying our present tax and transfer-payment systems.

2) Public advocates should support more flexible working conditions.

The demands of a parent's employment should conflict as little as possible with the needs of the family.

Working hours should be made flexible whenever possible so that parents can sometimes manage family affairs during the day, and so they are not forced to leave their children in the care of others at times when they would rather not.

"Flexitime"—the system under which employees can determine the hours they work on any given day so long as the weekly hours add up to a required total in any given period—is one innovation that government and private employers should try more widely. Part-time jobs should be upgraded and structured with full guarantees of job security benefits, and they should provide equal wages for equal work. Federal and state legislation should require governments to set an example by creating both flexitime scheduling and part-time jobs for their workers.

Pregnancy leave should be expanded and protected. American employers should be required to grant mothers, and possibly fathers, a twelve-week leave of absence to be used in any proportion they choose before and after the birth of a baby, without losing seniority, advancement privileges, or job security.

Longer leaves for child rearing need to be protected, too; whenever possible, parents should not lose seniority when they take several years off for child rearing. The easier it is to reenter a job after time off, the freer parents will feel to choose whether to stay at home with their children or go out for wages on the basis of what suits the family best.

3) Public advocates should support an integrated network of family services.

All families need services. The nation needs to help families get them.

Services should have black and white children, middle-class and poor in the same program as often as possible. The services should be easy to find and get to. There should be a wide range of services for families to choose from, and parents should play a strong role in the services themselves. Above all, family services should stress prevention, making it as easy for a family to go to a clinic for a mild problem as to go to an emergency room after the problem has become serious, and as easy for a court or government agency to provide a homemaker to help a troubled family with its children as it is to put the children in foster care or an institution.

Federal standards for quality and fairness should be enacted for all services, public or private. To see that they are meeting these standards, services should be subject to "quality audits" commissioned by local consumers' councils. The councils would also survey needs and coverage in their areas. Both at this local level and above, data on service needs and coverage must be radically improved, as must state plans for services.

Government does not need to provide all services directly to all families. But it does need to pay for surveys of needs, coverage, and impact, for start-up costs in many cases, for test programs, for the consumers' councils to monitor local services, and for establishing services in areas that cannot afford to set them up.

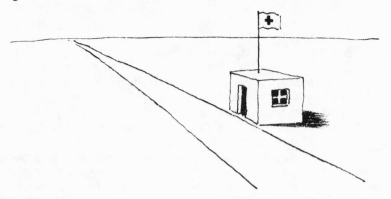

4) *Public advocates should support proper health care for children.*

We need to recognize that children's health depends as much on income, environment, and diet as it does on hospitals, nurses, and pediatricians.

We need national health insurance to guarantee that all children get health care, and we need to reorganize the system to emphasize prevention and primary care—the simplest kind of checkups and treatment.

Federal and state legislation should create a network of community health agencies (CHAs), built on existing public health departments or the recently created state Health Service Agencies, and dominated by laymen. CHAs should be given the authority to coordinate both private and public health services, preventing overlaps, controlling costs, maintaining consistent records, and holding service providers to account for what they do.

We need better public data on health-care providers, so parents can select care more thoughtfully and so that monitoring groups can keep services up to the mark. Education for parents and children should be increased so they can interpret their own medical records and learn to perform minor health procedures such as taking throat cultures and doing ear exams. Communities should have twenty-four-hour telephone services to answer medical questions, and health professionals should be trained to increase their collaboration with parents.

5) Public advocates should support improved legal protection for children outside and inside their families.

The law should make every effort to keep families together. No child should be removed from home at either the court's request or a parent's without a clear showing that the child will be better off elsewhere and that less drastic solutions, such as therapy or special education, would not relieve the problem. Courts and social agencies must make every effort to return a child who is removed; or, when this is still impossible after over a year, speed adoption procedures in a new family.

Placement of any child in any institution should be reviewed regularly, with the burden of proof always on those who argue for maintaining the child at the institution. All institutions should ensure children reasonable civil rights as well as rights to treatment, rehabilitation, protection, and a minimum standard of care.

Children's rights to make their own decisions about health care and whether to leave school to work should be expanded.

Students' rights in relation to schools need protection. Schools should seek the return of truants instead of accepting their absence, and truants should not be referred to juvenile court. Restless older adolescents should be allowed to drop out of school for a year and come back without penalty, at least up to the age of twenty-one. School suspensions should be severely limited and permanent expulsion eliminated altogether. Students' privacy should be protected and their records should be open only to them and their families. Schools' ability to assign students to special classes or require that hyperactive children be given drugs should be restricted.

We need to develop various ways to protect children from the assaults of the technological environment, including children's compensation laws and child-impact statements.

Finally, we need to give all the support we can to lawyers, ombudsmen, agency monitors, and children's advocates, who are often pursuing at a broader level the goals we commend to all individual adults, parents or not, who care about children.

A Vision of the Possible

We have tried, in defining our policy objectives, to think in terms of what could actually be achieved within a decade. But we cannot and do not wish to conceal the vision of a better society that has animated our entire work.

The society we imagine would be one that put children first, not last, that saw the development of a vital, resourceful, caring, moral generation of Americans as the nation's highest priority. The devotion that individual parents now feel to their own children would be broadened to include everyone's children. The next generation's strength and well-being would become everyone's responsibility. "How will it affect all our children?" would be the first question we ask of every new technology, each innovation, all policies.

The society we want would be one where no parent able to work suffered the stigma and degradation of not being able to provide for his or her family.

It would be a society where being a parent would be seen as an honorable calling, a form of work as worthy of public support as the defense of the nation or the construction of superhighways.

It would be a society where every child would have a chance, a realistic basis, to imagine herself or himself a decent future, limited only by ability and aspirations.

It would be a society where parents could choose to be both effective mothers and fathers and productive workers, even when their children were young.

It would be a society where more children survived to adulthood, and where adults enjoyed more robust physical vitality.

It would be a society where parents had available to them the kinds of help they needed and where they had a powerful voice in every institution affecting them and their children.

It would be a society where present excessive inequalities of income, power, and dignity were much reduced.

It would be a society where the rights of parents and children were more adequately represented in the courts and throughout the land.

It would be, in short, a society that took seriously and had translated into its basic outlooks and policies today's rhetoric that claims children to be our "most precious natural resource" and calls families "the building blocks of our society." Such a nation would, we believe, be a better society for all Americans, which is precisely as it must be if we are to do a better job for all our children.

Council Members

Kenneth Keniston, chairman and director of the Council, has undertaken extensive studies of social change, social protest, and alienated youth: *The Uncommitted* (1965), *Young Radicals* (1968), and *Youth and Dissent* (1971). Formerly a professor of psychology in the department of psychiatry at the Yale Medical School, he is now Mellon professor of human development at the Massachusetts Institute of Technology, where he is exploring the impact of modern society on patterns of human development.

Catherine Foster Alter, a social worker, is planning director of federally supported social and nutrition services for elderly people in a three-county area surrounding Davenport, Iowa. She has worked with the League of Women Voters and with state and county governments to assure the rights of students and to set up youth advocacy agencies and home-based day-care arrangements.

Nancy Buckler was formerly a child-care worker in a residential treatment center for disturbed children. She is now master teacher at the Loyola University Day School in Chicago, a center working with severely disturbed children and their families, and is an adjunct faculty member at Stritch Medical Center and at the National College of Education.

John Putnam Demos, a professor of history at Brandeis University, is the author of *A Little Commonwealth* (1970) and other studies of family life in the American past. Formerly acting director of the Center for Psychosocial Studies in Chicago, he is trained in psychology as well as history. His current research interests include witchcraft in early America and the human life cycle in relation to historical change.

Marian Wright Edelman practiced law in Mississippi during the early 1960's, where she worked with the NAACP Legal Defense Fund. In addition to handling test cases involving children, she now directs the Children's Defense Fund of the Washington Research Project, a group she founded to document and challenge unfair treatment of children in schools, courts, and the welfare system.

Robert J. Haggerty, a pediatrician, is professor of health services and pediatrics at the Harvard School of Public Health and Harvard Medical School. While at the University of Rochester, he pioneered a child health program involving many disciplines and community agencies. The senior author of *Child Health and the Community* (1975), he is now helping plan new integrated health services for several New England communities.

William Kessen, professor of psychology at Yale University, has conducted numerous studies of how young children develop the abilities to perceive and think, and has written about the history and philosophy of how social science approaches children. He is the author of *The Child* (1965), and he recently edited *Childhood in China,* the account of thirteen American social scientists who spent three weeks in China in 1973.

Laura Nader, professor of anthropology at the University of California at Berkeley, has studied law among the Zapotec of Mexico and the Shias in Lebanon. She has investigated extrajudicial complaint handling in the United States and is the editor of a forthcoming book on the subject. The author of *Talea and Juquila: A Comparison of Zapotec Social Organization* (1964), she has produced a film on Zapotec court procedure (1966) and edited several books on conflict, social control, and health. She is currently working on the human factors involved in energy planning.

Faustina Solis, deputy director of the California state health department's Public Health Division, is on leave from her post as associate professor of community medicine at the medical school of the University of California at San Diego. A social worker, from 1967 to 1971 she directed the first major expansion of state health services for migrant workers in California.

Patricia McGowan Wald * is an Assistant Attorney General in charge of legislative affairs for the Department of Justice. Previously, as a public interest lawyer, she was litigation director of the Mental

---

* Patricia Wald, who participated in the final decisions concerning this volume, resigned from the Council upon appointment to her post in the Justice Department in February, 1977.

Health Law Project in Washington, D.C. She served as a consultant to the National Commission on Civil Disorders and the National Commission on the Causes and Prevention of Violence, as co-director of the Ford Foundation Drug Abuse Research Project, and as a member of the American Bar Association's commission developing new guidelines for children's rights.

Harold W. Watts, director of the Center for the Social Sciences and professor of economics at Columbia University, formerly headed the Institute for Research on Poverty at the University of Wisconsin. He supervised the evaluation of the federally sponsored test in New Jersey of a negative income tax as an alternative to the welfare system.

Council Staff

Executive Director: Kenneth Keniston

Associate Directors: Peter O. Almond, Joan Costello, Richard H. de Lone

Senior Editor: Jill Kneerim Grossman

Director of Public Affairs: Christopher T. Cory

Research Associates: Peter O. Almond, Robin Boger, Susan Bucknell, Alison Clarke-Stewart, Joan Costello, Richard H. de Lone, Peter Garlock, Mark Gerzon, John Gliedman, Rochelle Kessler, Michael A. Lerner, Katherine Messenger, John U. Ogbu, Hillary Rodham, William Roth, Elga Wasserman

Research Assistants: Chris Buckley, Deborah R. Chernoff, Ellen Chirelstein, Laura Eby, Francesca Gobbo, Georgia Goeters, Susan Hunsinger, Vera Wells Jones, Nina Kraut, Felicity Skidmore, Phyllis Holman Weisbard

Statistical Analysis: Georgia Goeters

Dissemination Staff: Adelina Diamond, Virginia Fleming, Kathryn K. Toll

Administration: Darlene Copeland, Susan Ellison, Arlene Gurland, Ethel Himberg, Jane Hyland, Margaret Jackewicz, Karin Kaminker, Marion Lincoln, Sheila Meyers, Susan Mulford, Donna Piazza, Sylvia Rifkin, Laurie Rosenbaum

Television Planning: Donald Dixon

Television Writers: Barbara Gordon, Richard McCutchen, Larry Neal, Mort Silverstein

---

For this book: Editors: Jill Kneerim Grossman, Christopher T. Cory

Design: Bob Ciano

Illustrations: Guy Billout

227

Notes

Chapter 1

The Transformation of the Family

1. *Toward a National Policy for Children and Families,* the report of the Advisory Committee on Child Development of the National Academy of Sciences, Washington, D.C.: National Academy of Sciences, 1976.

2. U.S. Department of Labor, "Married Persons' Share of the Labor Force Declining, BLS Study Shows," *Department of Labor News,* No. 77191, March 8, 1977.

3. National Academy of Sciences, *op. cit.,* for 1948 figure; U.S. Department of Labor, *op. cit.,* for 1976 figure.

4. Howard Hayghe, "Families and the Rise of Working Wives—An Overview," *Monthly Labor Review,* May, 1976, U.S. Department of Labor, Bureau of Labor Statistics. During the year 1975, about two-fifths of all children under age 18 were in families where both husband and wife worked, i.e., 22 million children (p. 16).

5. Kingsley Davis, "The American Family in Relation to Demographic Change," in *Demographic and Social Aspects of Population Growth,* Vol. 1, Charles R. Westoff and Robert Parke, Jr., eds., Commission on Population Growth and the American Future. Washington, D.C.: Government Printing Office, 1972.

6. Mary Jo Bane, "Marital Disruption and the Lives of Children," *Journal of Social Issues,* Vol. 32, No. 1, 1976, pp. 109–110. Bane estimated that in the 1970's, between 20 percent and 30 percent of all children under 18 will experience the divorce of their parents; an additional 3 percent to 5 percent can be expected to be affected by an annulment or long-term separation; and about 9 percent will lose one or both parents by death. Thus, between 32 percent and 44 percent will be involved in marital disruption. Another 2 percent will spend a substantial period of time in a single-parent home with a never married mother, bringing the total to between 34 percent and 46 percent.

Americans marry at earlier ages than people in any other Western industrialized country; they marry more often and at any given time; more of them over the age of 14 are counted as married than their counterparts in other countries. Today 4 out of 5 divorced Americans eventually remarry; the average time between divorce and remarriage is 3 years. As noted, age for age, the marriage rate is higher among the divorced population than it is among the single population. In 1970, about three-fifths of all children of a divorced parent were living in husband-wife families in which one was a stepparent.

For a discussion of the American habit of changing marital partners and its impact on children, see Davis, *op. cit.;* Paul Glick, "Some Recent Changes in American Families," *Current Population Reports,* Special Studies, Series P–23, No. 52, U.S. Department of Commerce, Bureau of the Census, Washington, D.C.: Government Printing Office, 1976; and Alexander Plateris, "100 Years of Marriage and Divorce Statistics, United States 1867–1967," Department of Vital and Health Statistics, Series 21, No. 24, National Center for Health Statistics, U.S. Department of Health, Education and Welfare, December, 1973.

7. Glick, *op. cit.,* p. 3.

8. *Ibid.,* p. 13.

9. Even when other adults are living with husband-wife families, they are more than likely to be found in the labor force. In 1975, of the 23 million families in which both husband and wife worked, 17.4 percent (almost a fifth) had a third worker in the family (*Monthly Labor Review,* May, 1976, U.S. Department of Labor, Bureau of Labor Statistics, p. 14, Table 3). That this trend will continue is evidenced by the numbers of young people aged 16–19 seeking work. But many are unable to find jobs. Unemployment rates for this group grew from 14 percent in 1973 to 20.5 percent in 1975. Of these 2 million young people, 89 percent were living at home or with a relative who was head of the household (*Monthly Labor Review,* January, 1976, U.S. Department of Labor, Bureau of Labor Statistics, p. 14, Table 3; p. 50, Table 1; p. 54, Table 7).

10. Paul Bohannan, ed., *Divorce and After.* New York: Doubleday, 1971.

11. Burton L. White, *The First Three Years of Life,* Englewood Cliffs, N.J.: Prentice-Hall, 1975.

12. Jerome Kagan and R. E. Klein, "Cross-Cultural Perspectives on Human Development," *American Psychologist,* Vol. 28, 1973, pp. 947–961.

13. Orville G. Brim, Jr., *Education for Child Rearing,* New York: Russell Sage Foundation, 1959.

14. John P. Demos, "The American Family in Past Time," *Contemporary Marriage: Structure, Dynamics and Therapy,* Henry Grunebaum and Jacob Christ, eds. Boston: Little, Brown & Co., 1976, p. 434.

15. *Ibid.*

16. This is a rough and conservative estimate based on the U.S. Department of Agriculture's standard estimations of raising children from under 1 year of life to age 18 in 1971, reported in Ritchie H. Reed and Susan McIntosh, "Costs of Children," *Economic Aspects of Population Change,* Vol. 2, Elliott R. Morse and Ritchie H. Reed, eds., Commission on Population Growth and the American Future. Washington, D.C.: Government Printing Office, 1972.

Based on the U.S. Department of Agriculture's data derived from the 1960–61 Consumer Expenditure Survey, the costs were estimated for families with from 2 to 5 children who have disposable family incomes which fall between $10,500 and $12,500, depending upon region and type of residence. The cost for 1 child ranged from $29,470 for a farm family to $32,830 for an urban family. Suburban costs were slightly higher at $32,990. These latter 3 figures do not take into account the initial cost of childbirth, which was estimated to be between $853 and $1,500, including hospital and medical care, basic nursery supplies, and maternity clothes.

For a family with from 2 to 5 children who had disposable family incomes of $7,000 to $8,000 (which characterized about one-third of the families in 1971), costs of raising a child ranged from $20,000 to $21,630, not including the cost of childbirth.

Edith Taittonen, chief of the Budget Standard Service for the Community Council of Greater New York, reported that 2 decades ago, it would have cost a New York City worker's family of 4, on a moderate income, $27,578 to raise a child born in 1958 up to 18 years of age. (This is a slightly lower figure than that estimated by the USDA.) Her projections show, however, that for the same family, a child born in 1976 and reared to age 18 would now cost

230

a whopping $84,777. Excluded in this estimate are such costs as extraordinary medical or dental expenses, i.e., orthodontics; educational opportunities for a talented child; and music or art lessons (Research Note No. 22, Sept. 15, 1976, Community Council of Greater New York, New York City).

17. Demos, *op. cit.* See also testimony of Vincent P. Barabba, Director, Bureau of the Census, before the Senate Subcommittee on Children and Youth of the Committee on Labor and Public Welfare, the Ninety-third Congress, First Session, Sept. 24, 1973. Subject: "American Families, Trends and Pressures, 1973."

18. Between 1950 and 1974, the median annual income of families more than doubled when the wife was in the paid labor force and rose by only about four-fifths when she was not (figures adjusted for inflation) (*Monthly Labor Review,* May, 1976, U.S. Department of Labor, Bureau of Labor Statistics, p. 15).

19. Since 1950, the number of persons employed in the service sector has more than doubled, while the number working in the goods-producing sector rose by only about a fifth. By 1975, 82 percent of all women working in nonagricultural industries were employed in the service sector, where they held about 45 percent of all jobs. The proportion of wives who work even though their husbands are employed full time has increased from 36 out of 100 families in 1950 to 49 out of 100 in 1975. The contribution of their earnings to the family income, however, is proportionately the same as in 1920, 26 percent (*Monthly Labor Review,* May, 1976, U.S. Department of Labor, Bureau of Labor Statistics, pp. 13–15).

20. Theodore Lidz, *The Person: His Development Throughout the Life Cycle.* New York: Basic Books, 1968.

21. Alimony and support payments help very little, however. In a recent study of alimony and support payments for mothers (of children under 18) who were divorced or separated, Isabel Sawhill and her co-researchers found that, on the average, only 3 percent received enough alimony and support payments to bring them up to or above the official U.S. poverty line without their going to work. Sixty-one percent did not receive anything, 24 percent received less than half the amount of the official poverty figure, and 12 percent received something over half but below the full poverty amount. Hence, the financial effects of divorce on children are particularly hard on those women who cannot work—because they lack skills demanded in today's economy—or who should not work—because they prefer to continue housekeeping and child rearing in their homes. (Carol Adair Jones, Nancy M. Gordon, and Isabel V. Sawhill, "Child Support Payments in the United States," Working Paper 992–03, October 1, 1976. Washington, D.C.: The Urban Institute, p. 74, Table IV.)

Chapter 2

The Stacked Deck: Odds Against a Decent Life

1. "Characteristics of the Population Below Poverty Level: 1974," *Current Population Reports, Consumer Income,* Series P–60, No. 102, U.S. Department of Commerce, Bureau of the Census. Washington, D.C.: Government Printing Office, January, 1977.

2. Lee Rainwater, "Poverty, Living Standards and Family Well-Being," Subcommittee on Fiscal Policy of the Joint Economic Committee,

Congress of the United States, the Ninety-third Congress, First Session, Dec. 3, 1973, Paper No. 12, Part 2, *The Family, Poverty, and Welfare Programs: Household Patterns and Government Policies.* Washington, D.C.: Government Printing Office, 1973.

3. *Current Population Reports, op. cit.,* Table 45.

4. "Consumer Income: Money Income in 1974 of Families and Persons in the United States," *Consumer Population Services,* Series P–60, No. 101, Table 26, U.S. Department of Commerce, Bureau of the Census, 1976.

5. "Three Budgets for an Urban Family of Four Persons, 1969–70, Autumn, 1971, 1972, 1973, 1974," Urban Family Budgets and Geographical Comparative Index, Supplement to Bulletin 1570–5, Supplement to Bulletin 1570–6, U.S. Department of Labor, Bureau of Labor Statistics.

6. The figures in this table represent extrapolations of the budget shares of the two lowest Bureau of Labor Statistics budgets, using constant expenditure elasticities. (The higher of these two budgets is the one shown in Table 1.)

7. John Gliedman and William Roth, *Handicapped Children in America, a* report to the Carnegie Council on Children. New York: Academic Press, 1978.

8. "Consumer Income: Money Income in 1974 of Families and Persons in the United States," *Consumer Population Services,* Series P–60, No. 101, U.S. Department of Commerce, Bureau of the Census. Washington, D.C.: Government Printing Office, January, 1976.

9. Infant Mortality Section, Department of Vital and Health Statistics, National Center for Health Statistics, U.S. Department of Health, Education and Welfare, 1975.

10. "Profile of American Health, 1973: Based on Data Collected in the Health Interview Survey," Public Health Reports, Nov.–Dec., 1974, pp. 504–523.

11. *Minority Health Chart Book,*

American Association of Public Health, U.S. Department of Health, Education and Welfare, Contract No. HRA 106–74, October, 1975, p. 63.

12. Phyllis Weisbard, "The Delivery of Child Welfare Services to Minority Group Children," staff report, Carnegie Council on Children, May, 1975.

13. William H. Sewell and R. M. Hauser, "Causes and Consequences of Higher Education: Models of the Status of Attainment Process," in *Schooling and Achievement in American Society,* William H. Sewell, R. M. Hauser, and David L. Featherman, eds. New York: Academic Press, 1976.

14. *Current Population Reports,* Series P–60, No. 102, Table 4, U.S. Department of Commerce, Bureau of the Census. Washington, D.C.: Government Printing Office, 1976.

Note that the advantage of whites over blacks in family income, which decreased during the 1960's, has been increasing since 1969 (*Current Population Reports,* Series P–60, No. 97, p. 5, 1975.) The median income for black families was 61 percent of the white family median income in 1969 but decreased to 58 percent in 1974 (*Current Population Reports,* Series P–60, No. 101, Table 13, 1976).

15. Infant Mortality Section, *op. cit.*

16. *Minority Health Chart Book, op. cit.*

17. Weisbard, *op. cit.*

18. Nicholas Hobbs, ed., *Issues in the Classification of Children: A Sourcebook on Categories, Labels, and Their Consequences,* Vol. II, San Francisco: Jossey-Bass, 1975.

19. *Statistical Abstract,* U.S. Department of Labor, Bureau of Labor Statistics, 1974.

20. *Manpower Report to the President,* U.S. Department of Labor. Washington, D.C.: Government Printing Office, 1973.

21. "Consumer Income," *op. cit.,* Table 58.

22. Carol B. Stack and Herbert Semmel, "The Concept of Family in the Poor Black Community," *Studies in Public Welfare,* Paper 12, Part 2,

"The Family, Poverty and Welfare Programs: Household Patterns and Government Policies," Joint Economic Committee, the Ninety-third Congress, First Session, Dec. 3, 1973.

23. Henry Goddard (1913) quoted in Leon Kamin, *Science and Politics of IQ.* New York: Halsted Press, 1974.

24. Sydney E. Ahlstrom, *A Religious History of the American People.* New Haven: Yale University Press, 1972, p. 789.

25. Oscar Lewis, *Five Families: Mexican Case Studies in the Culture of Poverty.* New York: Basic Books, 1959.

26. Daniel Patrick Moynihan, "The Negro Family, The Case for National Action," U.S. Department of Labor, Office of Policy Planning and Research, March, 1965.

27. Horace Mann, *Twelfth Annual Report to the Massachusetts Board of Education,* Boston, Mass., 1848.

28. Figures as of 1974, *Current Population Reports,* Series P–60, No. 99, U.S. Department of Commerce, Bureau of the Census. Washington, D.C.: Government Printing Office, July, 1975.

29. Joseph A. Pechman and Benjamin A. Okner, *Who Bears the Tax Burden?* Washington, D.C.: Brookings Institution, 1974.

30. For a review and brief summary of major studies, see Peter Henle, "Exploring the Distribution of Earned Income," *Monthly Labor Review,* December, 1972, U.S. Department of Labor, Bureau of Labor Statistics, pp. 16–27; James D. Smith and Stephen D. Franklin, "The Concentration of Personal Wealth, 1922–1969," *The American Economic Review,* Vol. 64, No. 2, May, 1974.

31. Lee Soltow, *Men and Wealth in the United States 1850–1870,* New Haven: Yale University Press, 1975;

Stanley Lebergott, *Wealth and Want,* Princeton, N.J.: Princeton University Press, 1975; and Robert Gallman, "Trends in the Size Distribution of Wealth in the Nineteenth Century: Some Speculations," in Lee Soltow, ed., *Six Papers on the Size Distribution of Wealth and Income,* National Bureau of Economic Research, Studies in Income and Wealth, Vol. 33, New York: Columbia University Press, 1969.

32. William Miller, "The Business Elite in Business Bureaucracies: Careers of Top Executives in the Early Twentieth Century," and Frances W. Gregory and Irene D. Neu, "The American Industrial Elite in the 1870's: Their Social Origins," in William Miller, ed., *Men in Business.* Cambridge, Mass.: Harvard University Press, 1952.

33. Samuel Bowles and Herbert Gintis, *Schooling in Capitalist America: Educational Reform and the Contradiction of Economic Life.* New York: Basic Books, 1976.

34. *Manpower Report to the President, op. cit.*

35. Pechman and Okner, *op. cit.;* and Richard A. Musgrave and Peggy B. Musgrave, *Public Finance in Theory and Practice,* 2nd ed. New York: McGraw-Hill Book Co., 1976.

36. James Coleman, *Equality of Educational Opportunity,* U.S. Office of Education, Washington, D.C.: Government Printing Office, 1965; and Christopher Jencks et al., *Inequality: A Reassessment of the Effect of Family and Schooling in America,* New York: Basic Books, 1972.

37. John U. Ogbu, *Minority Education and Caste: The American System in Cross-Cultural Perspective.* New York: Academic Press, 1978.

Chapter 3

The Technological Cradle

1. The Jamaica Bay (New York) Environmental Study Group report to the National Academy of Sciences, in

James D. Miller, *Effects of Noise on People,* National Technical Information Service report.

Washington, D.C.: U.S. Department of Commerce, December 31, 1971, p. 56.

2. These figures always fluctuate somewhat according to factors in living styles. But the change has been sharp since 1900 when, according to Alice Gerard, nearly all babies were breast-fed. In 1921, 96 percent of American babies were fully breast-fed; in the next 15 years, the percentage dropped to 38 (Alice Gerard, *Please Breast-Feed Your Baby,* New York: New American Library, 1971). By 1972, all but 5 percent of new mothers chose to bottle-feed their babies for the first six months of life. After sinking to this low, breast-feeding has since begun to regain in popularity (Consumers Union, "Is Breast-Feeding Best for Babies?" *Consumer Reports,* March 1971, p. 152).

3. Urie Bronfenbrenner, *Two Worlds of Childhood: U.S. and U.S.S.R.* New York: Pocket Books, 1973, p. 106.

4. Robert Choate, "The Selling of the Child," testimony before the Consumer Subcommittee of the U.S. Senate Committee on Commerce, Ninety-third Congress, Second Session, February, 1973.

5. Evelyn Kaye, *The Family Guide to Children's Television.* New York: Pantheon Books, 1974, p. 37.

6. United Methodist Women's Television Monitoring Project, *Sex Role Stereotyping in Prime Time Television,* New York: United Methodist Church, 1976, p. 8; Aimee Dorr Leifer, Neal J. Gordon, and Sherryl Browne Graves, "Children's Television: More Than Mere Entertainment," *Harvard Educational Review,* May, 1974, p. 221.

7. The final installment of *Roots,* telecast on January 30, 1977, received a 51.1 rating by the A. C. Nielsen research company, making it the highest-rated program in television history. The show reached an estimated 36,000,000 to 38,000,000 homes, 2.4 million more than "Gone With the Wind," which drew record audiences the previous fall. A. C. Nielsen Co: *Nielsen National*

Television Ratings, February 1, 1977.

8. Leifer, et al., *op. cit.,* p. 214.

9. Kaye, *op. cit.,* p. 37.

10. Choate, *op. cit.*

11. *Ibid.*

12. Charles Kuralt, CBS news commentator, quoted in Ross Hume Hall, *Food for Nought: The Decline in Nutrition.* New York: Harper and Row, 1974, p. 183.

13. Mark Gerzon, *A Childhood for Every Child: The Politics of Childhood.* New York: E. P. Dutton & Co., 1973, p. 114.

14. Ross Hume Hall, *Food for Nought, op. cit.*

15. Robert Choate, "Dry Cereals: Hearings," testimony before the Consumer Subcommittee of U.S. Senate Committee on Commerce, Ninety-first Congress, Second Session, July 23, Aug. 4 and 5, 1970, Serial No. 91–72.

16. *Ibid.*

17. Bronfenbrenner quoted without reference in *Reader's Digest,* March, 1972.

18. A. C. Nielsen Co., *op. cit.,* March 4–31, 1976.

19. *Ibid.,* Sept. 1975–April 1976.

20. David Potter, "Television: The Broad View, The Historical Perspective," in Stanley R. Donner, ed., *The Meaning of Commercial Television.* Austin: The University of Texas Press, 1967.

21. Harry J. Skornia, *Television and Society.* New York: McGraw-Hill Book Co. 1965, p. 73.

22. Erik Barnouw, *History of Broadcasting in the United States,* Vol. 1. New York: Oxford University Press, 1966.

23. Beatrice Trum Hunter, *Food Additives and Federal Policy: The Mirage of Safety.* New York: Charles Scribner's Sons, 1975, p. 5.

24. *Ibid.*

25. R. L. Hall, "Food Additives," *Nutrition Today,* 8(4), 1975, pp. 20–28.

26. James Turner, *The Chemical Feast.* New York: Grossman Publishers, 1970.

27. Figures from two surveys of household food consumption conducted by the U.S. Department of

Agriculture, one in the spring of 1955 and the other in the spring of 1965. In judging the quality of diets, the USDA relied upon the Recommended Dietary Allowances (RDA) for each of 22 different sex and age groups. These guidelines were established by the Food Nutrition Board of the National Academy of Sciences, National Research Council (USDA Yearbook, *Food for Us All,* Washington, D.C.: Government Printing Office, 1969). Between 1945 and 1972 the GNP rose by $437 billion—yet per capita consumption of milk products dropped by 10 percent. (Stanley Lebergott, *The American Economy: Income, Wealth, and Want,* Princeton, N.J.: Princeton University Press, 1976, p. 81. (See also USDA report, "Dietary Levels of Households in the United States, Spring, 1965," No. 6, Table 13, 1965.)

28. The USDA 1965 survey showed that 14 percent of American families with incomes below $3,000, and 10 percent of American families with incomes above $10,000 failed to get the RDA. USDA report No. 6, *op. cit.,* Table 7.

29. *Journal in Nutrition Education,* Vol. 1, No. 2 suppl., Fall 1969, p. 54.

30. See the American Heart Association pamphlet "Diet and Heart Disease," 1968; T. Leary, *Bulletin of the New York Academy of Medicine,* Vol. 17, Dec. 1941, p. 387; J. P. Strong and H. C. McGill, Jr., *Experimental Molecular Pathology Supplement,* No. 1, August 1963, p. 15; L. K. Dahl et al., *Experimental Hypertension and Death from Chronic Consumption of Processed Baby Foods,* Upton, N.Y.: Brookhaven National Laboratory, Medical Research Center, 1968; and Samuel J. Fomon, *Infant Nutrition,* Philadelphia: Saunders, 1967.

31. For a detailed discussion of these issues among government leaders, private food industries, and scientists, see *Hearings before the Select Committee on Nutrition and Human Needs,* U.S. Senate, Ninetieth and Ninety-first Congresses, Part 13A, "Nutrition and Private Industry," July 15, 17, 18, 1969; Part 13B, "Nutrition and Private Industry, Federal Regulation—New and Fortified Foods —Overseas Experience," July 22–24, 1969; and Part 13C, "Nutrition and Private Industry," July 28, 30, 1969. Washington, D.C.: Government Printing Office, 1969.

32. Weston A. Price, *Nutrition and Physical Degeneration,* Redlands, Calif.: Weston A. Price, 1945; Dr. Harris J. Keene, Chief of Epidemiology Division, Naval Dental Research Institute, Great Lakes, Ill., Address to the American Association for the Advancement of Science, Philadelphia, Dec. 28, 1971. See especially testimony of Samuel J. Fomon, M.D., Professor of Pediatrics, University of Iowa, *Hearings before the Select Committee on Nutrition and Human Needs,* Part 13A, *op. cit.,* pp. 4048–53.

33. "Water Quality Impacts of the Uranium Mining and Milling Activities in the Grants Mineral Belt, New Mexico," Environmental Protection Agency. Washington, D.C.: Government Printing Office, July, 1975.

34. See Favus, et al., *New England Journal of Medicine,* Vol. 294, May 6, 1976, p. 1910.

35. Quoted in Leo Marx, *The Machine and the Garden: Technology and the Pastoral Ideal in America.* New York: Oxford University Press, 1964, pp. 182–3.

36. *Ibid.*

Chapter 4

Premises for Change

1. Alison Clarke-Stewart, *Child Care in the Family: A Review of Research and Some Propositions for Policy,* a report to the Carnegie Council on Children, New York: Academic Press, 1977.

Chapter 5

Jobs and a Decent Income

1. *Employment and Earnings,* May, 1976, Vol. 22, No. 11, U.S. Department of Labor, Bureau of Labor Statistics, pp. 99–100.

2. Richard H. de Lone, "Work, Employment, and Equality: Full Employment and Family Welfare," Carnegie Council on Children working paper, April, 1975.

3. See James Tobin and Leonard Ross, "Living with Inflation," *New York Review of Books,* May 6, 1971; also James Tobin, "Unemployment and Inflation: The Cruel Dilemma," in A. Phillips, ed., *Price Issues in Theory, Practice, and Policy.* Philadelphia: University of Pennsylvania Press, 1967, pp. 101–107.

4. Richard A. Musgrave and Peggy B. Musgrave, *Public Finance in Theory and Practice,* 2nd ed. New York: McGraw-Hill Book Co., 1976, p. 672.

5. *Manpower Report to the President,* U.S. Department of Labor. Washington, D.C.: Government Printing Office, 1973.

6. *Employment and Earnings,* Vol. 24, No. 1 (January, 1977), Table A–4, U.S. Department of Labor, Bureau of Labor Statistics.

7. *Handbook of Labor Statistics 1975–Reference Edition,* Bulletin 1865, Table 20, U.S. Department of Labor, Bureau of Labor Statistics; also *U.S. Working Women: A Chartbook* (1975), Bulletin 1880, Table 14, U.S. Department of Labor, Bureau of Labor Statistics.

8. Rhona L. Pavis, "Towards the Equalization of Income and Occupational Distribution of Blacks and Whites and Males and Females," Working Paper 113–27 of the Urban Institute, Washington, D.C., November 28, 1969.

9. "Money Income of Families and Persons in the United States," *Current Population Reports, 1957 to 1975,* U.S. Department of Commerce, Bureau of the Census; also *Handbook of Labor Statistics 1975,*U.S. Department of Labor, Bureau of Labor Statistics.

10. *Current Population Reports,* Series P–60, No. 101, U.S. Department of Commerce, Bureau of the Census.

11. John U. Ogbu, *Minority Education and Caste: The American System in Cross-Cultural Perspective.* New York: Academic Press, 1978; and Richard H. de Lone for the Carnegie Council on Children, *Small Futures: Inequality, Children and the Failure of Liberal Reform,* New York: Harcourt Brace Jovanovich, 1978.

12. See Equal Employment Opportunity Commission Rules and Regulations, Subpart G, Section 1601, pp. 50–58.

13. For a discussion of the history of executive orders, see Michael I. Sovern, *Legal Restraints on Racial Discrimination in Employment,* New York: Twentieth Century Fund, 1966.

14. See "Income Security for Americans," U.S. Congress Joint Economic Committee, Dec. 5, 1974.

15. See Joseph A. Pechman and Benjamin A. Okner, *Who Bears the Tax Burden?* Washington, D.C.: Brookings Institution, 1974.

16. The prototype sketched here in its basic features resembles those advocated by Lee Rainwater, James Tobin, and Harold Watts, among others. Two other models have been proposed by Martha Griffiths' Subcommittee on Fiscal Policy of the Joint Economic Committee (which advocated a small tax credit combined with nationalized Aid to Families with Dependent Children that also reached the working poor) and the Income Supplement Program put forward by HEW in 1974 in its Technical Analysis Paper No. 11.

17. Leonard Goodwin, *Do the Poor Want to Work?* Washington, D.C.: Brookings Institution, 1972.

18. See John Gliedman and William

Roth, *Handicapped Children in America.* New York: Academic Press, 1978.

19. See, for example, Richard Goods, *The Individual Income Tax,* revised ed. Washington, D.C.: Brookings Institution, 1976.

20. James D. Smith, "The Concentration of Personal Wealth in America, 1969," in James D. Smith,

ed., *The Personal Distribution of Income and Wealth.* New York: Columbia University Press, 1975.

21. Lee Soltow, *Men and Wealth in the United States 1850–1870,* New Haven: Yale University Press, 1975; and Stanley Lebergott, *The American Economy: Income, Wealth and Want,* Princeton, N.J.: Princeton University Press, 1975.

Chapter 6

Family Work and Wage Work

1. See Stanley Lebergott, *The American Economy: Income, Wealth and Want.* Princeton, N.J.: Princeton University Press, 1975.

2. Harold Wilensky, "Work as a Social Problem," in Howard S. Becker, ed., *Social Problems: A Modern Approach.* New York: Wiley Press, 1966.

3. Alvar O. Elbing, Herman Gadon, and John R. M. Gordon, "Flexible Working Hours: It's About Time," *Harvard Business Review,* January–February, 1974.

4. Susan Bucknell, "Flexible Work Practices," Carnegie Council on Children working paper, April, 1975.

5. Elbing, et al., *op. cit.*

6. *Ibid.;* K. E. Wheeler, "The Four Day Week," New York: American

Management Association, 1972.

7. Bucknell, *op. cit.*

8. S. Darrow and S. Stokes, "Part-Time Professional-Administrative Employment at the University of Michigan," study for the University of Michigan Hospital, Ann Arbor, Mich.: January, 1973.

9. Mark Goldsmith, "A Radical Work Plan to Free Both Husband and Wife," *San Francisco Chronicle,* February 6, 1976.

10. Evelyne Sullerot, *Women, Society and Change.* New York: McGraw-Hill Book Co., 1971.

11. *Work in America,* report of a Special Task Force to the Secretary of Health, Education and Welfare. Cambridge, Mass.: MIT Press, 1973.

Chapter 7

Services Families Need

1. Sheldon H. White, et al., *Federal Programs for Young Children.* Washington, D.C.: Department of Health, Education and Welfare, 1972, Appendix IIIC, pp. 2–3.

2. *Ibid.*

3. Program categorization and budget estimates were derived from unpublished materials developed at the Congressional Budget Office for a "Children's Budget" for fiscal year 1976. All calculations were done by the Carnegie Council on Children.

4. These data are from federal

reports on the progress of states' implementation of Early and Periodic Screening, Diagnosis and Treatment (EPSDT) and from a year-long field study of how the program is working by the Children's Defense Fund, reported in *EPSDT: Does It Spell Health Care for Poor Children?* Washington, D.C.: Children's Defense Fund, 1977.

5. 20 U.S.C.A. §1262 (b) (3) and U.S. Department of Commerce, Bureau of the Census, *Statistical Abstract of the United States, 1975,*

96th edition. Washington, D.C.: Government Printing Office, Table 62, p. 45. There is also some question as to whether the 10 percent set aside is actually reaching handicapped and retarded children who are in public schools because the Office of Education has not monitored or reported the results publicly.

6. From research conducted for *Children Out of School in America.* Cambridge, Mass.: Children's Defense Fund, 1974.

7. Nathan Glazer, "Paradoxes of Health Care," *The Public Interest,* Winter, 1971, pp. 62–77.

8. *Public Assistance Statistics, June, 1976,* SRS, National Center for Social Statistics, Nov. 1976, p. 1.

9. Paul E. Mott, "Foster Care and Adoptions: Some Key Policy Issues," prepared for the Subcommittee on Children and Youth of the United States Senate Committee on Labor and Public Welfare. Washington, D.C.: Government Printing Office, 1975, pp. 1–2.

10. Unpublished preliminary figures for Fiscal Year 1976, Child Welfare Expenditures under Title IV–B. Washington, D.C.: Social and Rehabilitation Service, October, 1976.

11. *Public Assistance Statistics, April 1976.* Washington, D.C.: National Center for Social Statistics, August, 1976, Table 12, p. 22.

12. Statistics on incidence of lead-paint poisoning come from Frederick Green, M.D., "Getting Ready for National Health Insurance: Shortchanging Children," statement before the Subcommittee on Oversight and Investigations of the United States House Committee on Interstate and Foreign Commerce, October 7, 1975; see also *Catalog of Domestic Assistance,* program number 13.266, 42 U.S.C. 480.

13. *Monthly Vital Statistics Report, Summary Report, Final Natality Statistics,* National Center for Health Statistics, U.S. Department of Health, Education and Welfare, Washington, D.C.: Government Printing Office, 1973, p. 8; and *America's Children, 1976, A Bicentennial Assessment.* Washington, D.C.: National Council of Organizations for Children and Youth, 1976, p. 34.

14. Compare the fiscal year 1977 appropriation of $56.5 million with an authorization for fiscal year 1977 of $266 million (Title IV–B, § 420, Social Security Act). This trend has continued since the budget authorization for Title IV, Part B was increased in 1969; see *More Can Be Learned and Done About the Well-Being of Children.* Washington, D.C.: U.S. General Accounting Office, April 9, 1976, pp. 4–5.

15. In Title I funding, the proportion of the authorized funding for local school programs actually appropriated is called the "rateable reduction." That figure was projected to be 39 percent for fiscal 1977 by HEW's Office of Education. It has never exceeded 46 percent since 1970 census data was first used as the basis of distribution (in 1973). Figures were supplied by Caroline Horner of the Title I staff of the Office of Education. A National Institute of Education survey in 1976 indicated that school districts actually spread the limited funds more thinly over the eligible population, so that 50 to 70 percent of eligible children receive some diluted Title I services.

16. Public Law 94–142 established a very complex formula for determining the amount of federal aid provided to the local schools of each state for the education of handicapped children. For fiscal year 1978, the first year of full operation of this law, the following rough calculations will apply: the law authorizes 5 percent of the national average per-pupil expenditure (in the preceding year, fiscal 1977) per handicapped child *served* by the schools in the previous year. The average per-pupil expenditure in fiscal 1977 will be about $1,400, so the authorization will be 70 federal dollars per child previously served. Half of this amount is reserved for the continuation of older state-selected research and demonstration projects, so only about $35 per child served in 1977 will be available to local schools in fiscal 1978.

238

The most recent estimates of the percent of all handicapped children served by public school programs (Nicholas Hobbs, *The Futures of Children: Categories, Labels, and Their Consequences*, report of the Project on Classification of Exceptional Children. San Francisco: Jossey-Bass, 1975) are that only 51 percent of the retarded, 40 percent of the emotionally disturbed, 24 percent of the learning disabled, and 20 percent of the hearing impaired are reached. Assuming that at least half of all handicapped children were served in 1977 (which is very optimistic in the light of the OCD figures just given), in 1978 the $35 of federal aid will have to be spread over two children—one served the previous year, and one not yet reached. About 50 percent of the funds must be spent to seek out the least served, according to a recent Bureau of the Education of the Handicapped ruling, in any case.

Thus there will be about $17.50 per handicapped child available in the first year of this program. The P.L. 94–142 formula will gradually increase this amount over the following four years to a rate equal to 30 percent of the average per pupil expenditure (if all handicapped children are finally reached), but the very low funding in the first year of the program will have already set a precedent for inadequate levels of service.

17. *Children Out of School in America, op. cit.,* Appendix J, p. 226.
18. See correspondence of Rims Barber, David Rice, and Charles E. Jenkins, Directors, Mississippi Head Start, to Senator Jacob Javits cited in *Children Out of School in America, op. cit.,* p. 108.
19. The importance of public standards applying to private service programs cannot be underestimated. In 1972, during a five-day period, of 2,084 requests to social welfare agencies for services from families with children under eighteen, 1,663 (79.8 percent) were directed to private voluntary agencies. (Barbara L. Haring, *1972 Census of Requests*

for Child Welfare Services. New York: Child Welfare League of America, Inc., December, 1972, p. 8.)
20. The exception is the Current Population Reports of the Bureau of the Census for which the family-income reporting surveys (series P–60) do make a strong effort to identify sources (including federal sources) of income received by low-income families. It is no coincidence that many family-oriented policy analyses and proposals draw upon the Current Population Reports for their cost and incidence estimates.
21. See, for example, National Center for Health Statistics, *Vital and Health Statistics,* "Visual Acuity of Children," Series 11, No. 101, Washington, D.C.: Government Printing Office, February, 1970.
22. See, for example, Sidney Abraham, *Preliminary Findings of the First Health and Nutrition Examination Survey, United States, 1971–72: Anthropometric and Clinical Findings,* Washington, D.C.: Government Printing Office, April 1975.
23. *BLS Handbook of Methods for Survey and Studies,* Bulletin 1711, Bureau of Labor Statistics, Washington, D.C.: Government Printing Office, 1971, Chapter 1. Also see any issue of the Bureau's monthly *Employment and Earnings.*
24. See, for example, Wayne A. Clark, *Discrimination in General Revenue Sharing in the South,* Atlanta, Ga.: Southern Governmental Monitoring Project, Southern Regional Council, Dec., 1975, pp. 5–6.
25. Morton H. Sklar, "The Impact of Revenue Sharing on Minorities and the Poor," in *Revenue Sharing: A Selection of Recent Research,* Subcommittee on Intergovernmental Relations of the U.S. Senate Committee on Government Operations. Washington, D.C.: Government Printing Office, March 1975.
26. Richard P. Nathan, et al., *Monitoring Revenue Sharing.* Washington, D.C.: Brookings Institution, 1975, pp. 211–213.

Chapter 8

Children's Health

1. *Health, United States 1975,* Publ. no. HRA 76–1232, Washington, D.C.: U.S. Department of Health, Education and Welfare, 1976, pp. 223, 224, and 349. Adult rates are for 1972, infant rates for 1973.
2. *Vital Statistics of the United States, 1973,* Vol. I, Natality (in press), National Center for Health Statistics, U.S. Department of Health, Education and Welfare; and Tables CD II.11 and CD II.14 in *Health, United States 1975, op. cit.,* p. 365.
3. Myron E. Wegman, "Annual Summary of Vital Statistics—1975," *Pediatrics* 58: 793–799 (1976), p. 797.
4. David M. Kessner, *Infant Death: An Analysis by Maternal Risk and Health Care.* Washington, D.C.: Institute of Medicine, National Academy of Sciences, 1973; and *Doctors and Dollars Are Not Enough: How to Improve Health Services for Children and Their Families,* Washington, D.C.: Children's Defense Fund, 1976, pp. 11–13.
5. *Health, United States 1975, op. cit.,* Table CD II.33, p. 409.
6. M. S. Mueller and R. M. Gibson, "Age Differences in Health Care Spending, Fiscal Year 1975," *Social Security Bulletin,* Vol. 39, No. 6, June, 1976, p. 23.
7. *Trends Affecting the U.S. Health Care System,* prepared by the Cambridge Research Institute, U.S. Department of Health, Education and Welfare Publ. no. HRA 76–14503, January, 1976.
8. Victor Fuchs, *Who Shall Live? Health, Economics and Social Choice,* New York: Basic Books, 1975; Ivan Illich, *Medical Nemesis: The Expropriation of Health,* New York: Pantheon Books, 1976; Spencer Klaw, *The Great American Medicine Show,* New York: Viking Press, 1975; and Rick J. Carlson, *The End of Medicine,* New York: John Wiley & Sons, 1975.
9. Fuchs, *op. cit.,* p. 37.

10. Richard H. de Lone for the Carnegie Council on Children, *Small Futures: Inequality, Children and the Failure of Liberal Reform.* New York: Harcourt Brace Jovanovich, 1978.
11. *Health, United States 1975, op. cit.,* Table A.21, p. 47.
12. *Ibid.,* Tables A.21 and A.25, pp. 47, 54–55.
13. *Ibid.,* Table A.24, p. 53.
14. Karen Davis, "A Decade of Policy Development in Providing Health Care for Low-Income Families." Washington, D.C.: Brookings Institution, July, 1975.
15. A. M. Rivlin and P. M. Timpane, eds., *Planned Variation in Education.* Washington, D.C.: Brookings Institution, 1975, pp. 25, 94.
16. Davis, *op. cit.* EPSDT was probably too ambitious to succeed. A more realistic goal would have been to offer comprehensive services from conception to 5 years of age, so that total preventive care could have been provided in the crucial years of development.
17. Spyros Andreopoulos, ed., *National Health Insurance: Can We Learn From Canada?* New York: John Wiley & Sons, 1975.
18. *Ibid.,* pp. 241–3.
19. *New York Times Magazine,* Sunday, January 9, 1977; also see *National Health Insurance Proposals: Provisions of Bills Introduced in the 94th Congress as of February 1976,* U.S. Department of Health, Education and Welfare, Office of Research and Statistics, Publ. no. (SSA) 76–11920, 1976. The most directly focused are the Scheuer-Javits Bills (H.R. 12937 and H.R. 14309) and the Hart Bill (S 3897) introduced in 1976.
20. Children's Defense Fund, *op. cit.,* p. 17.
21. Mueller and Gibson, *op. cit.,* p. 20.
22. R. J. Haggerty, K. Roghmann, and I. B. Pless, *Child Health and the Community.* New York: John Wiley

& Sons, 1975, p. 176.

23. Mueller and Gibson, *op. cit.,* p. 20.

24. Lisbeth Bamberger Schorr, "Issues in National Health Insurance from a Child Advocacy Perspective," open letter to Joseph A. Califano, Secretary, U.S. Department of Health, Education and Welfare, February 24, 1977, p. 4.

25. Karen Davis and Ray Marshall, "Rural Health Care in the South," draft report, Task Force on Southern Rural Development, 52 Fairlie Street, N.W., Atlanta, Ga. 30303, October, 1975.

26. See Children's Defense Fund, *op. cit.,* for extensive documentation of health-care programs throughout the country that are already using parts of this humane approach to child health care.

27. C. E. Lewis, R. Fein, and D. Mechanic, *A Right to Health.* New York: John Wiley & Sons, 1976, p. 13.

28. See C. Arden Miller, "Societal Change and Public Health: A Rediscovery," *American Journal of Public Health,* 66:54–60, 1976; Davis, *op. cit.*

29. C. Altenstetter, J. W. Bjorkman, A. Fultz, and G. A. Silver, *Politics and Social Policy: Failures in Child Health Services.* New Haven: Yale Health Policy Project, August, 1976.

30. *A Proposal for New Federal Leadership in Maternal and Child Health Care in the United States,* draft, November 1, 1976, U.S. Department of Health, Education and Welfare, Office of the Assistant Secretary for Health, Office of Child Health Affairs.

31. The recent Project on Classification of Exceptional Children, sponsored by HEW, outlined a cogent series of recommendations regarding safeguards in the use of records, which we endorse. (Nicholas Hobbs, *The Futures of Children: Categories, Labels, and Their Consequences,* report of the Project on Classification of Exceptional Children. San Francisco: Jossey-Bass, Inc., 1975.) The project recommends a national set of comprehensive guidelines for the "maintenance, protection, and disposal of records on children," with each institution or agency that keeps such records (this would include Health Service Agencies) to have a Records Policy Board with professional, legal, and parent representatives to carry out and monitor these guidelines (p. 243). The group further suggests:

1) The existence of personal record-keeping systems may not be kept secret and must be made a matter of public knowledge. Parents or guardians of exceptional children should be notified periodically of information collected and kept about their children, why the information is kept and how it will be used, how long it will be retained, and what persons or agencies will have access to it.

2) Parents or guardians of exceptional children should be given access on reasonable terms to records maintained about their children, and they should be afforded reasonable opportunities to contest the accuracy or completeness of the records. Records should be withheld from parents or guardians only under the authorization of the Records Policy Board.

3) Information about a child obtained for one purpose should not be used or made available for other purposes without the consent of the child's parents or guardians or, when appropriate, by the child himself.

4) Records regarding exceptional children should be disseminated outside the agency or office that maintains the record only with prior consent of the parents or guardians of the child, or, when appropriate, by the child himself. Exceptions should be made only if convincing evidence is presented of benefit to the child, and only if consistent with the policies of the relevant Records Policy Board.

5) Computer-based registries of

children should provide protection against inappropriate or unauthorized linking of information with the names of individual children in ways that would violate confidentiality. Normally, information about a specific child should be made available only to the agency supplying the information in the first instance, or to a new agency upon formal authorization by the child's parents or, when appropriate, by the child himself.

6) Record systems should be designed to permit their routine use in research and epidemiological studies without the violation of confidentiality.

7) Guidelines and procedures should be developed to render records inactive and unavailable ("expunging the record") with respect to an individual child, when they are no longer of service to him, while preserving the records for research and epidemiological studies.

8) Where appropriate to their age and circumstances, children should be afforded some or all of the rights described above, independently of their parents or guardians (pp. 244–245).

32. H. Jack Geiger, "The Illusion of Change," *Social Policy,* Vol. 6, No. 3, Nov.–Dec., 1975, pp. 30–35; and R. R. Alford, *Health Care Politics: Ideological and Interest Group Barriers to Reform,* Chicago: Chicago University Press, 1975.

33. For a fuller representation of the argument in favor of this position, see Budd N. Shenkin and David C. Warner, "Giving the Patient His Medical Record: A Proposal to Improve the System," *New England Journal of Medicine,* Vol. 289, 1973, pp. 688–692; Children's Defense Fund, *op. cit.,* provides a list for groups interested in health record keeping issues.

34. M. A. Lewis, "Child Initiated Care," *American Journal of Nursing,* April, 1974, pp. 652–54.

Chapter 9

Protection of Children Under the Law

1. Twenty-three reports are in preparation by the Juvenile Justice Standards Project, Cambridge, Mass.: Ballinger Publishers, in press. See especially the 8 reports by Committee 1 of JJSP.

2. Figures cited in Robert H. Mnookin, "Foster Care—In Whose Best Interest?" *Harvard Educational Review,* Vol. 43, 1973, pp. 599, 606.

3. Young, in Mnookin, *op. cit.,* p. 624.

4. Foster-care figures in Mnookin, *op. cit.,* pp. 610–613.

5. See Diane Divoky, "Child Abuse— Mandate for Teacher Intervention," *Learning,* April, 1976, p. 14:

What began as an intensive but very limited movement in the early '60s to save physically battered and ravaged children—usually preschoolers—from death or permanent physical damage is suddenly a national social welfare system, complete with data banks, a whole new army of social workers, and enormous legal authority, capable of subtly and not so subtly directing parents and guardians as to how they will raise and treat their children.

6. Joint Commission on the Mental Health of Children, *Crisis in Child Mental Health: Challenges for the 1970's,* New York: Harper and Row, 1970.

7. President's Committee on Mental Retardation, Fred Cohen, "Advocacy," in *The Mentally Retarded Citizen and the Law,* New York: Free Press, 1976.

8. National Association for Retarded Citizens, *Residental Services,* Position Statement No. 9, 1968, National

Association for Retarded Citizens, 2709 Avenue E East, Arlington, Texas 76011.

9. "The Detention and Jailing of Juveniles," Hearings before the Subcommittee to Investigate Juvenile Delinquency of the Senate Committee on Judiciary, Ninety-third Congress, First Session, March 8, 1973.

10. See data collected by the Advisory Committee on Child Development, Assembly of Behavioral and Social Sciences, the National Research Council of the National Academy of Sciences report, *Toward a National Policy for Children and Families,* Washington, D.C., 1976.

11. A comprehensive review of medical laws pertaining to children is contained in Harriet F. Pilpel, "Minors' Right to Medical Care," *Albany Law Review,* Vol. 36, 1972, pp. 462, 467.

12. *Children Out of School in America,* Cambridge, Mass.: Children's Defense Fund, October, 1974.

13. Ad Hoc Committee on the Effect of Trace Anesthetics on the Health of Operating Room Personnel, American Society of Anesthesiologists, "Occupational Disease Among Operating Room Personnel," *Anesthesiology,* Vol. 41, October 1974.

14. I. Landcranjan, "Genital System —Men," *Occupational Safety and Health Encyclopedia,* Vol. 1,

Geneva: International Labor Organization, 1971.

15. M. Wasserman, "Oestrogens," *Occupational Safety and Health Encyclopedia,* Vol. 2, Geneva: International Labor Organization, 1971.

16. Andrea Hricko, "Two-Fifths of the Nation's Workforce," *Journal of Current Social Issues,* Spring 1975.

17. B. McMahon, "Prenatal X-ray Exposure and Childhood Cancer," *Journal of the National Cancer Institute,* Vol. 28, 1962.

18. Landcranjan, *op. cit.*

19. G. Schwanitz, G. Lehnert, and E. Gebhart, "Chromosomal Injury Due to Occupational Lead Poisoning," *German Medical Monthly,* Vol. 15, 1970.

20. *Lead: Airborne Lead in Perspective,* Washington, D.C.: National Academy of Sciences, 1972.

21. I. Landcranjan, et al., "Reproductive Ability of Workmen Occupationally Exposed to Lead," *Archives of Environmental Health,* Vol. 30, August 1975.

22. See, for example, a recent lawsuit against Baker/Beech-Nut Corporation for sending personalized letters to 760,000 mothers warning of an esoteric acid and rare disease (methemoglo-binemia) traceable to homemade baby food. Robert Rosen, "Crying to the Sheep; Notes on *Freitas et al. v. Baker/Beech-Nut,*" unpublished paper, 1976.

Chapter 10

Converting Commitment into Politics

1. For a well-reasoned case for a national children's policy, see *Toward a National Policy for Children and Families,* the report of the Advisory Committee on Child Development of the National Academy of Sciences,

Washington, D.C.: National Academy of Sciences, 1976.

2. See Gilbert Y. Steiner with Pauline H. Milius, *The Children's Cause,* Washington, D.C.: The Brookings Institution, 1976.

Index

A

Absent parents, designing means to assume child support by, 113–15
Abusive parents, 136, 191–92
Accessibility
  of health care, 162–67, 170–71
  of all services, 142–43
Accountability
  of health agencies, 171–78
  of services, increasing parent control over, 145–50
  of states for children in their care, 198
Addams, Jane, 38
Adolescents
  alcoholism among, 199, 200
  black, unemployment among, 35, 92
  dealing with dropouts, 203
  suicide among, 199, 200
  See also Delinquency
Adoption
  foster care and, 188
  of minority children, 33
  services for adopted children, 136
  subsidies for, 190
Adult roles available to poor children, 34, 35
Advocacy
  of family policy, 216–21
  parental, 178–81, 214–16
AFDC (Aid to Families with Dependent Children), 100–3, 109, 111, 116, 141
Affluent, the
  diet quality of, 57n
  taxes paid by, 45, 105
  See also Wealth
Agee, James, 1
Agricultural families
  children as economic assets in, 13–15
  effects of mechanization of agriculture on, 14
  self-sufficiency of, 10, 13
Aid for the Education of Handicapped Children, 148
Aid to Families with Dependent Children (AFDC), 100–3, 109, 111, 116, 141
Alcoholism
  adolescent, 199, 200
  programs for prevention of, 138
Alger, Horatio, 36
American Indians, *see* Native Americans
Appalachian Child Development Program, 139
Atomic weapons, 66, 70; *see also* Radiation

B

Barter economies, 10, 13
Beecher, Henry Ward, 38
Birth defects
  anesthetic gases and, 207
  food additives and, 56
Black
  "culturally deprived" as euphemism for, 39
Black adolescent unemployment, 35, 92
Blacks
  damage and deprivation suffered by children of, 33, 34, 35
  discrimination against, 78
  economic mobility of, 45
  as excluded from U.S. society, 36, 37
  health care for, 156, 162
  job discrimination against, 92–93

Blacks (*cont.*)
  median income of, 35
  poor children of (1974), 27, 28
  unemployment among, 35, 89, 92
Blaming the individual, 22, 37–38,
  214
Block grants for family support
  services, 138, 148
Bohannan, Paul, 7*n*
Breast-feeding, 51
Bronfenbrenner, Urie, 54
Budget of urban families, 28–29

C

Camus, Albert, 73
Cancer
  chemotherapy for, 88
  food additives and, 56
Capitalism
  basis of faith in, 69
  corporations and, 66
  free market, 64–66, 137
  ideological justification of, in
    nineteenth century, 65
  stopping pollution under, 67–68
CDI (childhood disability insurance),
  115–16, 137, 150, 151
Ceiling effect in health services, 166
CHAs (community health agencies),
  174–78, 219
Chemicals, 66
  food additives, 56
  harmful effects of, 206–8
Child abuse and neglect, 136, 137
  children's rights in cases of, 189–92
Child Care Food Program, 174*n*
Child development, 51
  in day care, 6–7
  role of television in, 7; *see also*
    Television
  workshops on how to stimulate, 8
Child-initiated care (experiment in
  health care), 180–81
Child labor laws, 77
Child Lead-Based Paint Poisoning
  Control Program, 141
Child rearing
  costs of, 14–15
  of difficult children, 76
  effects of changing family values
    on, 3–6; *see also* Families
  inadequacy of support programs
    and costs of, 78
  income, employment and, 84
  as job, 98, 99*n*, 103, 104, 112

and organization of work, 79,
  121–22, 127–30
  parents and, *see* Parents
  by working mothers, 31; *see also*
    Working women
Child support, 109, 113–16
  designing means to assure, by
    absent parent, 113–14
  for handicapped children, 115–16
  supplementary, 114–15
Childhood disability insurance (CDI),
  115–16, 137, 150, 151
Children
  See Families; Parents; Rights
    of children; *and specific groups
    of children; for example:* Blacks,
    children of; Handicapped
    children; Adolescents; Poor
    children
Children and youth projects, 163
Children's allowance, 116–17
Children's compensation laws, 209
Coal, as source of energy, 60–61
Cognitive development, effects of
  airport noise on, 51
Coleman, James, 45
Communes, 5, 76
Community health agencies (CHAs),
  174–78, 219
Community participation in
  health-care system, 178–81
Community services, 193, 194
Compulsory education (public
  education), 15–16, 77; *see also*
  Schools
Confidentiality, CHAs and need for,
  176, 177
Consumer movement, praised, 71
Consumers
  free choice argument and, 54–55,
    58–59
  technological innovation and
    powerlessness of, 69
  ultimate responsibility resting
    with, 64
Consumer's councils, 145–47, 174, 221
Corporations
  corporation-consumer relations, 69
  socioeconomic background of
    executives, 44–45
  laissez-faire economy and, 66
  social responsibility of, 70, 71
Costs
  of child rearing, 14–15
  of flexitime, for employers, 125
  of full-employment policy, 90–91,
    117

inadequacy of income supports and
costs of child rearing, 78
of income-support programs,
117–18
of lunch programs (1976), 139
of NHI, 166–67
of services, 139, 150–52
of television commercials (1950's),
53
See also Funds
Credit income tax, 104–12, 123, 217
Crime, see Delinquency
Cultural deprivation, 38, 39
Culture of poverty, 38

D

Day-care centers, 141
bonds formed in, 76
for handicapped or retarded
children, 194
shift in health-care system and,
168, 169
types of, 6–7
Deaths
accidental, 160
after first year of life, 168
infant mortality, 32, 33
traffic accident, 50
Degenerative diseases, 57; see also
Cancer
Delinquency
delinquency prevention services, 149
and nature of work, 130
services needed, 137
status offenders compared with
delinquents, 195
See also Adolescents
Dental care, 32, 169, 170
Detention homes, 195–96
Diet
decline in quality of (1955–65),
56–57
food additives, 56, 207
health and, 56–57, 60
high-salt, high-fat, high-sugar, 57–
58
poverty and malnutrition, 32, 33
technological innovation in food
and, 56–59, 67–70
Difficult children, 76
Disability insurance
for children, 115–16, 137, 150, 151;
see also Handicapped children
paid maternity leave as, 127, 128
Disabled, see Handicapped

Disadvantaged families, see Poor, the;
Poverty
Discrimination, 78
job, 85, 92–99, 122
Diseases, degenerative, 57; see also
Cancer
Disruptive children, rights of, 205
Divorce, 4–6, 20–22
changes in marital expectations and,
20–21
designing means to assure child
support by absent parent in
cases of, 113–15
effects of, on children, 6, 21–22
effects of, on nuclear family, 4–5
Dropouts, 203
Drug abuse, 199, 200
programs for prevention of, 138

E

Early and Periodic Screening,
Diagnosis and Treatment
program (EPSDT), 139, 164
Earnings, see Income
Ecological reappraisal of health
priorities, 160–61
Economic development programs,
full employment and government
supported, 87
Economic mobility, 45
Economic system
barter as, 10, 13
changes in, and changes in family,
12–15
perpetuation of poverty and, 118
See also Capitalism
Education
costs of, 14–15
formal, and transformation of
family, 15–16
of handicapped children, 138, 204
and myth of equal opportunity,
41–42
poverty and chances for higher, 32
on television, 55
See also Scholastic achievement;
Schools
Elderly, the
as exempted from work
requirement, 112
family function in care of, 14, 16
poverty among, 27
Eligibility for income support, 104;
see also Income-support programs

Emancipation, legal, 199, 200
Employee benefits in part-time jobs, 126
Employee participation, flexitime and, 125
Employers
    cost of flexitime to, 125
    subsidies for, to hire low-skilled workers, 90
Employment
    and ability to purchase services, 136, 137
    discouraged by AFDC, 101
    self-esteem and, 79
    See also Fair employment; Fair employment laws; Full-employment policy; Jobs; Labor market; Self-employed, the; Unemployment; Wage labor; Wages; Work; Workers; Working women
Energy
    lack of planning in policy on, 70
    sources of, 60, 61, 69
    See also Nuclear energy
EPSDT (Early and Periodic Screening, Diagnosis and Treatment program), 139, 164
Equal opportunity, 39–47
    importance of, as promise, 46–47
    myth of, 39–46
Equality
    abundance and, 63
    nineteenth-century economic realities and ideal of, 40, 41
Ethnicity, health care and, 162–67
Exclusion from U.S. society
    political change to eliminate, 217
    poverty and, 35–38, 84
    real forces behind, 43
Expenditures, see Costs
Experimental research, rights of children volunteered for, 200, 201
Experts, see Professionals
Extended families, 17

F

Fair employment, 98, 137, 217
Fair employment laws, 93–99
Families
    effects of economic pressures on, 31; see also specific kinds of economic pressures; for example: Unemployment

effects of transformation of, 3–23
    See also Child rearing; Children; Parents
Family income
    distribution of, 44
    necessary for parents to participate in work-sharing plan, 127n
    percentage of, spent on health care (1970), 163
    what is a decent, 26–27
    See also Median family income
Family planning
    abortions, 199
    contraceptive devices, 51
Family planning services, 157, 168, 170
Family policy, national, 216–22
    commitment to comprehensive, 214–15
    proposal on, 76–78, 216–21
    See also Full-employment policy
Family support services, 133–52
    accessibility of, 142–43
    accountability of, 145–50
    available to middle-class families, 133–35
    community, 193, 194
    costs of, 150–52
    existing, 138–42
    need to change and strengthen, 79–80
    principles for changing, 142–44
    public advocates in support of, 216–220
    types of, 135–36
Family work
    flexitime scheduling and, 79, 85, 123–25, 151, 218
    part-time jobs and, 125–27; see also Part-time jobs
    time out for children and, 79, 127–30
    wage work and, 121–30
Fathers
    1800's ideal, 10, 11
    time out from work for, 128n, 129
Federal government
    assessing risks connected with technology as responsibility of, 69–71
    assessment of services by, 145–47
    establishment of maternity benefits and, 128
    funding and operation of services by, 138–39; see also Costs; Funds
    regulation of agriculture by, 59

responsibilities of, for services,
151–52
role of, in providing services,
136–38
states and role of federal
government in providing
services, 149
upgrading of part-time jobs and,
126, 127
*See also specific programs and
policies*
Female-headed households
number of, 5
poverty in, 20, 27–28, 82
working women in, 19
see also Unwed mothers
Fiscal and monetary policies, *see*
Monetary and fiscal policies
Flexible scheduling (flexitime), 79,
85, 123–25, 151, 218
Follow Through program, 163
Food, *see* Diet
Food additives, 56, 207
Food stamps, 91, 102, 139
Ford, Henry, 50
Foster care, 136, 190
bonds formed in, 76
disruptive effects of, 141
Native American children in, 33
number of poor children in, 32
operation of, 138
services for children in, 135n
"4/40" work week, 124, 125
Four-person families
credit income tax for, 104–7, 109
income, 28–31, 150
income supports for, 113
Free choice of consumers, 54–55,
58–59
Free education, *see* Compulsory
education; Schools
Free market, 64–66, 137; *see also*
Capitalism
Frictional unemployment, defined, 86
Fuchs, Victor, 160
Full-employment policy, 79, 84–91,
137, 216–17
and changes in wage-work practices,
122
costs of, 90–91, 117
credit income tax and, 109, 111
defining ideal of, 86
fair employment and, 98
income-support programs and, 85
inflation and, 88–90
job-creation programs and, 87–88,
91.

labor market and, 89–90
public advocates in support of,
216–17
services and, 150, 152
time out for children possible
under, 130
upgrading part-time jobs and, 147
work requirements and, 112
Full-time jobs, restructuring part-time
jobs as miniatures of, 126
Funds
for Child Lead-Based Paint
Poisoning Program, 141
for family-planning services, 157
for services, as insufficient, 141–42
for special educational services,
140
See also Costs

G

Genetic abnormalities, occupational
exposure and, 208; *See also*
Birth defects
Geographic mobility, 17
Grievance mechanisms in schools, 205
Gross National Product (GNP)
effects of full-employment policy
on, 90
job of child rearing not included
in, 99n
percentage of, spent on health care,
136, 155
Group homes
for handicapped or mentally
retarded children, 194
rights of children in, 196
for status offenders, 196

H

Handicapped, the
as excluded from U.S. society,
36, 37–38
as exempted from work
requirement, 112
unemployment among, 92n
Handicapped children, 187–88
child support for, 115–16
day-care centers for, 194
educational program for, 136, 204
future of, 33–34
high cost of raising, 31–32
in Head Start, 142
number of, 31–32

Handicapped children (*cont.*)
  rights of, 192–94
  services for, 136
  vocational programs for, 140
Head Start, 7, 138, 142, 163
Health
  impact of technology on, 51
  nutrition and, 58–59, 160
  poverty and, 32
  work and problems of, 130
Health care, 78, 102, 155–81
  accessibility of, 162–67, 170–71
  accountability of agencies, 171–78
  changed family function in, 16
  children's rights to make decisions
    about their, 198–202
  disparities in, 156–57, 162–67
  goals for change in, 159–81
  parental advocacy in support of,
    178–81
  poverty and, 32
  public advocates in support of,
    219–20
  for school-age children, 139, 140
Health-care team, 169
Health foods, 57–58
Health insurance, 126, 163
  national, 115, 151, 158, 164–67,
    170
Health Service Agencies, 219
Higher education, poverty and
  chances for, 32
Hiring practices, job discrimination
  and need to change, 93–99
Home Start program, 8
Hospitals
  health-care system centered on,
    168
  rights of children in mental, 196
Household heads
  guaranteeing jobs to, 113, 123
  unemployment among, 86, 91
Housework (homemaking), 112
Housing subsidies, 102

I

Illegitimate births (1950s; 1971), 5
Immigrants, 11, 36–38
Implicit tax rate, 101, 111, 117
Income
  inequality of, 44, 92–93
  and quality of diet, 57*n*
  See also Family income; Wages;
    Median family income

Income distribution, 42–46, 117
Income floor of SSI, 116
Income maintenance experiment
  (New Jersey; 1968–72), 111
Income supplement, 78–79
Income-support programs, 77–78, 85,
  99–118, 217
  and ability to purchase services,
    136, 137
  adequate level of supports, 113–16
  benefiting poor children, 100–3,
    109, 111, 116, 141
  changes in wage-work practices
    and, 123
Income supports
  costs of, 117–18
  credit income tax as sample,
    104–12, 123, 219
  services and, 150–52
  work requirements and, 111–12
Income tax, credit, 104–12, 123,
  217–18
Industrialization, 10–11, 14, 15;
  see also Pollution; Technological
  society
Inequality, 41
  in health care, 156–57, 162–67
  of opportunity, absolute, 43–44
  See also Affluent, the; Income;
    Poor, the; Poverty
Infant care projects, 163
Infant mortality, 32, 33
Inflation, full employment and, 88–90
Information, parents as caretakers
  and need for health care, 178–81,
  219–20
Inoculations against epidemics, 137,
  138
Institutionalization, 135*n*, 141,
  192–94, 196–98
Insurance
  childhood disability insurance
    (CDI), 115–16, 137, 150, 151
  health insurance, 126, 163
  National Health Insurance plan,
    115, 151, 158, 164–67, 170
  unemployment insurance, 77, 89,
    91, 100
  See also Disability insurance;
    Health insurance; Social Security;
    Unemployment insurance

J

Jails, status offenders in, 195
Jefferson, Thomas, 62

Jencks, Christopher, 45, 46
Job ceiling, 35n, 92–93
Job-creation programs, 87–88, 91
Job discrimination, 84, 92–99, 122
Job qualifications, as basis for
    discrimination, 97–98
Job sharing (work sharing), 127
Jobs
  child rearing as, 98, 99n, 103, 104,
    112
  children's rights to make decisions
    about, 202
  full-time, 126
  part-time, 79, 85, 125–27, 218
  public, 86, 91
  See also Employment
Johnson, Lyndon B., 94
Justice, see Laws; Rights of children

K

Kaemmerev, Christel, 124
Kagan, Jerome, 8
Kepone incident, 206–7

L

Labor laws, child, 77
Labor market, 89–91; see also
    Workers; Working women
Laws
  child labor, 77
  fair employment, 93–99
  need for change in, 79
  See also Rights of children
Lawyers, children's, 211, 214, 220
Lead, 138, 208–9
Legal protection of children, 183–85;
    see also Rights of children
Lewis, Charles, 180
Lewis, Mary Ann, 180
Local governments
  responsibility of, for services,
    167–68
  services operated by, 138
Locke, John, 65

M

Malnutrition, 32, 33
Mann, Horace, 15, 41
Married women (1948; 1976), 4
Maternity benefits, 122, 127–30, 218
Median family income
  black and white, compared, 35

credit income tax based on half of,
    106, 109
  for four-person family, 150
  income floor set at 40% of, 104,
    113
  in 1974, 19
  poverty line as half, 27, 29–32
  standard of living afforded by
    (1974), 28–29
Medicaid, 102, 138, 163, 164, 174,
    176
Medical sciences, technological
    innovations in, 67, 68
Mental health services, 168
Mentally retarded children
  day-care centers for, 194
  rights of, 192–93, 196
  vocational programs for, 140
Mexican-Americans, 11, 35, 92
Middle-class children, 22, 37, 38, 139
Middle-class families, services
    available to, 133–35
Minority children
  adoption of, 33
  health care for, 156–57
  subsidies for adoption of, 190n
  suspended from schools, 203n
  See also specific minority group
    children
Monetary and fiscal policies
  full employment and, 87
  See also Tax system; Taxes
Moral danger concept, as justification
    for removing a child from home,
    187
Mothers
  1800's ideal, 10–11
  See also Female-headed households;
    Unwed mothers; Women;
    Working women
Mutations, food additives and, 56

N

National Health Insurance plan
    (NHI), 115, 151, 158, 164–67,
    170
National security, premised on
    balance of terror, 71
Native American children
  damage and deprivation suffered
    by, 33
  future of, 35
Native Americans
  full citizenship denied, 36

Native Americans (*cont.*)
 myth of self-sufficiency and, 11
 unemployment among, 92
Natural gas, exhaustion of, 60
Natural resources
 exhaustion of, 60
 in laissez-faire economy, 69
Neighborhood health centers, 163
Newborn care, 169–70
NHI (National Health Insurance
  plan), 115, 151, 158, 164–67, 170
Non–English-speaking children, right
  of, to education, 204
Nuclear energy, 59–62
 assessing risks connected with
  power plants run on, 60, 68–69
Nutritional counseling services,
  168–70
Nutritional programs, 157

O

Occupational exposure to harmful
  substances, 207–8
Oil, 60, 69
Old Age, Survivors, and Disability
  Insurance, *see* Social Security
Ombudsmen, need for in schools, 205
On-the-job training, 98
Orphans, services required by, 137
Overtime, voluntary, 125

P

Paraprofessionals, 144
Parent education, types of, 7–8
Parent participation
 accountability of services and,
  145–50
 in health care, 178–81, 219–20
 in services, 136, 144
Parental autonomy, doctrine of, 198
Parents
 absent, designing means to assure
  child support by, 113–15
 abusive, 136, 191–92
 as advocates, 178–81, 214–16
 as caretakers, and need for health-
  care information, 178–81,
  219–20
 as coordinators, 17–18, 122
 effects of employment on, 79, 85
 effects of unemployment on, 88–89
 as experts, 76
 new role of, 12–13, 17–23, 122

removing external barriers to
  responsibility of, 76–77
rewards of parenthood, 77
in technological society, *see*
  Technological society
ultimate responsibility for
  child rearing resting with, 9;
  see also Child rearing
See also Children; Divorce;
  Families; Fathers; Mothers
Partially emancipated children,
  defined, 199
Part-time jobs, 79, 85, 125–27, 218
Physicians
 need for ecological reappraisal of
  health priorities by, 161–62
 parents as health caretakers and,
  179–80
 and public health-care system, 177
 shifting present emphasis of
  health-care system and, 169
 shortage of, 137, 157–58
Political action, need for, by
  children's advocates, 214–15
Political change, 213–21
 need for, 214
 practical aspect of, 215
 price of resisting, 215–16
 proposed family policy, 216–20
 vision of the possible and, 221
Pollution, 160
 air, 50, 56
 atmospheric, 67, 68
 noise, 51
 water, 56, 60, 67, 206–8
Pollution tax, 67
Poor, the
 access of, to health care, 162–67
 diet quality of, 57*n*
 health care for, 162–67
 Home Start program for, 8
 myth of self-sufficiency and, 11
 See also Poverty
Poor children, 27–38
 damage and deprivation suffered by,
  31–33
 as excluded from U.S. society,
  35–38
 full-employment practically
  eliminating poverty of, 86–87;
  see also Full-employment policy
 future of, 33–35
 income-support programs benefiting,
  100–3, 109, 111, 116, 141
 number of, 26–29, 32
 *See also specific groups of poor
  children and specific programs*

Potter, David, 55
Poverty
  basis for perpetuation of, 118
  child neglect and, 188
  defining limits of, 26–32
  and exclusion from U.S. society,
    35–38, 84
  in female-headed households, 20,
    27–28, 92
  health care and, 32; *see also*
    Health care
  myth of equal opportunity and,
    39–41
  wealth distribution and, 42–46
  See also Poor, the
Poverty line, 27
Prejudices, 37–38
Prenatal care
  emphasis on, 168, 170
  funds for, 157
  infant mortality and, 156, 160–61
  poverty and, 32
Preschool children, working mothers
  with (1948; 1976), 4
Preservatives, food, 56
Preventive family services, 136, 141,
  144, 218
Preventive health care, 167–71
Primary health care, 167–71
Privacy, CHAs and, 176, 177
Production, social costs of, 67–68
Professionals
  law of supply and demand as
    applied to, 137–38
  parents' relations with, 17–18, 122
  See also Physicians
Promotions
  maternity leaves and, 127
  in part-time jobs, 126
Protective services for children, 141
Public advocates, *see* Advocacy
Public education (compulsory
  education), 15–16, 77; *see also*
  Schools
Public health-care system, *see* Health
  care
Public interest, laissez-faire
  economy and, 64–65
Public jobs, 86, 91
Puerto Ricans, 35, 92

R

Race and access to health care,
  162–67
Radiation, 60, 66, 70, 208

Reading undermined by television, 54,
  55
Rebellious children, rights of, 194–95
Recessions (1970's), 98
Reproductive function, effects of
  occupational hazards on, 207–8
Revenue-sharing program, 148
Rich, the, *see* Affluent, the
Rights of children, 186–211
  to decide about health care,
    schools and jobs, 198–206
  without families, 176–98
  fighting for, 211
  new belief in, 186
  public advocates in support of,
    220
  in relation to the family, 185–96
  in technological society, 206–10
Runaway children, 138, 194–96
Rural families, poverty line for, 27

S

Scholastic achievement
  birth status and, 45–46
  of poor children, 33–35
  programs to help low achievers,
    139
School-age children
  health-care services for, 139, 140
  of working mothers (1948; 1976), 4
School Breakfast Program, 174*n*
School lunch programs, 138, 139
Schools
  as agents of change, 20, 41–42,
    45–47, 85–86
  children's rights in, 202–6
  federal expenditures for (1976),
    139
  health-care system compared with,
    171–72
  role of, in changed health-care
    system, 169, 170
  as services, 80, 135, 137
Secondary support services, 143
Selection of employees, criteria
  for, 97–98
Self-concept
  basis of low, 84
  of poor children, 33
Self-employed, the, 112, 124
Self-sufficiency
  ideal of, historical development
    of, 9–11
  myth of, 7–12

Seniority system, 98, 127, 128
Separations
    marital, *see* Divorce
    voluntary, of parents and children,
        194–96
Services, *see* Day-care centers; Family
        support services; Health Care;
        Protective services for children;
        Secondary support services;
        Special educational services
Single-parent families
    credit income tax for, 106, 107,
        109, 111
    income supports for, 151
    number of, 5
    sense of commitment in, 76
    See also Divorce; Female-headed
        households
Six-person families, credit income
        tax for, 110, 111
Slavery, 11, 13
Smith, Adam, 65
Social costs
    of full-employment policy, 90
    of economic production, 67–68
    of technological innovations, 67, 70
Social responsibility of corporations,
        70, 71
Social Security, 77, 90, 100
Solar energy, 60, 61, 69
Spanish-speaking minorities
    access to health care of, 162
    Mexican-Americans and Puerto
        Ricans, 11, 35, 92
    number of poor (1974), 27
Special educational services, 140
Special Supplemental Food Program
        for Women, Infants and Children
        (WIC), 174n
SSI (Supplemental Security Income),
        101n, 116
Staggered working hours, 124
Standard of living
    afforded by half the median family
        income (1974), 29
    afforded by median family income
        (1974), 28–29
    public advocates in support of
        decent, 216–17
State governments
    responsibility of, for services,
        50, 149
    services operated by, 138
Status offenders, 195–96
Stereotypes, 37–38
Students' rights, 202–6, 220

Subsidies
    adoption, 192
    for employers, to hire low-skill
        workers, 90
    housing, 102
    services, 138
    tax, for the rich, 105
Suicides, teen-age, 199, 200
Supplemental Security Income (SSI),
        101n, 116
Supplementary child support, 114–15

T

Tax system, 45
    income supports and revamped, 103
    need to reform, 116–17
    replacing transfer payments with
        revised, 105
Taxes
    credit income, 104–12, 123, 217
    full employment and lowering of,
        87
    implicit tax rate, 101, 111, 117
    paid by the affluent, 45, 105
    pollution, 67
Technological society, 49–50
    children's rights in, 206–10
    laissez-faire economy and, 62–66
    problems posed by, 60, 66–70
    solutions to problems posed by,
        70–71
    television in, 7, 22, 51–56, 70
    See also Diet; Energy
Teen-agers, *see* Adolescents
Television, 7, 22, 51–56, 70
Totally emancipated children, defined,
        199
Tracking, 204–5
Training schools, 195, 196
Truancy, provisions to deal with, 203

U

Unborn children
    effects of lead on, 208–9
    effects of parent's occupational
        exposure to harmful substances
        on, 207–8
Unemployment
    among blacks, 35, 89, 92
    to check inflation, 87, 88
    distribution of, 91–92
    effects of, 84, 85

Unemployment insurance, 77, 89, 91, 100
Unionization of part-time workers, 126
Unwed mothers, 201, 202
  neglected children and, 189
  number of illegitimate births (1950s; 1971), 5
  prenatal care for, 156n
Urban families
  budget of, with median income (1974), 28–29
  poverty line for, 27

V

Veterans' programs, 100
Violence on television, 52, 53, 55
Vocational Education Act, 148
Vocational Educational Amendments (1968), 140
Vocational programs, 140
Volunteers in services programs, 144

W

Wage labor, 13–14; see also Family work
Wages
  inflation and wage-price controls, 89
  in part-time jobs, 126
  prices and, 91
  recommended, for low-skill public work, 86
Wealth
  distribution of, 42–46, 117–18
  personal worth and, 42

Webster, Daniel, 63
Welfare, 77, 91, 130, 137
  AFDC, 100–3, 109–11, 116, 141
  disruptive effect of, 140–41
  need to reform, 116–17
  rights of children in, 196
White, Burton, 8
Women, discrimination against, 78; see also Mothers; Working women
Work
  family life and, 13, 14; see also Family work
  incentives to, 104, 109
  life-cycle patterns of, 123n
  valued in terms of cash income, 15
  work requirements, 111–13
  See also Employment; Workers; Working women
Work schedules, flexible, 79, 85, 123–27, 151, 179, 218
Work tests, 112, 113
Workers
  credit income tax for poor, 108
  guaranteeing jobs to low-skill, 86
  myth of self-sufficiency and, 11
  subsidies to hire low-skill, 90
Working women, 19–20, 22, 45, 79, 123
  with children, effect on children, 5, 31
  job discrimination against, 92–98, 122
  maternity benefits for, 122, 127–30, 218
  number of (1948; 1976), 4
  unemployment among, 89, 92
Workmen's compensation, 100, 127
Work sharing (job splitting; job sharing), 127

HQ536 .K43 1977
Keniston, Kenneth.
All our children : the
American family under
pressure

APR 2 7 2006

~~MERCYHURST~~

~~COLLEGE LIBRARY~~

~~ERIE, PENNSYLVANIA 16501~~

DEMCO